S0-AQI-805

The Fear Factor

Also by Colin Read

GLOBAL FINANCIAL MELTDOWN: HOW WE CAN AVOID THE NEXT ECONOMIC CRISIS

INTERNATIONAL TAXATION HANDBOOK: POLICY, PRACTICE, STANDARDS AND REGULATION (edited with G. Gregoriou)

The Fear Factor

What Happens When Fear Grips Wall Street

Colin Read

palgrave
macmillan

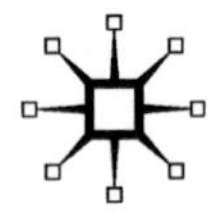

First published 2009 by
PALGRAVE MACMILLAN

Palgrave Macmillan in the UK is an imprint of Macmillan Publishers Limited, registered in England, company number 785998, of Houndmills, Basingstoke, Hampshire RG21 6XS.

Palgrave Macmillan in the US is a division of St Martin's Press LLC, 175 Fifth Avenue, New York, NY 10010.

Palgrave Macmillan is the global academic imprint of the above companies and has companies and representatives throughout the world.

Palgrave® and Macmillan® are registered trademarks in the United States, the United Kingdom, Europe and other countries.

ISBN-13: 978–0–230–22846–7 hardback

This book is printed on paper suitable for recycling and made from fully managed and sustained forest sources. Logging, pulping and manufacturing processes are expected to conform to the environmental regulations of the country of origin.

A catalogue record for this book is available from the British Library.

A catalog record for this book is available from the Library of Congress.

10 9 8 7 6 5 4 3 2 1
18 17 16 15 14 13 12 11 10 09

Printed and bound in Great Britain by
CPI Antony Rowe, Chippenham and Eastbourne

I dedicate this book to my fiancé and wonderful partner, Natalie, and my mother, Gail

Contents

Figures

Preface

Over the months between writing *Global Financial Meltdown* and completing this book, the economies of the world have been shocked in a manner without parallel. Families around the world have become fearful for their financial future. As of today, these fears remain unabated.

Just two years ago, if one were to spoil the economic party by pointing out the fragilities of our global economy, there would be no warm reception. Now, one cannot watch a newscast or open a newspaper without seeing numerous stories of fear and misery. Unlike two years ago, almost all are calling for very significant reform to prevent this misery from ever occurring again.

We have seen our worst economic fears. And we now understand that these fears translate into action designed to protect our collective economic future.

Time is ripe to better understand the nature of our economic fears. In doing so, we can also understand how our fears are manipulated by others in their pursuit of profits. By understanding how some can capitalize on our fears, we will be better able to create the reforms and institutions that can rebuild our confidence in markets and investments.

In the process of writing this book, I also conclude that there is a need to reemphasize the pursuit of true production rather than the mere production of paper profits. Greed and excess has replaced toil and sweat, and has our brightest young minds aspiring to Wall Street rather than Main Street. A consequence of fear-driven markets is a renewed recognition of the value of true production. Just as we recall those circumstances that have placed us in peril before, our memories of these economic perils will hopefully motivate us to demand reform and not repeat excesses.

I view the messages and the focus on market fear as productive. Information is power, and an understanding of markets and of our human response to threats will allow us to better cope with the gyrations of markets and the uncertainties of economic life. An embracement of economic fear, through understanding, can be empowering rather than debilitating.

I hope as you read this book you will try to integrate the lessons on these pages into your own economic life. Our economic challenges will abate, and our fears will pass. We will be left with an emotional memory of circumstances that have placed us all in great discomfort. And our fears will allow us to recognize, right in the solar plexus, those economic circumstances that can threaten our economic security.

Colin Read
Plattsburgh, New York
April 21, 2009

About the Author

Colin Read is a professor of economics and finance, former dean of the School of Business and Economics at SUNY College at Plattsburgh, and a columnist for the *Plattsburgh (New York) Press-Republican* newspaper. He has a PhD in economics, a JD in law, an MBA, a masters in taxation, and has taught economics and finance for 25 years. Colin's recent books include *Global Financial Meltdown: How We Can Avoid the Next Economic Crisis* and a book on international taxation. He has written dozens of papers on market failure, volatility, and housing markets. He writes a monthly column in a business trade journal, and appears monthly on a local PBS television show to discuss the regional and national economy. He has worked as a research associate at the Harvard Joint Center for Housing Studies and served the Ministry of Finance in Indonesia under contract from the Harvard Institute for International Development. His consulting company can be found on the Internet at www.economicinsights.net. In his spare time he enjoys floatplane flying from his home on Lake Champlain that he shares with his partner, Natalie, daughter, Blair, and dog, Walter.

Introduction

Not since the Great Depression have Wall Street and Main Street been so gripped in fear. The lives of those who lived through the Great Depression in the 1930s were forever changed. Only two generations of almost unbroken prosperity since the 1960s have allowed us to shake the fear of loss created by the pain of the Great Depression. Fear and despair have returned. This is a book about the fear that drives troubled economies. I also explore how fear is manipulated, in politics and in financial markets, to benefit hundreds but cost billions.

It is the realization and manipulation of our basic emotion that plays such a crucial role in otherwise rational decision making. While the dismal science of economics has been used to great effect to yield consistent returns for some investors, it is psychology that, at times like these, plays the critical role in our collective economic future.

The uncomfortable reality that fear and other psychological influences can move markets is most troubling to economists, politicians, and technocrats. They understand, more or less, how to manipulate a modern economy that is humming along smoothly. Their models break down when the animal spirit of fear grips our modern economy.

Few still harbor an idolatry of unfettered market. Most have finally come to accept the importance of the interplay between economics, finance, and psychology. This realization of the role of fear demonstrates that our analyses remain incomplete until we can more successfully combine our economic theories with new theories that integrate psychology and economics. I motivate this integration by describing how the psychology of fear currently pervades our political economy. While the doctrinal application of conventional economics works well most of the time, these are not normal times. From this pain of economic breakdown comes the fear that reduces our economic models to esoteric studies of better times.

I come to this book from an academic background. My university studies began with a Bachelor of Science degree in physics, followed by a PhD in economics. I slowly realized that the analytic tools of physics that so pervaded modern economics has strayed too far from explaining this important dimension of human nature. To better understand the interplay between scientific methods, the dismal science, human behavior, and public policy, I continued on in my studies toward a masters in taxation, an MBA, and a JD in law. It was not until my frustration with the recent Global Financial Meltdown that I became convinced this once-in-a-lifetime event when fear grips the market necessitates a less doctrinal discussion of the free market.

So I devoted my research to the explanation of market failures to the public. I stepped down from my job as the dean of a school of business and economics at the State University of New York to write a regular business column and a book that documents the unraveling of the current economic crisis. The book, entitled *Global Financial Meltdown: How We Can Avoid the Next Economic Crisis,* described the events that gave rise to the most significant economic crisis in a lifetime. As I do here, I try to explain modern economic theory to the intelligent lay reader, while at the same time critiquing our theoretical economic models when they fail to adequately explain our macro economy.

My background as a dean of a business school and as a researcher who devoted a career in modeling information failures gives me a unique perspective. I recognize the incredible advantages of free markets and capitalism, when they work well. I am also quick to judge these same markets harshly when they fail to perform as promised. Unfortunately, market failures are now colossal, and the pain inflicted when markets fail so dramatically and quickly outstrips the goodwill generated when the markets work well.

My previous book reinforced in me the importance of an economically literate citizenry. I hope to provide you here with a primer on the U.S. and world economies, from an academic and practical perspective, while at the same time challenge you to become a participant in our collective future. I realized that our political leaders can only lead if we all collectively understand where they are going.

All too often, however, our leaders merely reflect our own level of sophistication. If we cannot provide our leaders with a thoughtful policy debate, we should not be surprised if they lead us astray. And if we expect little thoughtful economic analysis from our political leaders, they will too easily live up to our low expectations.

I also hope that this book will provoke you to formulate new questions that you may not have asked before. Understanding how much we do not know is a measure of our wisdom. And our blissful ignorance over the past couple of decades allowed others to successfully usurp billions of dollars from us, while costing us trillions. A healthy political economy requires us to participate in our own economic future. We fail to do so at our peril. The current Global

Financial Meltdown provides a timeless lesson of how some will capitalize if we ever drop our economic guard.

We now realize from this Global Financial Meltdown of 2008 that markets must be watched – like a hawk. While it may be true that an ideal market is the aggregate of a multitude of tiny economic actors, each operating in relative anonymity, it is this same blind faith in the collective assembly of individual actors that fatally obscures the workings of the economic black box.

I write this book in an interdisciplinary manner because we are now discovering that markets fail most dramatically when our models are narrow and doctrinal. I begin with a description of the important evolutionary role of fear in human survival. In the first part of the book, I recognize that fear is multifaceted. While we all recognize its uncomfortable qualities, it also serves an essential purpose of focusing our attention on what is most immediately important. The fear that grips the market as we move through the five stages of economic grief – anger, denial, bargaining, depression, and acceptance – provides us with motivation to change. It also motivates us to avoid similar harmful circumstances in the future.

In Part II, I provide a brief primer on the workings of financial markets. I then describe in Part III how fear is incorporated into our economic models. Economists rarely speak of fear directly. However, we do discuss the cost of uncertainty, our aversion to risk, and the consequences of making decisions based on false assumptions.

In Part IV, I show how fear, risk, and uncertainty are distorted by the incentives used to make our modern economy function. It is important to understand concepts such as moral hazard and adverse selection if we must measure the costs of our mistaken assumptions about the nature of risk in our economy. If we collectively label these tendencies to make poor decisions under poor information as noise, I show in Part V how increased noise in the economy increases market volatility and decreases its predictability. I look at the pattern of market returns across generations to establish how markets perform in turbulent times.

I pay particular attention in Part VI to the most significant historical economic traumas. I review past crashes and panics, but I devote particular attention to the Roaring Twenties, followed by the Great Crash and the Great Depression. This crash, which contributed to the first global economic crisis of the modern economic era, gave us the first opportunity to experiment with the newly developed tools of Keynesian economics. I also document in Part VII how the tools of modern economics can help shorten the duration of an economic depression, even if they have been unable to eliminate our economic fears.

In Part VIII, I ask whether there is a certain social responsibility on the part of those that benefit from free markets to assist in making free markets work better, more efficiently, and more transparently. I then outline in Part IX how politics, the media, our economic players, and even our political leaders play into the problem. If we are able to understand their roles more fully, they may emerge as part of the solution.

I end with a number of chapters that describe how we might use our fears to motivate our understanding and reform of our economy so that we need not suffer the same traumas – at least until we become so comfortable that our fear subsides, once again.

Ultimately, it is the fear derived from pain that has brought us to where we are today. It is also fear that will motivate us to ensure we do not make the same mistakes tomorrow. If we can harness fear for our own economic benefit, the hard lessons learned today will hopefully benefit many generations to come, just as we retained the lessons learned from the Great Depression until two generations of affluence and excesses caused us to forget.

Part I
The Nature of Risk

In this part, I describe the nature of risk from a biological and an economic perspective. I conclude that an appropriate level of fear is healthy, but too much fear, and lack of control, can be debilitating. I also discover that the economy can behave in a distinctly emotional way at times, necessitating the incorporation of psychology into our future economic models.

1
The Biology and Psychology of Fear

Fear is an essential animal emotion. Its triggers, and the associated symptoms of anxiety or aggression fear can cause, have evolved to serve a number of very important purposes, and have served us well.

Scientists and psychologists have long postulated the essential role of fear in human survival. For instance, neuroscientist Jaak Panksepp identified fear and panic as two of the seven basic emotional systems, together with seeking, rage, play, lust, and caring. These emotions are protective mechanisms that have been programmed into our genes to produce a profound biological response when we are confronted with threats.[1]

The emotional system associated with fear is complex. When threatened, the body exhibits a number of symptoms of stress. Blood pressure and the heartbeat rises, breathing becomes more pronounced and hormones such as epinephrine and adrenaline are released. These biological changes prepare us to respond to external stimuli that are sufficiently important to require our immediate and focused attention.

The anxiety that we associate with fear has evolved over millions of years. If we did not experience such anxiety, we would be ill-prepared to respond immediately to fast moving situations. A small amount of anxiety keeps us focused at work, attentive while driving home, and engaged in important conversations. Of course, too much anxiety can be debilitating. But without some anxiety, we would wander through our days with little sense of immediacy or priority, and little preparation for danger.

Scientists are discovering that fear, and the anxiety it produces, has even deeper biological roots than previously imagined. Recent discoveries of receptors in the brain point to a strong chemical pathway that gives rise to our fears and anxiety.

One particular receptor, beta-CCE, comes from the family of alkaloids that have long been known to produce a variety of strong neurological responses. Scientists have discovered that the injection of beta-CCE into monkeys and human subjects creates severe anxiety almost instantaneously.

Fortunately, the discovery of these biological roots of anxiety also permitted the design of antidotes to control excessive anxiety. Such common sedatives as Valium and sleeping pills are now known to quell these anxiety receptors and place the patients in a more tranquil state. Some who suffer from such severe and nonproductive anxiety require medical antidotes to avoid the debilitating effects of constantly exaggerated threats.

A right amount of fear

While there can be too much anxiety and fear, we know that there can also be too little. Fear is in balance when it provides us with sufficient guard and responsiveness to address those external forces provoking our fear, but without an unnecessary response that focuses an inordinate amount of attention on trivial threats.

Fear becomes counterproductive whenever it debilitates our necessary responses. To balance our response to external threats, we must place our fear in some sort of rational perspective. It is, however, not necessarily easy to balance a primordial emotion with rationality and logic. Nonetheless, the more we temper our emotion of fear with logic and reason, the more likely we can put fear in perspective and muster an appropriate response to those external forces that threaten us.

Our earliest fears were much more immediate than those that may trouble us now. Millennia ago, we were most likely concerned about animals that may threaten us, the natural elements that may do us harm or cause discomfort, and the loss of the resources we accumulate to sustain us through lean times. If our lives are no longer filled with primordial fear, it might appear we have come far. Even so, such natural threats from our environment still invoke strong fear and anxiety in us, as do the many new and varied forms of loss we now experience. Our lives have become significantly more complex than that of the hunter/gatherer, but our most basic fears remain.

If some of our most basic fears may be less common or essential now, they have been replaced by other fear triggers that could not have existed 10,000 years ago. Certainly our natural fear of predatory or self-protecting animals is much less commonly invoked now than it might have been before civilization. Indeed, this fear and anxiety is now cultivated, through zoos and horror films, provoking our primordial response in an environment everybody understands is safe.

But while we may no longer face the primordial fears of animals, other natural fears, of hurricanes, floods, tornados, and fire, still inflict many of us on occasion. Even those who do not experience the fear directly can now vicariously feel the anxiety by watching the evening news. The common media expression "if it bleeds, it leads" reinforces our fascination with fear inflicting others, viewed from the comfort and safety of our own environment.

These traumas of the most basic type inflicted on others may even have a somewhat cathartic effect. If we realize that the world remains a dangerous place, but this danger is instead experienced by others, we are consoled that danger is directed elsewhere. The odds shift in our favor.

Maslow's hierarchy of wants and needs

However, the fear of loss seems much more prevalent and ubiquitous than it has ever been. In 1943, the psychologist Abraham Maslow created a hierarchy of human wants and needs, with basic physiological needs at its base, followed by the need for safety and economic security. Anything that threatens Maslow's lower wants and needs of food, shelter, safety, and security can invoke fear and anxiety. As Maslow shows, only after we satisfy our basic physical and security needs can we be free to satisfy our higher psychological and emotional needs. It is this world, the economic world of providing for our basic needs, literally and figuratively, that has become easier in some respects, but much more complex and uncertain in others.[2]

These new reasons to fear are the subject of this book. Though gone are the fears of predatory animals, falling from trees, or unannounced disasters, we are still left with a multitude of fears of the unknown. As our sphere of the known has dramatically expanded, so too has the range of possible unknowns. Fear of animals has been replaced by fear for our economic and social security.

For instance, James F. Mattil, managing editor of *Flashpoints: Guide to World Conflicts,* writes:

> People are social beings who come together in groups with shared values, religion, culture, language, tradition, heritage, or location in hope of survival and prosperity. Whenever the core characteristic that bonds a group together comes under threat, the group will inevitably fear for its very survival. They'll attempt to change the situation that poses the threat, or, failing that, they will attempt to repel the threat and strengthen their group cohesiveness. Occasionally, leaders who seek to exploit popular fears for personal advantage by exaggerating threats.[3]

The reach of these varied interactions is now so much broader and amplified. While natural disasters are perhaps less dangerous now and encounters with dangerous animals more rare, the threats to our economic security are almost infinitely more profound. A single human being now has the ability to harm hundreds, thousands, or even millions of people. And while civilization has developed these weapons of mass fear and destruction over the past century, we have not developed their antidotes.

Our fear of threats to our economic security has been magnified as the economy has become more complex. Those living a thousand generations ago had to protect their cache of food, shelter, and fire. They developed strategies to preserve this economic security so that they need not depend on others. Now, though, our economic security is tied up in an intricate web called the modern economy. And we must rely on the protection of our economic security from those we do not know and perhaps do not trust are concerned for our welfare.

This new fear of threats to our economic security has become heightened of late. The reasons "why" constitutes the balance of this book. We cannot underestimate either the importance of these threats or the anxiety they cause.

Our increasingly complex world also introduces a new fear that did not afflict us until now. Humankind has increasingly become aware of a growing fear of loss of control. As so much of what we do, produce, and save is subject to the stewardship or cooperation of others, we are left with a general anxiety that our own economic destiny is fast escaping us. This is one element that is an unavoidable consequence of a modern economy, society, and civilization. And the only antidotes to this fear are information, education, understanding, coordination, and cooperation.

A brave new world

Step back and imagine for a moment the uncertainties that riddle us now but did not exist just a century ago. We face risk by traveling in cars, airlines, and ships, undertaking elaborate medical procedures, and even in our dependence on a computer hard drive that might wipe out a year's work. Increasingly, a broadened scope of horror films offer us an opportunity to vicariously view the misery of those inflicted by airline, ship, or automobile disasters, and thereby make us feel somewhat safer in the comfort of our sofa or movie theater.

Whole industries also cater to alleviating us of our other technologically based fears. Companies will protect our data, protect our computer from viruses, and even insure our car for some of the losses of an automobile accident. All the while, computer hackers, identity thieves, and terrorists play against our fears, rational or not, to heighten our anxiety and extract from us whatever they seek in the process. While the lives lost to such terrors are comparatively small in number, their real goal is economic terrorism. Globally, we now consume hundreds of billions or perhaps more than a trillion dollars a year for protections from these new perceived threats.

The media too plays a role, as we shall describe in depth later. It brings these calamities into our living room each evening and creates an exaggerated sense of their probabilities. For instance, one of the deepest fears a parent can have is of harm befalling their children. Perhaps there is more deviancy in the world today that fuels such concerns. Certainly we are much more aware of almost every tragic incident in our narrow or broadest communities. And while our children may be safer than ever before, this perception that it could happen in any neighborhood may create an exaggerated estimate of its probability.

I recall when I grew up almost every family had a car, but few children were driven to school. Something has changed since then, with few children walking to school and so many parents hovering over their children to such an extent that the new term "helicopter parent" has been coined. While the calamities that could beset a child could not be significantly different, and in many cases may be significantly less, than just a generation or two ago, our belief in the frequency of such calamities was either dramatically suppressed then or significantly amplified now. It seems likely that the small world modern media has created explains some of this newfound anxiety today.

Too much information?

While I argue that education and information reduces the anxiety induced by an increasingly uncertain world, there are perhaps two unfortunate side effects of this increased education.

An increased level of awareness can inflict upon us a heightened sense of what could lurk around every corner. Certainly life in simpler times justified an ignorance that was blissful. While knowing all the things that could go wrong might allow one to dwell on every possibility to the point of emotional incapacitation, we must be able to translate this knowledge into wisdom. Just as the Serenity Prayer[4] guides us to differentiate between issues we can control and issues we cannot, we can use our experience and education to discern between those economic issues which we can positively affect the outcome and those which we cannot.

The last artifact of modern civilization is the fear of losing what we have worked a lifetime to accumulate. It is this latter threat to our economic security that has helped precipitate the current Global Financial Meltdown. Increasingly, our personal well-being is bound to our current possessions and savings, and our fears are bound around losing what we have worked so hard to create.

At one time, our economic security rested with the clothes on our back and the ability of our hands to produce. Some of our security was also wrapped up in the health and productivity of our offspring who could support us for those years in which we were no longer productive. Except for calamitous threats to our long-term health, if we had our hands and our land, we could always reacquire the clothes on our back.

As our economic well-being becomes more complex, the market for our services becomes more removed and specialized. And as the extended family is replaced by the nuclear family, or smaller yet, the basis for our economic security becomes more fragile. To recall the lyrics of Kris Kristofferson in the song

"Me and Bobby McGee": "Freedom is just another word for nothing left to lose." We rely on wealth accumulation to soothe our fear of economic entrapment. We then become fearful of any loss in our wealth, and we become less free to explore new opportunities. Even the fear of loss of health care makes some fearful of changing jobs. The trapping of our fear of loss of economic security is our loss of economic freedom.

This fear seems to pervade all of society in these perilous times. And, for this fear there seems to be few antidotes. Not even a good understanding of what brought us here or where we must go from now will soothe the pain brought on by this threat to our long-term economic security.

A rational response to threats

Ultimately, we must find the proper balance between healthy fear and pathological fear. Healthy fear is constructive. It offers us the proper perspective in making decisions that protect us. Unhealthy fear is destructive and often leads to either undue and debilitating anxiety or unproductive or exaggerated responses to threats.

Sometimes, though, there is a fine line between an appropriate and an exaggerated response, as we shall see later. We also find that there is a difference between an appropriate response for an individual and the optimal response for an entire economy or society. We shall see that individual and uncoordinated responses can collectively bring about a self-fulfilling prophecy and bring down an entire economy. It is in such times that strong leadership may be necessary to guide us down the safe path, despite our worst fears.

The need for economic leadership as an antidote to destructive fear will be a major theme of chapters to follow. Unfortunately, in the most perilous times we often find leadership is the most lacking. After all, if strong benevolent leadership existed in the first place, it would be less likely that dramatic economic perils, like the current Global Financial Meltdown, would befall us.

The five stages of economic grief

As so many now face our worst fears of economic loss, we find we go through an almost universal response process. This process can be summarized by Elizabeth Kübler-Ross's five stages of grief. In facing a traumatic event, we pass through denial, anger, and bargaining, followed by depression and acceptance.[5]

We follow this grief cycle even for our individual and collective economic losses. Consider the current Global Financial Meltdown brought about by the follies of greed and mismanagement. This event did not happen overnight, and indeed took a decade to brew. But for much of the grief cycle, we remained in blissful denial, afraid that any overt acknowledgment might bring an early end to our artificial economic buoyancy and security.

We even failed to listen to the prophets who warned us that the end of the financial house of cards was near. Economists such as Dean Baker of the Center for Economic and Policy Research, and recently deceased Provost Ed Gramlich of the University of Michigan and past member of the Federal Reserve Board of Governor, tried to warn us of the instability of our housing markets and the overly risky nature of new financial instruments du jour on Wall Street. Rather than heed their call, Federal Reserve Board Chairman Alan Greenspan kept the economic spigot open full tilt and interest rates artificially low, even though many economists expressed concern that returns were no longer related to economic risk.

We moved from denial to anger once we saw our economic future threatened. Some were angrier than others. Those on the verge of retirement had to reevaluate their strategy, while many of those in retirement faced ruin. We let our collective anger be known to the politicians, in part resulting in the earth-shaking election of the first African-American president of the United States. And we let our elected officials know that this financial calamity cannot be papered over with feel-good policies that do nothing or bailouts for those who got us into this mess in the first place.

This anger was soon transformed into bargaining. We harbored the belief that the inevitable recession would be short and shallow, circumvented by a small tax rebate or two. We went from bank bailouts to bailouts of major manufacturers. None of these actions provided that desperate quick fix, even though they collectively cost the global economy a few trillion dollars in investment and about twenty five trillion dollars in lost wealth. As our realization of the seriousness of the problem set in, our bargaining was quickly replaced by a depression and funk that brought the economy down still further.

By late 2008, as the initial extent of the Global Financial Meltdown became obvious, we found ourselves wavering between a collective depression and hope for our economic salvation. As with most depressions, the root of our trauma was duly and indelibly etched into our psyche, and we finally began to accept the economic reality.

It is in this final stage of grief, our process of acceptance, that fear gives way to resolve. We cannot put the economic genie back into the bottle, but we can roll up our sleeves and make the economy more productive and perhaps even more lean and efficient.

As with every productive trauma, we remember. We will hopefully stand vigilant to make sure there are processes in place to prevent this type of downturn from occurring again. And we become wary of false economic idols that provide us with artificial solace and security.

In the end, I am confident that this economic trauma and fear will accomplish something. It may well demonstrate our global resilience and foster a new spirit of global cooperation. And it will remind us that economic security flows not from mischievous games, but through hard work and production that is the foundation of all durable and sustainable economies.

This crisis points out the important psychological role of fear. Our fears should warn us of present danger, and guard us against circumstances that could bring harm to us in the future. Fear, and proper perspective, is an essential evolutionary tool that is as important today as it has ever been – and perhaps even more so.

Converging economic worlds

Unfortunately, if fear is the basic emotional response to threats to our security and well- being, then the world is fast becoming a more fearful place. The irony is that technological progress has for hundreds of years advanced the financial security of most of the First Economic World. This group, the main recipients of the fruits of technology flowing from the Industrial Revolution, has increased its wealth manyfold. At the same time, though, and for the same reasons, so much more of our own livelihood has passed beyond our individual control. The very tools of technology and markets that have harnessed the individual self-interest of millions of producers and consumers have also made each of us more dependent on a well-functioning market for our skills. And the wealth this creates from these millions of producers and workers alike is channeled into financial markets.

Our wealth has ultimately constrained our freedom and autonomy. The extreme specialization that has produced such wealth has also made us more dependent on each other. While a century ago we were rural and provided for much of our own food, cared for our extended families, and traded with our own community, few of the residents of the First Economic World have such self-sufficiency. We have grown absolutely dependent on the electricity and fuel that runs our homes, the gasoline that runs our cars, the employer that rents our skills, and the processors that make our food. Without any of these provisions from the free market, most of us in the First Economic World would be lost, many of those living in the rapidly developing Second Economic World would be inconvenienced, and the lives of the vast majority in the Third Economic World of sub-Saharan Africa would continue without a hiccup. Perhaps their disengagement from a rapidly changing world is indeed bliss.

This increase of wealth produced as our First Economic World and Second Economic World converge also creates more fear – of the unknown, of cultures converging, of shifts in wealth and ownership, and of change. There is more wealth to protect, more forces competing for our wealth and our jobs, and more disparate groups to demonize for an increasingly risky world. If risk is the unavoidable uncertainty that can harm us and affect our life, liberty, and pursuit of happiness, and if fear is that uncomfortable primitive discomfort we experience when our security is threatened, then we all live in increasing fear.

This fear is fueled by one additional reason. It is natural for us to fear the unknown. What we do not or cannot know creates a risk that we cannot easily mitigate. Through education, though, we can better understand and control the external factors that could do us harm, assess the risk of that which we cannot control, and incorporate our assessments into action. Through education, we reduce uncertainty, risk, and fear.

We must also separate our human fears of all sorts from the fear that threatens our economic security. We next define what we mean by the economic risk that gives rise to our fears.

2
An Economic Definition of Fear and Risk

Life is uncertain by its very nature. In many ways, it is becoming less and less certain all the time. Our economic life is amazingly more complicated than what it was just a century or even half a century ago. Each of these complications brings not only more that can go right but also more that can go wrong. With progress, our economic well-being has been most enhanced while our economic security is most diminished.

Humans, of course, are hardwired to create economic security. The need to amass surpluses for the harsh winter, or to preserve food and meat between the harvests or the hunts, meant that our very survival depended on our ability to maintain a relatively even flow of consumption over days, months, and, increasingly over years. Because any threat to our basic needs affects the security that Abraham Maslow, in his hierarchy of wants and needs, claims is the foundation of our well-being, we by our very nature strive to accumulate wealth, and from that the consumption necessary to thrive.

Also from the need to create economic certainty comes our abhorrence of risk. Even uncertainty that yields an equal probability of benefit or loss is considered a threat, as we shall see later.

Uncertainty and risk

Threats to our economic security can elicit a range of responses. If the threat is not so severe that it affects our fundamental economic security, we might meet the threat with mild annoyance or even amusement. If the threat can likely be met successfully with quick action, it might elicit from us some anger that motivates us to action. But if the threat is more fundamental, more difficult to overcome, more uncertain, or more elusive, we often meet it with fear, and sometimes panic.

Note that we are not talking here of upside uncertainty. Of course, we consider a random world that bestows upon us pleasant surprises as a bountiful and generous world, even if it is uncertain. Instead, we define risk as the uncertainty that can cause us damage and invokes fear for our economic or bodily security.

Nor are we describing the amusing fear conducted in a safe environment that we may actually enjoy. We are even willing to pay to be scared by horror films or on a fast roller coaster ride at the amusement park. Some consider themselves thrill seekers, enjoying their ability to control what would otherwise be fearful environments.

This points to an associated characteristic that differentiates uncertainty and fear. We are fearful when we are exposed to risk, defined as an uncertain outcome that deprives us of our economic security, combined with a lack of control of the outcome.

Fear implores us to assess the uncertainty, recognize the downside danger, and determine the probabilities of each. However, because fear often induces us to spring to some action, we may not always have time to fully access the dangers and then formulate a suitable response. Instead, our biology forces us to react to the risk, sometimes in a rational manner, but sometimes, too, in an irrational manner.

It is fear that can lead to an emotional response that is not adequately modeled in our economic understanding. And it is the nature of risk and fear in economics that is described in this book. We must begin by delving into the workings of financial markets and the role that fear, risk, and volatility play in their failure.

Part II

The Supply and Demand of Loanable Funds

In this part, I describe the workings of financial markets and the various entities that compete for investment funds. Those familiar with financial markets in general may wish to skip to Part III that describes the reasons why risk so profoundly affects our economic decision making.

I begin by describing the demand for loanable funds by consumers, producers, and government. I also describe the supply of loanable funds from those who are willing to save and postpone today's consumption for an increased consumption tomorrow. I end in Chapter 5 with a discussion on the balance of global capital and the effects of financial markets that are increasingly linked around the world. These links cause the exuberance or fear of one market to infect others, with booms and busts sometimes circling the world at literally the speed of light.

3
The Demand Side

Humans are by nature risk-averse. This is a simple consequence of the way we derive pleasure, and is well explained by economic theories that allow us to model human economic satisfaction and happiness.

Economics had until about 150 years ago been unable to model human satisfaction. The reasons for the initial failure of economic theories to model this most fundamental of human striving are a lesson in the limitations of a theory in general.

Economists have long understood what we all know – more of something that is good is a good thing, plainly enough. However, this conclusion is subtler than it might first appear.

Let's suspend our disbelief for a moment and assume that we could actually measure human satisfaction. Like us, economists too recognize that it may never be possible to actually measure satisfaction, and even if it were, would our scales of human satisfaction be comparable at all? Even if we could make these measurements, they would probably prove unhelpful.

Postulating that we could measure satisfaction does nonetheless provide for us some understanding of how humans make decisions. It also helps us understand how humans ought to process risk.

Let's first develop a scale of human satisfaction for each good, service, or interaction we enjoy. If these various economic activities are good, then having more of the activity should give us a higher level of satisfaction. In other words, if we graphed our level of satisfaction against the quantity q of consumption of the good, the graph would be upward sloping.

Economists traditionally label the horizontal axis the quantity axis that denotes the number of units of the good we enjoy. The vertical axis is labeled the utility scale, derived from the admittedly awkward term (utility) meant to be synonymous with satisfaction or happiness. The graph demonstrates that greater consumption of a good yields greater utility.

We might already be sensing a certain slipperiness in our economic concept of utility. Something can be good one moment and bad a while later. For

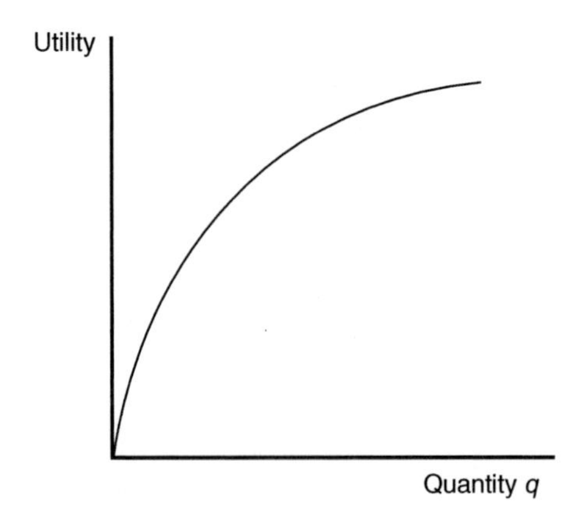

Figure 3.1 An Upward Sloping Utility Curve

instance, the first glass of wine over dinner may be very pleasant indeed. With too much consumption we can reach a point where the last glass could be bad rather than good. In other words, while more sometimes means better, at some point additional consumption makes us no better at all, and may even make us feel worse.

Consequently, the increase in our utility with additional consumption of a good is positive, but could become negative once the good becomes a bad. Beyond the peak in Figure 3.1, the good provides us with no further enjoyment and is no longer good. Because economists assume rationality, we, perhaps erroneously, assume that we would never consume till a point where a good becomes a bad.

Marginal utility

It turns out that our utility or satisfaction does not dictate our decisions. Instead, we are interested in the additional utility we get through our purchases. Economists label this increase in the utility for each additional unit of consumption as marginal utility. Marginal utility should be positive for each increment of a good and negative for each increment of a bad. Our total utility is simply the sum of our marginal or incremental utility from the first bit of consumption, plus the second, and so on.

Another artifact we would hope to capture from our utility curve is the notion that our first sip of lemonade on a thirsty day may be most satisfying, but with the subsequent sips our additional increment to utility or satisfaction diminishes. This very important observation constitutes the Law of Diminishing Marginal Utility.

When we accept that our utility of a good rises with each additional unit of consumption, but at an ever decreasing rate, we can draw an important conclusion, and at the same time resolve a paradox that confused philosophers for centuries. We can conclude that the utility curve starts off upward sloping and steep at first, and gradually flattens as it peaks out, much like climbing a hill that starts off steps. At the peak of the utility graph, we have obtained as much utility as possible. Any further consumption will actually decrease our utility and satisfaction. as the good is transformed into a bad.

The paradox of value

Let's see how this conclusion resolves a vexing paradox. The "paradox of value" explains why a diamond, though frivolous, gives us more satisfaction than a glass of water that is essential for human life. To understand this simple paradox, we observe that a diamond had better give us a big boost in satisfaction because we must sacrifice so much money in exchange for a diamond. This money could have been used to purchase other goods that would have given us much satisfaction. A diamond must then be equivalent to all that we had to sacrifice to purchase it. In other words, its marginal utility must be very high, and we will own and enjoy relatively few, commensurate with its high price.

However, water is cheap and plentiful. We have to sacrifice little more than a walk to the kitchen or water fountain to obtain a glass of water. We are unwilling to pay much for water, designer water being the exception. As a consequence, we consume water to the extent that we are no longer thirsty, and hence belittle the value of another glass of water.

Of course, if we were dehydrated and desperate for water, we would be willing to sacrifice all the diamonds in the world to quench the thirst. It is not that water is not valuable. Rather, the low value we place for water is for the last glass of water "at the margin," and not indicative of the total value this abundant good provides us.

We can now draw three very important conclusions. Satisfaction diminishes with every additional consumption of a good (diminishing marginal utility), we consume a good until the diminished marginal utility is proportional to its price, and high priced goods command high marginal utility (and hence low consumption), while low priced goods provide low marginal utility (and hence a high level of consumption). This final observation also allows us to draw the often invoked demand curve.

High prices result in low consumption (but high marginal utility), while low prices allow us to consume more until our marginal utility drops commensurate to the price paid. Graphically, this means that a demand curve, which graphs the price p of a good compared to its quantity q consumed, must slope downward.

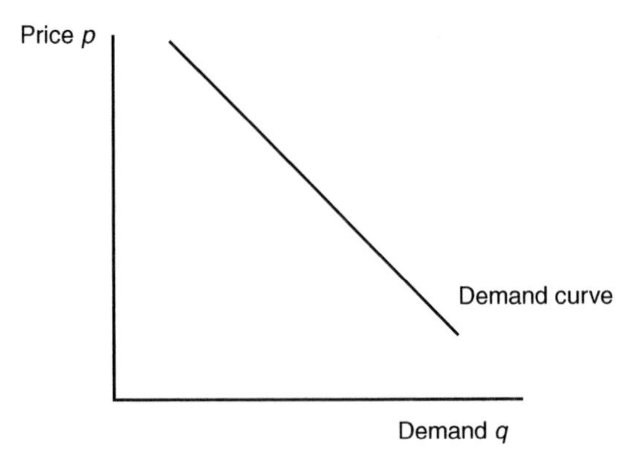

Figure 3.2 Demand Curve

Market demand

While each of us formulates our own individual demand curve based on our willingness to purchase various quantities of a good, depending on its price relative to its marginal utility, the market must aggregate these individual demand curves to come up with an overall market demand curve.

To see how this works, let us add up the demand for a favorite bottle of wine. One low-income pasta lover might be willing to buy ten such bottles of wine per year if the price is $10 per bottle, or five bottles of wine if each bottle costs $20. Someone who is wealthier or a wine lover might be willing to buy twenty such bottles at $10 each, or ten bottles per year at $20. The total demand from these two consumers is thirty bottles at $10 and fifteen bottles at $20.

Each additional demander moves the demand curve out further as the demand curve represents the horizontal sum of each individual demand at each price.

We can use this approach to model the demand for loanable funds. Borrowing money creates demand for consumption today, at the expense of an even greater reduction in consumption tomorrow. The sacrifice of even greater consumption tomorrow arises because we must pay interest for the right to borrow so we may shift consumption from tomorrow to today.

Individualized preferences for borrowing from our future

Why would we be willing to sacrifice tomorrow's consumption and wealth for todays'? There are a number of reasons.

Some goods may provide us with a flow of consumption, today and tomorrow. For instance, purchase of a house, a stock or bond, or, to a lesser extent, a car or a consumer durable like washing machine, provides a flow of services over time. The benefit that accrues on the purchase of a stock is the satisfaction

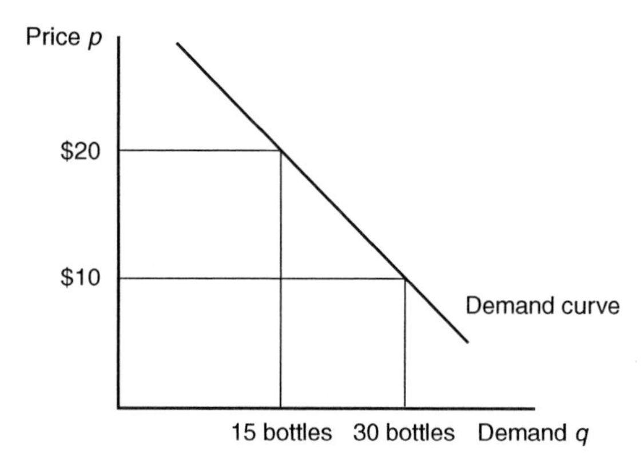

Figure 3.3 Aggregate Demand

of a capital gain and the security of storing and growing wealth, usually. A car or washing machine spreads its consumption benefits over years, justifying borrowing wealth from the future for the upfront cost today. A home provides us with long-term consumption but also acts as an investment because it is an asset that typically rises in value over time.

Just as individuals may differ in their preferred consumption of a good such as wine, many individual factors also influence our willingness to borrow from tomorrow to consume today. All must pay a premium, in the form of an interest rate, in even greater sacrificed consumption tomorrow if we borrow and spend today. For instance, if the interest rate is 10% for a one year loan, we must sacrifice the equivalent of $110 worth consumption tomorrow if we instead choose to consume today.

This may not be a bad trade-off for some. If we believe we will have a larger income in the future, we can afford more consumption tomorrow, but at a lower marginal utility because of our greater consumption. We may prefer to sacrifice some of this low utility consumption later for some highly valued consumption today. In other words, if we expect to have increasing wealth over our lifetime, we can smooth out our consumption by borrowing.

As another example, consider loans to pay for college. A student is willing to borrow today, knowing that the funds are invested in their own human capital. Our model would then predict that a younger person would be more willing to use student loans at a given interest rate. The students' ability to repay the loans will be based on the number of years they will take to pay the dividends in the form of higher earnings from the increased value of their human capital. We return to this concept in the next chapter and in chapters 6 and 8.

Our individual reasons to borrow and invest today and repay tomorrow give rise to our demand for loanable funds and for the existence of financial

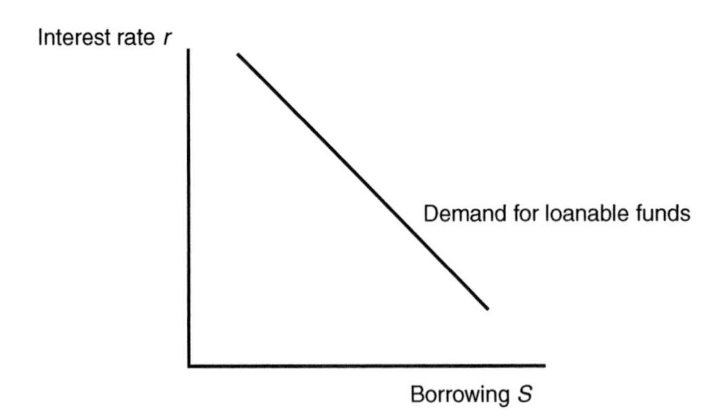

Figure 3.4 Demand for Loanable Funds

markets. Of course, higher interest rates mean fewer activities that can offer returns sufficient to cover the interest payments.

Just as with any demand curve, the demand for loanable funds is simply the horizontal sum of the amount each of us would be willing to borrow at each interest rate.

The graph of the demand for loanable funds is downward sloping, indicating greater demand for borrowing when interest rates fall. As this borrowing is based on our perceived ability to repay the loan, a number of factors affect this relationship. For instance, we can expect an increased willingness to borrow if we expect the assets we plan to purchase to appreciate. Students expecting growing salaries in their field of choice will be more inclined to borrow at a given interest rate.

Alternately, if we expect home values to increase at a more dramatic pace in the future, we would be more willing to borrow to buy now so we can better capitalize on its appreciation later. We may even want to borrow now if we expect an increase in the cost of future borrowing or in the cost of the goods we intend to purchase later.

Borrowing to produce

Adding to the demand for loanable funds are the capital needs of commerce. Production of goods and services requires investment in factories, supply and distribution chains, inventories, and retail outlets.

These investments in productive capacity are investments in the economists' sense, but not investments in the financial sense. While households usually refer to investment as putting money into financial markets for speculative purposes, economists reserve the term for spending used to expand the productive capacity of the economy, through new factories, equipment, homes, and the like.

Each such production activity can be ranked based on its investment needs and its expected returns. This comparison of interest rates to the efficiency of capital investments is sometimes labeled the Marginal Efficiency of Capital model. If expected returns exceed investment needs and the borrowing costs to cover interest payments, the activity is profitable. As interest rates increase, fewer activities are profitable, and fewer investments are made. As interest rates decline, more activities are profitable and the demand for loanable funds increases so that producers can take advantage of profitable opportunities.

Just as consumers demand fewer loans as the interest rate increases, so do producers. The sum of these two demands represents the domestic private demand for loanable funds from households and firms.

The budget deficit

There is one additional item that has commanded an increasing share of the demand for loanable funds. The funds required to fuel the budget deficit, mostly through the sale of Treasury bills, notes, and bonds, have become an increasingly important factor in the loanable funds market.

While we might assume that the government is as likely to save for a rainy day as spend during the rainy day, government has increasingly run a deficit of late. The U.S. government has become a perennial borrower. Actually, no American president has run a budget surplus in the past 80 years, as the following table demonstrates.

Presidencies and Federal Deficits

Year	Presidency	Average Surplus/Deficit as % of GDP
1929–1932	Hoover (R)	–1.3
1933–1945	Roosevelt (D)	–8.4
1945–1952	Truman (D)	–9.0
1953–1960	Eisenhower (R)	–0.5
1961–1963	Kennedy (D)	–0.9
1963–1968	Johnson (D)	–1.1
1969–1974	Nixon (R)	–0.9
1974–1976	Ford (R)	–3.8
1977–1980	Carter (D)	–2.6
1981–1988	Reagan (R)	–4.2
1989–1992	G.H.W. Bush (R)	–4.0
1993–2000	Clinton (D)	–0.8
2001–2008	G.W. Bush (R)	–5.0
2009–2012	Obama (D)	–9.0 est.

Note: D refers to Democratic Party and R refers to Republican Party. GDP refers to Gross Domestic Product.

The table above shows that the U.S. government and a good share of governments abroad have competed for loanable funds in the modern economic era.

The difference between public and private borrowing

There are a couple of significant differences between government borrowing and the process that determines the borrowing by households and firms. Government borrowing is not so strongly interest sensitive, and is instead driven by political considerations and by the gap between tax revenue and government spending.

Government typically raises money through taxation and borrowing. Their borrowing is done through fixed income securities, commonly called bonds. These bonds specify the amount that will be paid to the recipient upon maturity, and the fixed income payments they make, typically every six months, until they mature. Bonds issued by government differ from other bonds in that the debt they issue is considered almost completely risk free.

U.S. treasury bonds, defined as debt obligations lasting more than ten years, T-notes, of a duration between one and ten years, and the short-term T-bills of one year or less, are considered some of the safest debt obligations in the world. Treasury securities differ from other loans in that they are also considered very safe, with almost no default risk. Consequently, their interest rates at each moment often determine what we call the risk-free rate of return for the economy overall.

These instruments differ in their years to redemption (their maturity date) and their pattern of payment of a return to the lender. Short-term notes of one year or less do not have time to issue the traditional semiannual interest payment. Instead, they are "discounted" from face value. Instead of issuing coupons that permit the bearer to receive an interest payment every six months, they sell a note valued at $1,000 upon maturity for an amount less than $1,000. For instance, if I can pay $950 today for $1,000 a year from today, I am earning a return of $50 on a $950 investment, equivalent to a simple interest rate of $50 / $950 = 5.26%.

This same principle can be applied to any fixed income security issued by governments or businesses. At the time of issue, the underwriter must specify the bond's terms and provide the coupons that will be redeemed each period to provide the regular flow of fixed interest payments that the buyer seeks. This way the purchaser can calculate the effective interest rate this periodic income provides. If the predetermined payments are not competitive with other comparable fixed income securities, bidders will offer a price lower than the face value of the bond.

For instance, if the Treasury offers a 30-year bond with the face value of $1,000 and annual payments of $100, the effective interest payment is 10%. If the prevailing return on other comparable fixed income securities is 20%, the bond is worth approximately half of the face value. By bidding $500 for the $1,000 bond and the right to receive $100 payments each year, the purchaser receives an effective yield of 20%, competitive with other fixed income opportunities.

However, if the bond newly issued by the Treasury offers 10% annual payments when the going return on long-term bonds is only 5%, the new bond issue will be worth approximately twice its face value.

All bonds are priced to create an equivalency between its face value, its coupon payments, the length of time to maturity, and the going yield on similar fixed income securities. Corporate and other bonds depart from this formula based on the market's perception of risk for each bond, as we shall see later.

Fixed income volatility

While bonds are often viewed as stodgy and safe fixed income securities, they can actually be quite volatile. As debt instruments, they are more secure than stock, which only offers shareholders any remaining equity after debt is paid. But while fixed income securities provide a flow of interest payments (fixed income) until maturity, their value in trade fluctuates dramatically with their coupon interest rates, in comparison to prevailing market interest rates. These fluctuations are more pronounced, the greater the length to maturity because bond holders will either suffer of benefit from the interest rate gap longer.

As a consequence of the perceived safety of U.S. treasury issues, these fixed income instruments tend to segment the loanable funds market into two sectors: one seeking very low-risk investments, at a return sufficiently attractive to raise the necessary funds at each issue and another market offering a higher return but with commensurately more risk.

Ratings agencies to the rescue?

It would be costly for every investor to try to assess the risk of these fixed income assets. Rating agencies come to our rescue by researching the viability of projects and assessing a ranking for marketed debt ranging anywhere from AAA (triple-A) to junk status. U.S. treasury securities are considered safest, and are considered the gold standard worldwide.

Bonds issued by jurisdictions with the power to tax are also considered safe because government can always raise taxes to pay the bond. Revenue bonds are also considered quite safe because their annual payments and principal returns come from a dedicated flow of revenues from projects such as toll roads. As long as the governmental jurisdiction is sound, or the project remains viable, these bonds earn a high rating. This high rating allows the issuer to offer a lower interest rate commensurate with its lower risk.

More speculative corporate bonds are typically more risky. The longer the duration of the fixed income security, the more industry conditions can change, and the higher the interest rate the issuer will have to offer to raise the capital necessary. Worsening industry conditions or rising interest rates can also cause a precipitous drop in the value of such commercial paper that had previously been auctioned. The bonds of bankrupt companies may be rated junk status because they claim only a share of any liquidated corporate assets.

While ratings agencies will evaluate and reevaluate Treasury, municipal and revenue bonds, and commercial paper alike, the market constantly reevaluates the value of these instruments based on its perceptions of market conditions and prevailing interest rates.

Ratings agencies are crucial in the cost of borrowing. States that run budget deficits aspire for the highest triple-A ratings so that they can raise funds at the lowest possible interest rate. A worsening deficit or a drop in tax revenues can cost a state government billions of dollars. As bonds mature and must be reissued, though the total value of government debt changes more slowly, governments must constantly reissue bonds to replace maturing bonds. If a ratings agency downgrades a state because of its belief, the state will have a more difficult time repaying debt, and the cost of this ongoing borrowing can rise substantially.

Pricing of bonds

This fear of downgraded debt, and the associated increase in cost of their interest burdens, forces governments and corporations alike to do whatever they must to maintain their strong bond-rating. This includes raising taxes or revenues, reducing spending, or any such measures that might convince ratings agencies to preserve their bond ratings.

The value of existing bonds can fluctuate dramatically with changing market conditions and prevailing interest rates. The fear generated by the recent Global Financial Meltdown has even forced effective interest rates to be negative. During the recent Global Financial Meltdown, many have been so willing to let the government hold their money temporarily for safekeeping that they have been willing to pay more than $1,000 for the right to receive $1,000 on maturity of a note without any coupon payment. This is equivalent to a negative yield.

For instance, on December 8, 2008, the U.S. Treasury sold $30 billion of four-week Treasury bills yielding a zero interest rate. The next day, the value of these T-bills rose in secondary markets, pushing the yield negative. Treasury bills rose beyond face value because people were desperate to park any cash they withdrew from the market at someplace safer than under their mattress.

Meanwhile, the bottom fell out of the commercial paper market. Competing for funds with their Treasury bill counterparts, these issuances by corporations are short-term (270 days or less) unsecured debt obligations that sell at a discount, like Treasury bills. They are used for short-term needs of corporations such as meeting payrolls, financing inventories, and covering accounts receivables.

Unlike treasuries, the worsening Credit Crunch made it very difficult for corporations trying to raise short-term funds in the commercial paper market. Only after major intervention from the Federal Reserve and other central banks did commercial paper markets worldwide begin to move toward any sense of normalcy, albeit with an uncharacteristically high premium compared with their treasury counterparts.

We will return to the most important element of the demand for loanable funds later. As not all instruments are considered safe, we must figure out how to factor risk into the equation. We will then see how market fear can significantly distort the traditional trade-off between return and risk, as the last example demonstrated.

We have literally described only half the picture. We have described the demand for loanable funds, and we must now provide for the supply of loanable funds.

4
The Supply Side

On the supply side of loanable funds, we must identify the factors that differentiate lenders from borrowers. Contrary to borrowers, lenders are willing to sacrifice consumption today for even greater consumption tomorrow. They make this intertemporal exchange for a number of reasons.

Perhaps lenders believe they will have so less wealth in the future and want to provide a nest egg for their future. Or perhaps they believe the rate of return, commensurate with the risk, will yield much greater consumption tomorrow that it outswamps our natural preference for consumption today. In other words, if the rate of return we receive by lending exceeds the rate at which we discount the future, we would find lending, or financial investment, attractive. Compared to the market interest rate, this "discount rate," which differs for each individual and is called the rate of time preference by economists, segments the market between borrowers and lenders.

Not all can afford to lend, even if they would otherwise be willing to sacrifice consumption today for even greater consumption tomorrow. Some individuals or households are simply capital constrained. Lenders must either have cash to lend or some long-term illiquid assets such as homes that can be converted to liquid assets such as cash to lend. Actually, few of us have liquid assets that are not invested elsewhere.

Most of us, however, hold some of our wealth in the form of cash to take care of our most immediate spending needs. For instance, if we are paid once a month, we hold a portion of this income in the bank to cover the transactions we make over the month. In turn, banks can pool these short-term transaction funds and lend them out to create longer-term loans. They make a profit as long as they can generate a positive spread between what they can earn from borrowers, net of default costs, and the rate they must pay to entice deposits from us.

By pooling these deposits and averaging them over the month, banks can create a steady and predictable supply of capital for loans. While the dynamics of determining lending and deposit rates are under the control of individual banks, prevailing market forces and competition tend to limit the rate at which they can lend, and thus constrain the rate they can profitably offer to depositors.

Money creation

Banks can also create money, and in turn create additional deposits and lending. It is this essential role banks play in creating the deposits, credit, lending, and spending that causes the economic system to hinge so precariously on the health of the banking industry.

To see this relationship, we must understand the role and regulation of commercial banks. I distinguish these from investment banks, which is described later. I will focus for now on the U.S. banking industry, though all banking systems worldwide function along similar lines.

To recall, a commercial bank can pool its deposits, knowing that deposits and withdrawals are spaced relatively evenly across the month. This means that it can rely on an average balance from each of its customers that is about halfway between a customer's high and low monthly balances. Banks realize that this deposit base is relatively constant and allows them to safely predict how much it can lend without using all of the bank's cash. This allows banks to create long-term loans from its short-term cash deposits.

It gets better for the banks than just that though. When a bank makes a loan, it typically does not simply handover a stack of cash. Instead, it deposits the loan to a customer's bank account, thereby increasing its deposits, at least for the moment, by the amount of the loan. It is true that the customer may then write a check on this new deposit, but that check is bound to be deposited at some other bank, thereby eventually creating a new deposit somewhere in the banking industry, and also creating an opportunity for a new set of loans.

Monetary authorities like the Treasury, a nation's central bank or bourse, or the Central Bank of the United States, the Federal Reserve, count these checking account deposits just like cash in their tally of a nation's money supply. Cash, checking account deposits, and such items as traveler's checks all can be readily converted to spending and all sum to the most liquid measure of our money supply, labeled M1. Much of the monetary measure M1 is actually created by banks in loans that flow into checking accounts.

Money supply gone wild

If gone unchecked, a bank could continue to create more and more money with each loan it makes. However, such rampant creation of loans, new deposits, and money would be dangerous on two reasons. First, just as there can be too much oil sloshing around in an engine, there can be such a thing as too much money floating around in the economic system. We see later that a great number of market panics were precipitated by either too little or too much money in economies, especially in the days before the creation of centralized monetary authorities.

Second, too many deposits on paper without sufficient backing of cash would be dangerous if customers all of a sudden demanded cash for their bank balances. We shall see, too, that these overextensions of banks, before the days of banking regulation, have invoked anxiety and fear on the part of banking customers and also instigated crashes of the banking and financial system.

Such bank runs, when many customers simultaneously try to cash out their bank accounts, can destroy a banking system. Such a run on the bank was illustrated most graphically in the memorable scene from Frank Capra's movie *It's a Wonderful Life* as savers clamored to withdraw their funds upon hearing their bank was under investigation.

If banks were required to keep all their deposits in cash, they could not make loans. And if banks were required to keep none of their deposits in cash, they would not be able to cover the needs of the occasional customer who wants to cash out his/her account. The first scenario means no profits for banks from lending activities; and the second scenario means no safety or convenience for customers who feel the need to cash out their account.

Deposit insurance and required reserves

The issue of deposit safety is relatively unimportant, now that bank deposits are insured as a consequence of reforms instituted following the banking crises of the Great Depression. For instance, in the United States, all deposits at commercial banks were insured up to $100,000 until recently. This insurance, provided by the Federal Deposit Insurance Corporation, was upped to $250,000 per account to prevent bank runs arising from the Credit Crunch of 2007 and the Global Financial Meltdown that followed.

If bank deposit safety is not an issue because of deposit insurance, certainly banks and regulators must find some sort of a happy balance between keeping all their deposits in cash and keeping almost all their deposits in the form of loans. This balance between two worthwhile goals created what is now known as the fractional deposit system. Banks are required to keep only some fraction of their deposits in the form of cash, and can lend out the rest, thereby creating more money in the form of new deposits somewhere in the banking system.

For example, let's see what would happen if banks were required to keep only 10% of their deposits in cash, and were permitted to lend out the remaining 90%.

A new customer comes along with $1,000 to deposit. An entry is made in the customer's account that $1,000 is held by the bank, which the customer could use to write checks. If the bank is required to hold 10% of this deposit in cash, it leaves $100 that can meet its cash requirement, and frees another $900 for the bank to use to make a loan. This $900 loan will also result in a new deposit somewhere, requiring a bank to hold an additional $90 in cash, and leaving a further $810 to lend out. This $810 again comes to the banking system as a new deposit somewhere, requiring the bank to set aside another $81 in cash, and leaving another $729 to lend out, and so on.

You can bring a horse to water...

As we can see, only after three rounds of deposits and lending, the bank has set aside $100 + $90 + $81 in cash, and has a total of $1,000 + $900 + $810 in deposits. This will continue, with each round getting slightly smaller, until in the end there is exactly $1,000 of cash supporting $10,000 of deposits, all flowing from the original $1,000 cash deposit. In a fractional banking system that is required to keep 10% of its deposits as cash, total deposits can eventually reach ten times (or 1 divided by 10%) the amount of cash in the system. This cash is actually held "in reserve" to maintain sufficient liquidity and confidence in the banking system. And the bank is able to lend out nine times the initial cash deposit.

This fraction, 10% in our current example, is called the reserve ratio (RR). The reciprocal of the reserve ratio 1/RR then gives the multiple of deposits that can ultimately be created through lending. The ratio 1/RR (in this case, 10) is called the deposit expansion multiplier, because it provides the theoretical upper limit of deposits that can be created as a multiple of cash held by the bank in reserves.

Another way to view this is that the banks can highly lever its loans arising from deposits at a rate of ten to one, if it wants to do so. I will describe a little later the reasons why it might not always want to be so highly levered. Suffice to say for now, that the fractional banking system is essential for bank profitability and loan creation. And too much leverage creates significant risk and makes much more likely panics and runs on the bank.

Banks will, of course, have to pay some interest on some of its bank deposits. However, it is also able to collect interest on many more loans than it would have been permitted to had fractional banking been prohibited. This is good for banks, but it is also good in expanding the supply of loanable funds that allow consumers to borrow to invest in homes, education, and cars; and corporations to invest in new plants, inventories, and supply chains. The fractional banking system and the role of banks are essential for spending and for investment throughout the economy.

While individual banks play an important part in the expansion of lending and credit in the economy, central banks also play an important role. On the regulatory side, the Federal Reserve, and their Central Bank counterparts worldwide, must monitor these commercial banks and the industry to ensure they protect the deposits of bank customers and prevent commercial banks from extending more loans than they should, based on the fraction of all loans that must be backed by cash. Central banks can also encourage more loans by injecting cash into the banking system.

... but you can't make it drink

It is this latter role, of injecting cash into the banking system to permit banks to extend a multiple of this cash in new credit, that has played a notorious role in the Global Financial Meltdown. If banks are fully loaned out, based on their mandatory cash reserves, further injections of cash to banks may allow for the creation of additional loans and credit. This, of course, permits banks to want to lend further.

These injections serve no such helpful purpose if the commercial banks have not fully used their existing cash reserves and capacity to lend. This caveat is central to the effectiveness of such central bank injections that have been so notorious in the recent global spate of bank bailouts.

Federal control over the money supply

The fractional banking system also affords government, through their monetary authorities, the opportunity to encourage lending if necessary. We will look at the reasons why central banks and treasuries may want to do this later. It is worthwhile first to discuss some of the precise mechanisms central banks can use to inject cash to encourage additional credit and lending.

Of course, the most obvious way the treasury can encourage lending is to directly lend cash to banks. While most immediate and direct, central banks can be subtler than that.

Let's assume the Fed wanted to increase banks' cash reserves by a million dollars, hoping to expand lending by a multiple of ten, or ten million dollars. The Fed could simply buy from banks some long-term assets. Perhaps these assets could be loan portfolios, if the Fed wanted to go into the business of servicing and ultimately collecting on loans. Or the Fed could buy buildings and property from banks. Either of these purchases would be complicated though, and would leave the Fed in a position of managing such illiquid assets. The Fed would rather purchase other assets that are easier to maintain.

The Fed could also have the banks issue some new shares which the Fed could purchase. This would give the banks cash and the Fed an ownership share in banks. While the Fed's motivation might be primarily to help expand the supply of loanable funds, the receipt of marketable securities in return may serve some purpose, at times. As the Fed is typically reticent to get into the business of investing in bank stocks, this approach would be employed in only the most desperate of circumstances.

We recently confronted such desperate times when the Congress passed the Troubled Asset Relief Program (TARP) in the United States and its inspiration, a similar program first proposed by Prime Minister Gordon Brown in the United Kingdom. By giving cash to banks in return for equity stakes in the banks, the Fed could, if willing, exert pressure on banks to pursue policies in the public interest. To do so, it required a violation of the principle of separation of banks and state, and transformed the potential for TARP to unfreeze credit markets into an ineffective bailout of banks, at least in the U.S. experience.

This policy had never been employed in recent U.S. economic history, and its anemic effectiveness this time around will probably prevent it from being implemented again in the future.

Daily monetary interventions

The Fed regularly employs Open Market Operations (OMO) to adjust banks' cash reserves. In this method, the Fed buys up Treasury bonds, notes, or bills in securities markets. By doing so, the Fed receives a safe and easily marketable government security, and the seller of the security gets a check from the Fed. When the seller deposits the check, the Fed moves some cash from its pile to the customer's bank's pile that it maintains at its regional branch of the Federal Reserve Bank. This infusion of cash then permits banks to further extend credit, if they wish.

When the banking system is running smoothly, the Fed employs this process daily or weekly to tinker with the level of cash reserves at banks and their ability to extend credit. If the Fed believes there is too much credit, it can even reverse this process by selling Treasury securities to banks' customers, thereby removing cash reserves from banks and forcing those banks fully lent out to call in some of their credit and loans.

Other tools

Of course, the Fed could tinker with the amount of credit that banks can create by adjusting the reserve ratio directly. This reserve ratio is currently approximately 10% of bank liabilities, and has remained at that level for decades. Changing the reserve ratio is confusing and complicated for regulators and banks alike, which partly explains why it is almost never adjusted.

The central bank could also directly lend cash to banks to augment bank reserves, or call in such short-term loans to contract reserves and force banks to cut back on lending. It is this process, of lending loans through the Federal Reserve discount window, that the Fed uses as necessary.

In response to the Credit Crunch of 2007, the Fed employed a number of these tools. By lowering the discount rate, the Fed offered banks loans to augment its cash reserves at very favorable interest rates. This only works, though, if the banks are willing to borrow.

Finally, the Fed can go on a government security buying binge to inject money into a banking system that needs inducements to lend. At the same time though, fear by individual investors and institutional investors alike forced trillions of dollars of former market investment onto the sidelines.

Their most common place to park cash is to purchase U.S. government securities. Treasury security purchases by the central bank and investors alike caused a bidding war on bonds, forcing up their price beyond the par value of even recently issued bonds. Such a negative interest rate is not only possible, but is becoming increasingly probable in the future.

A negative yield on bonds?

If we recently bought a $1,000 bond paying 5% interest each year for 20 years until its final $1,000 face value payout, this $1,000 bond would continue to be worth $1,000 as long as the 5% interest rate is consistent with the interest offered in other equally safe investments. Imagine if we desperately wanted to buy that bond because we were afraid to invest our wealth elsewhere, we were not confident about the safety of banks, and we had to park more money than the $250,000 limit a bank can insure. We may be willing to pay more for that $1,000 bond than its face value. As the price of an existing bond is bid up in the bond auctions, its effective interest rate falls.

These were instances in which the effective interest rate on some government securities fell to zero or lower as desperate investors fled stock markets. The Fed, traditionally a big purchaser of government securities, may not find the purchase of occasionally overpriced government securities an attractive method to prop up bank reserves. While the Fed's primary goal is to inject cash into the banking industry, it would prefer to do so by buying assets that are destined to drop in value should the bailout succeed.

For instance, in late 2008, the Fed had to shy away from its traditional method of open market operations as a consequence of the flood of funds that were already flowing into the government securities market. This left the Fed with little recourse but to buy preferred stock of sound banks directly through its troubled "Troubled Asset Relief Program," discussed in detail later.

The Fed, of course, hoped at the time that these mechanisms, loans through the discount window, open market operations, or direct purchases of bank stocks, would succeed in injecting cash into the banking system that would find its way into new loans and renewed credit. Certainly, there would not be any new credit if the Fed did not provide this new cash. However, the converse is not necessarily true. The Fed can inject new cash that does not result in new credit if banks refuse to expand lending and credit. While we can't win if we don't play, playing usually does not imply winning.

This was the perplexing and distressing dilemma of the bank bailout in 2008, and in many earlier similar bailouts, as we shall see in later chapters.

Other financial instruments for savings and investment

So far, I described the supply and the demand for loanable funds. These funds are typically used to build factories, construct new homes, buy new cars, or borrow student loans. Economists label borrowing for such expansions in our capacity to produce, to create new housing services, to create new transportation alternatives, or to provide expanded human capital. We can add to that the borrowing to cover government budget deficits.

Most people would consider investment more broadly than this narrow definition. While investment in the economic sense is limited to spending that expands our collective productive capacity, the term investment is used to describe a gamut of financial opportunities. Indeed, most would consider the purchases of stock, options or futures, bonds, swaps, or other such instruments as investment.

On a flow basis, the level of investment in new forms of physical capital such as factories and new homes is small compared to the actual investment in stock and other markets. The individual stocks on stock markets turn over many times in a year. For instance, the NASDAQ exchange was valued at $4.014 trillion at the end of 2007, but tallied trades worth $15.32 trillion the same year. Shares auctioned worlwide each day total about $4 trillion daily in a global financial market worth almost $60 trillion.

Similarly, flows through global markets in 2007 alone totaled over $100 trillion in 2007, about three times the total value of the stocks on these exchanges, and almost twice the approximately $60 trillion of global world production in the same year.[6] The average stock can be bought and sold between four and fifteen times in a given year. Trading is much more prevalent than the financial capitalization and investment that gave rise to financial markets in the first place.

These subsequent trades of existing stocks are not typically considered investment in the economic sense, because they may not actually expand the productive capacity of the economy. The reason is that the purchase of an existing stock is merely the exchange of a certificate from a buyer to a seller. Exchange of existing financial instruments does not directly result in the creation of new plants or factories.

The value of stocks can nonetheless indirectly translate into additional investment. Firms may retain some of their own shares, allowing the liquid assets of the firm to rise as its stock price rises. Bankers and bond rating agencies also look at the value of a company, as capitalized by the stock market, as a comparison to the health of the enterprise. A company is able to lend based on the level of its market valuation. As the stock price and market capitalization rise, companies are afforded easier and cheaper access to borrowed capital.

Finally, a company can issue additional shares at higher stock prices, thereby diluting the value of shares in the hands of the existing shareholders, but increasing the retained assets of the company. The capital so raised is an asset for the company, and it can then be employed to increase revenue and profits, and hopefully increase the value to shareholders.

It has been shown that, under certain restrictive conditions, such raising of investment capital by issuing new shares is financially equivalent to raising capital by issuing debt. Franco Modigliani, Nobel Memorial Prize in Economics winner in 1985, and Merton Miller, Nobel Memorial Prize in Economics winner in 1990, demonstrated that firms are indifferent to debt or equity financing of new projects under certain conditions when problems such as of adverse selection (described later) do not exist, and markets are working well.[7]

Is financial investment more than gambling?

If the simple exchange of shares in the absence of such new issues are not considered investments in the economic sense, does trading nonetheless serve any function but for the store of value and opportunity for capital gains? In other words, does the stock and securities market serve any purpose beyond gambling with others whether the market will go up or go down?

We should take a moment to note first that stock ownership in an incorporated company creates a right to profits but not an obligation to cover excessive liabilities. Stockholders share the right to a corporation's equity, defined as the difference between its assets and liabilities. The price of a stock is a market valuation of the value of a company's current and future equity. If a company has liabilities that exceed assets, it is insolvent and can petition or be placed into bankruptcy. Only after other creditors are fully satisfied will shareholders have the right to any remaining assets. However, nor are shareholders of a limited corporation required to make up any deficit of liabilities over assets.

Stockholders bid at auction for this right to a share of a corporation's equity. These auctions buy and sell shares worldwide valued at about $4 trillion daily, as reported by the World Federation of Exchanges representing a total market capitalization of $57.5 trillion before the Global Financial Meltdown of 2008.[8] However, almost none of the stocks auctioned is new issues. Instead, the same stocks are bought and sold, again and again, upwards of twenty times on average, in recent years.

To recall, it is the new issue of stock used to build plants, purchase equipment, or otherwise build up production capacity that economists define as investment. The marketability of such new issues depends critically on the continued marketability of these shares post-issue. The ability to exchange stocks also allows the best match between an individual's preference for risk versus return, as we shall see in a later chapter.

It is true that an individual could still privately sell shares of a company that is not publicly traded. However, such exchanges face significant transaction costs. These costs, in trying to assess the value of the shares, in matching a willing buyer and a willing seller, in preparing the contractual and legal documents associated with the exchange, and in exchanging the cash for shares, add a significant and costly burden to private stock exchanges.

These significant transaction costs inhibit their exchange and make stock much more costly to convert to cash, or vice versa. Significant transaction costs also drain capital from the market and discourage capital formation for investment in the economic sense.

The global bond market is of similar net worth, representing approximately $45 trillion U.S. in 2004.[9] Overall, market capitalization and corporate debt are of similar scales. Just as new issues of stocks allow firms to raise funds to embark on new projects, the sale of new bonds allows firms to borrow at market-determined rates. And just as markets assure buyers of stocks to easily sell these stocks if they require liquidity, bond markets permit bond buyers similar liquidity. While only the initial stock or bond issue raises funds directly for a firm to expand, the existence of subsequent markets lowers the transaction costs and the long-term risk to investors or lenders concerned about liquidity.

These markets also create avenues to price the risk of firms and hence create informational transparency. With many current and potential investors sharing a vested interest in the accurate reflection of the firm's health on its asset price, these thousand eyes on the firm help maintain a certain corporate discipline.

Derivatives – speculation everywhere and on everything

Financial markets have also created instruments that derive their value from the value and movements of stocks, bonds, other debt instruments, foreign exchange, and commodities such as corn, pork bellies, oil, and coffee. While these markets for assets that derive their value from other more fundamental assets have been an essential way to reduce risk, the derivatives market has been transformed of late into a tail wagging the dog. These markets are often little more than forums for legalized investment house gambling, with a level of activity thousands of times higher than that justified by the legitimate need to more efficiently match buyers and sellers of the underlying instruments.

The commodities market was originally designed to permit producers and consumers alike to lock in prices for the future delivery of farm products, minerals, and other commodities. A farmer might sell a contract for a thousand bushels of corn, and a food processor might bid on the contract to gain a reliable future supply. As both buyers and sellers are risk-averse and abhor uncertainty, this transaction works well for both parties.

Another important commodity is money. Importers and exporters need to obtain foreign currencies to conduct international trade. And those who want to invest in foreign stock or bond markets must also obtain foreign currencies. This would suggest that some portion of international trade in goods and services and in foreign investment would spur the exchange of foreign currencies. However, the foreign exchange required to trade goods, services, stocks, and bonds worldwide pale in comparison to the approximately $10 trillion in foreign exchange and its derivates traded on a typical day, as indicated by the Triennial Central Bank Survey.[10]

Other derivatives markets have been growing fantastically over the past decade. Commodities markets are no longer used primarily to provide certainty to farmers and processors hoping to lock in future prices. Speculation of investors who never intend to deliver or take delivery of the traded commodities now dwarf the legitimate needs of those who depend on the underlying commodities. Indeed, the trading of these so-called derivatives now dwarfs stock and bond markets combined. And they have been responsible for plunging global markets, from oil to corn, credit default swaps to bond and stock futures, into disarray and fear.

The level of trading in these derivatives markets has skyrocketed. The notional value of the instruments they bet against have risen from $220 trillion in 2004 to over $516 trillion at the end of June 2007. On an average day in April of 2007, shortly before the Global Credit Crunch hit in the summer of 2007, $3.2 trillion in foreign exchange derivatives, $4.2 trillion of over-the-counter derivatives, and another $6.2 trillion of interest rate and currency instruments were traded. It is almost mind-boggling that these trades, in excess of $13 trillion *each day*, are of a size comparable to the entire *annual* U.S. economy.

These derivatives rarely require the buyers and sellers to even own the underlying instruments. For instance, credit default swaps are essentially bets on whether a given credit instrument, such as a mortgage-backed security, will default. The world credit default swaps market was reported recently by the *Wall Street Journal* to be worth $65 trillion U.S., similar to the size of all the world's stock markets. These swaps are simply bets on whether a given credit instrument would default. Just as we can bet on a horse without owning it, we can also bet on the financial products owned by others. These swaps can represent a huge multiple of the actual credit from which these markets are derived.

The unreal economy

While we see that stock and bond markets help fund the real economy, defined as the production of goods and services, derivative instruments bear little relationship to the real economy. These instruments essentially act as bets on movements of real financial instruments. Some argue that these derivatives enhance market information by providing a forum to bet on the future value of stocks, bonds, or other instruments related to the real economy. If we accept some truth in this proposition, the theoretical benefits must be weighed against the risks such large-scale betting can impose on the economy.

We discovered from the Credit Crisis of 2007 that the scale of betting on derivatives markets is immense. Derivatives markets now dwarf the activity of the market for underlying securities, and dwarf the economic benefits that may be arguably derived from derivatives markets.

At best, the component of derivatives trading that does not contribute to additional economic production is simply a constant sum game, much like the game of poker. Winners gain as much as losers sacrifice. Unfortunately, creating an industry out of a constant sum game, and directing trillions of dollars of capital a day into such markets, simply throws good money after useless enterprise and diverts badly needed capital from more useful enterprises.

At worst, the large sums involved in such derivatives markets can actually be destabilizing, as evidenced by recent accusations that speculators have unnecessarily driven up oil prices to record and unjustifiable levels. This run up in oil prices raised inflation, significantly complicated the Federal Reserve's response to the looming Global Financial Meltdown, and may even have led to the fear and loathing in commodities markets, and in turn, in all markets.

There is another market we must consider that has also grown dramatically in recent decades. We find now that the financial markets are increasingly influenced by the twin deficits of foreign trade and federal spending.

5
Balance of Capital

International flows of capital have increased dramatically in recent years. This dramatic expansion of international trade in securities is a verification of globalization. It also creates a new investment landscape that has created both greater liquidity and some substantial new risks.

Net foreign purchases of stocks and bonds originating in the United States did not surpass the $100 billion mark until 1993. In 14 short years, it has increased ten times, peaking at almost a trillion dollars in 2007. This dramatic growth has added liquidity to U.S. markets and has strengthened conversion of foreign currencies to U.S. dollars. As a consequence of this demand for U.S. dollars, the currency has remained artificially strong.

One important source of these purchases of U.S. assets each year is the perception that U.S. markets are efficient and mature, and U.S. stocks and bonds are relatively safe. A second more problematic reason is the imbalance of trade with the United States and its trading partners.

U.S. financial markets have been the model of efficient markets worldwide. The Dow Jones Industrial Average continues to be regarded as the most recognizable measure of global financial health. While other markets rival the New York Stock Exchange in maturity and efficiency, and other measures, such as the Wilshire 5000 or even the Wilshire Global Total Market index, are more diversified and inclusive, the DJIA remains the gold standard of indices.

The Dow Jones Industrial Average has been recorded and in common use longer than any other index. Founded by *Wall Street Journal* editor Charles Dow, it was originally meant to represent the value of the 30 major manufacturers in the United States. It began with just 12 stocks in 1896, with only one of these stocks, General Electric, still surviving in its original form. As a consequence, the index needed to expand and adjust to maintain some semblance of consistency over its 113-year history.

Today the index contains 30 stocks, almost half of which are not manufacturers, and nearly a third from companies primarily in sectors that did not even exist when the index was formed. Despite the inaccuracy of its legacy name, the Dow Jones Industrial Average remains the most recognizable index calculated on the New York Stock Exchange of 11 Wall Street in New York City.

While Wall Street is regarded as the epicenter of global finances and of the recent Global Financial Meltdown, exchanges around the world now compete for trade in securities. Nonetheless, in an industry where reputation is an important component of the stock and trade, Wall Street finances and U.S. securities still retain the reputation as the world's most desirable and reliable.

Oil dollars

Until the 1970s, a modest share of the world's wealth found its way into New York financial markets, with U.S. companies representing the lion's share of worldwide market capitalization. However, with the formation of the Organization of Petroleum Exporting Countries (OPEC) in 1960, and its assertion of market power in 1973, huge amounts of wealth were diverted from the United States to the oil producing countries. A portion of this wealth was spent in these oil exporting countries. However, the bulk of the wealth found its way to London financial markets and back to the United States through the New York financial markets that could offer it the best return with low risk.

The United States was, and still is, the single largest importer of oil, by far. Rather than converting the U.S. dollars to oil exporter currencies, the sale of this commodity was denominated in U.S. dollars, which were then reinvested in U.S. financial markets. Those dollars not directed to the United States that found their way to London constituted U.S. dollars in Europe, or Eurodollars. Either way, the international wealth denominated in U.S. dollars reaffirmed the U.S. dollar as the international currency and U.S. markets as the world's preeminent financial forum.

The growth of the BRIC nations of Brazil, Russia, India, and China has renewed global demand for commodities, including oil, and has recently created even greater global wealth outside of the United States. The desire for wealth holders in these nations to invest in U.S. stocks, and in U.S. government securities still considered the safest in the world, has fueled continued investment flows into U.S. securities. It remains an open question, though, whether this pattern of repatriation of U.S. wealth will continue as convergence progresses.

A consumption nation

Another factor that has fueled the growing demand for U.S. financial capital is the U.S. penchant for consumption. The United States is the world's largest economy, representing almost a quarter of the world's gross domestic product.

Consumers in the United States represent 70% of the nation's spending and fuel almost 20% of global demand alone. Adding to this, U.S. spending abroad is the increasing tendency to outsource U.S. jobs to lower cost producers, most notably in China and India. Developing countries have grown to depend on the spending of U.S. consumers and manufacturers. As a consequence, when U.S. consumers and industry sneeze, the world catches a cold.

While it may seem that global markets that trade in goods and services remain distinct from the global trade in financial instruments, there is a very important link between the two. The dramatic increase of imports to the United States over exports from the United States also directs huge amounts of U.S. dollars abroad. And these dollars have to go somewhere.

U.S. trade in goods and services remained essentially balanced until the mid-1990s. With imports and exports at that time approaching $800 billion per year, the number of U.S. dollars used to purchase global goods and services was returned in the form of other country's purchases of U.S. goods. But when the United States begins to run up significant international trade deficits, these excess dollars from imports that exceed exports must have someplace to go. Either they pile up in foreign banks, are used to purchase U.S. goods and services in return, or are reinvested in U.S. financial markets. If there is not much produced in the U.S. that foreign countries want to buy or can afford, these dollars are repatriated in the form of investments in U.S. financial markets, through purchases of U.S. treasury securities, mortgages, stocks, and the like.

Since the mid 1990s, though, exports have approximately doubled while imports have tripled, as the graph in Figure 5.1 shows.

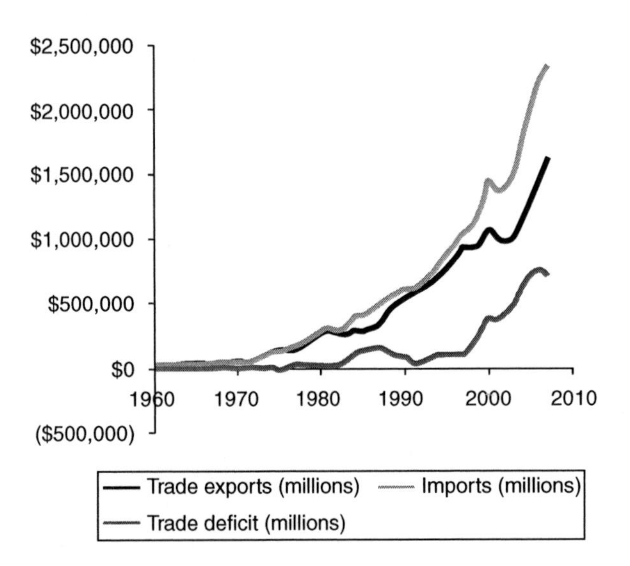

Figure 5.1 U.S. Imports, Exports, and the Trade Deficit 1960–2007 (millions)

The trade deficit began to accelerate rapidly over the past decade, surpassing $750 billion in 2006. This rapid expansion of the trade deficit tracks the increase in commodity prices over the last decade, just as emerging countries demand the commodities that fuel their development.

At the same time, the wealth created in these countries and the increased globalization of international financial markets also rose. Usually an increase in commodity prices for those goods the U.S. must import, and the resulting growing trade deficit, would mean more U.S. dollars going abroad than returning to purchase its exports. This would weaken the U.S. dollar, making U.S. imports more expensive, and its exports more attractive to countries with strengthening currencies. This weakening of the U.S. dollar would eventually reestablish balanced trade.

This traditional response of the U.S. dollar to a worsening U.S. trade deficit is no longer valid once financial investment goes global.

The twin deficits

The trade deficit should typically weaken a currency. However, the U.S. dollar did not weaken sufficiently under the weight of perennial trade deficits. Instead, the wealth abroad found its way back to the United States in the form of net purchases of U.S. securities. The trade deficit peaked at $759 billion in 2006, the same year in which net foreign purchases of U.S. securities peaked at just shy of a trillion dollars, at $987 billion in 2006. All those dollars drained by the trade deficit were returning in the form of purchases of U.S. securities.

The excess demand for U.S. dollars returning for net securities purchases over those leaving because of the trade deficit is explained in a couple of ways. First, U.S. dollars also leave in the form of profits to foreign firms operating in the United States. Second, central banks were stocking up on U.S. reserves. The net increase in demand for U.S. dollars since 2006 has also led to a strengthening of the U.S. dollar on world markets.

Part of the reason why foreign nationals, institutions, governments, and central banks remained interested in buying U.S. dollars is because of the perception of a safe and robust U.S. market for stocks and bonds. In addition, the U.S. offered sufficiently attractive terms to purchasers of U.S. treasury bonds in an effort to ensure sale of bonds to fuel the quickly mounting U.S. federal deficit.

China flexes its financial muscle

One country in particular was willing to support the accelerating U.S. debt and treasury bond issues for its own reasons. In 2007 alone, the United States ran a record trade deficit with China of $256 billion. These dollars were largely reinvested in U.S. debt to maintain a strong U.S. dollar and to earn a return on China's stockpile of excess U.S. dollars. Both of these effects are in China's interest. It must maintain a strong U.S. market so that it retains a healthy market for its exports.

Recently, though, China has begun to slowdown the reinvestment of their trade surplus with the United States.[11] They have a worsening domestic economy that requires investment to fill the gap as worldwide demand plunges.

Were China to become less willing to repatriate much of this dollar surplus, the U.S. dollar would weaken, and China's Remimbi would strengthen. The combination of these effects would reduce China's worldwide exports and hamper its growth. China was more than willing to become the largest foreign purchaser of U.S. government securities if it could preserve its growth. In doing so, China became the benefactor enabling the United States to spend out of control.

Been there, done that

This scenario, of one export-oriented nation indulging the excess spending of the United States, has happened before. In 1987, Japan was riding the wave of popularity of fuel-efficient Toyotas and innovative Sony Walkmen. And the United States was committed to a defense spending race it hoped would end the Cold War. Just as now, one country dominated purchases of newly issued U.S. treasury securities. The Nakasone government of Japan began to feud with the Reagan administration as the United States accused Japan of illegal dumping of computer memory chips.

In a pique of nationalism, Japanese citizens began to reduce their purchases of U.S. bonds, inducing Japan's treasury to pick up the slack by buying more U.S. securities to prevent a declining U.S. dollar. Like China, export-oriented Japan of the 1980s benefited from a strong U.S. dollar. The Treasury, too, helped sweeten the deal by offering higher interest rates on their bonds.

At the same time, the Federal Reserve Chairman Paul Volcker was increasing interest rates still further to curb inflation fears. This confluence of a growing federal deficit, rising interest rates, and the recognition of the vulnerability of the U.S. economy to another economic powerhouse willing to enable a U.S. addiction to spending shook the market. Yields on 30-year Treasury bonds rose to 10.2% on October 16, 1987, the Friday before the United States experienced one of the most dramatic stock market crashes in its history.

Monday, October 19, 1987,is known as Black Monday. It began in Asia, followed by dramatic plunges in South Asia and Europe, and ended with a 23% fall of the Dow Jones Industrial Average. By the end of October, Hong Kong had shed 46% of its value, New Zealand lost almost 60% of its value, and the U.S. and Canadian markets were down by almost 23%.

Plenty of blame to go around

This largest single day drop in the history of U.S. financial markets raised calls for many stock market reforms. The most significant was an automatic halt to trading when declines exceed certain preset levels. It was believed that the decline would have been much less significant were it not for programmed trading algorithms that major investment banks used to protect itself from huge swings. It was hypothesized that this algorithm resulted in mass simultaneous selling that caused secondary waves of declines. We return to this role of machines in magnifying market fear later.

Interestingly, markets recovered much of their losses in the ensuing months. By the end of 1987, the stock market was actually up for the year. We evaded that shot across our financial bow. However, while these events sound eerily like what world markets experienced two decades later, the rebound did not occur like it had before. There are some similarities between the causes and short-term consequences now and then, even though Black Monday in 1987 did not throw the global economy into the deep and severe recession that we experienced in the Global Financial Meltdown in 2008. Black Monday in 1987 did, however, herald in a new era of market volatility that we have not been able to shake ever since.

Part III

Measurement of Risk

We observed dramatic growth in financial markets in the 1990s and 2000s. Much of these new "investments" were not in commodities such as corn and wheat. Nor did they represent traditional stocks and bonds. Instead, these new "investments" were in foreign exchange and in the so-called derivatives that are sometimes difficult to comprehend, much less to assess their risk.

I next develop the tools to describe the significance of risk and fear on market participants. We begin to understand why humans are naturally adverse to risk, and how we are willing to accept some risk if offered a greater return.

I develop some economic tools in Chapter 6 to show how risk affects our level of utility or satisfaction. I describe the value of diversification and the pattern of diversification over a life cycle. Chapter 7 describes the fear premium, the cost of risk that is proportional to income, and motivates troubling behavior when markets decline dramatically. The final two chapters ask whether investors are cool and rational calculators of risk, or whether humans are by nature emotional in their investment decisions.

6
The Risk Premium – How Risk Affects Expected Returns

The utility curve readily tells us something about risk. It shows us why we value economic security and why any risk to our economic security creates discomfort. We will also see why declines in income from a market meltdown can breed fear and result in even greater subsequent declines.

To begin, let us explore our happiness levels in two scenarios – one risky, and one risk free. In the first scenario, we are offered ten units of food to last us a week. In the second scenario, we flip a coin. If the coin turns up heads, we get twice the allotment of food, or twenty units. But if the coin turns up tails, we get no food this week. Under either scenario, our average food allotment is ten units.

While our average allotment is preserved under either scenario, we are hardly indifferent to each. To see this, let's draw our utility graph running from zero, through ten, and to twenty units of consumption of food, or money, or whatever good we are willing to gamble.

As you can see from Figure 6.1, the average utility we would receive would be either U_0, with probability of 50%, or U_{20} with probability of 50%, or alternately U_{10} with certainty. The certainty equivalency is higher than the average of U_0 and U_{20} by an amount shown by the vertical arrows.

We confirm we are risk-averse because we incur a utility loss when our economic security depends on a fair coin toss. In other words, we would prefer to have an even flow income or consumption with certainty than risk feast and famine. This analysis simply confirms what we know intuitively. A bird in the hand is worth two in the bush.

While there appear to be exceptions to this postulate of human risk aversion, these exceptions are elusive. For instance, while some gamblers seem to thrive on risk, they may actually derive enjoyment not from the rolling of dice, but rather from the irrational enjoyment in their anticipation that they may hit the jackpot. This is despite their knowledge that the gambling house always skims its share of a few cents from the top for every dollar gambled. Indeed, lotteries are much worse, often retaining upwards of 50% of the proceeds.

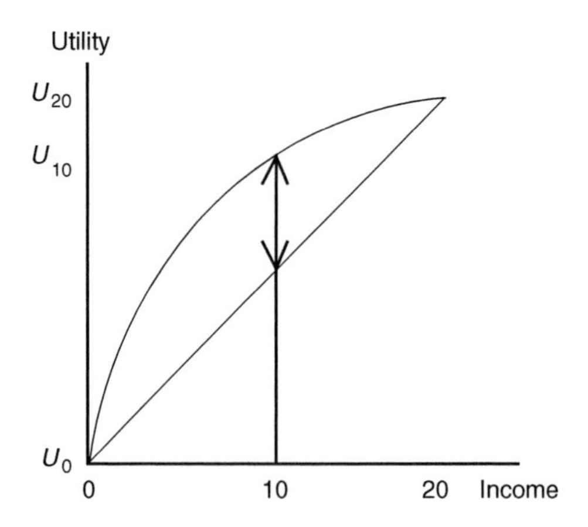

Figure 6.1 Average Utility

Are gamblers risk lovers?

Clearly, a rational gambler would not gamble to amass fortune and enhance consumption. To tolerate the house take on each transaction, a gambler must love risk rather than be risk-averse.

Diagrammatically, a gambler's utility curve is either upward sloping but at an increasingly steep rate, or the gambler is consuming two goods simultaneously – the value of his/her wealth and his/her intrinsic adrenaline fueled enjoyment in taking risks. Or, of course, the gambler may also be irrational, driven by addiction rather than common sense.

Indeed, the biological sciences have discovered this very fulfillment from taking risk. Some people derive enjoyment from that very anxiety that makes the rest of us feel uncomfortable. It is not necessarily that they enjoy life less than the rest of us, or they do not value their wealth or security. Rather, in addition to all this, they also enjoy the same hormonal rush that others prefer to avoid.

Even financial traders are not immune to this biological affinity toward risk. There have been a number of recent discoveries about the level of testosterone among aggressive traders of financial instruments.

Trading on testosterone

A couple of recent studies report that the largest risk takers have been found to have much higher morning levels of testosterone often associated with risk taking. In an article in the *Proceedings of the National Academies of Science,* researchers J. M. Coates and J. Herbert show that the levels of testosterone and cortisol, the stress hormone associated with anxiety and fear, are strongly correlated with traders' risk taking and profit. Those with high testosterone realized higher gains and losses, and produced more cortisol when the market was volatile.[12]

The researchers also observe that excessively high levels of testosterone can cause traders to take irrationally large risky positions. Somewhat provocatively, the researchers suggested that markets may be more stable if participants were women and old men because of their comparatively low levels of testosterone.

Subsequent research reported by the *Washington Post* even points to a correlation between testosterone exposure in the womb and risk-taking behavior in markets. Researchers discovered an indicator, a relatively longer ring finger than index finger on men's right hand, that is correlated to early exposure to testosterone. Those with greater exposure were found to earn six times as much on Wall Street as those with lesser exposure of testosterone. The difference in these profits was most pronounced when the market was most volatile, leading Prof. Andrew Lo of MIT to conclude that a greater understanding of fear and greed can allow us to more effectively avoid future panics.[13]

Differing risk tolerance and financial markets

If there is perhaps a biological explanation for some humans' willingness to override their natural inclination to risk aversion, the rest of us rely on our natural aversion to risk to direct us toward what is certain over what is speculative. However, we can also show that our income affects our willingness to take on risk. Differing incomes give rise to different risk tolerance for a given return. These differences act as the basis for transactions in financial markets.

To see this, notice that our risk aversion is derived from the curvature of our utility curve. We can use the same utility curve to show that a poor person is comparatively more risk-averse than a wealthier person.

For example, let us compare the risk premium between 0 and 10 and the risk premium between 10 and 20.

We can see that low-income investors suffer a larger risk premium than high-income investors. Intuitively, it makes sense that fear of risk tends to decrease with higher income. A starving person is less willing to gamble away a meal than a rich person may. If we already have a lot, a sacrifice in consumption because of a poor flip of the coin hurts us less, just as a boon in consumption from a favorable flip of the coin benefits us less.

The diagram shows that the wealthier among us are more willing to risk their income on more speculative ventures. They would be willing to lend to or insure those with less. Those living lower down on the utility curve have an opportunity to shed risk very costly to them as the wealthy absorb risk they find less costly. This is the nature of risk sharing and of financial markets in general that we describe next.

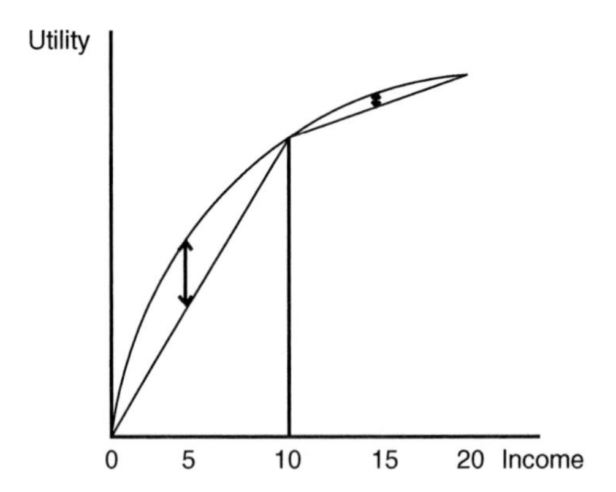

Figure 6.2 Decreasing Risk Aversion with Higher Consumption and Income

Risk diversification over time

Can we take advantage of our differing tolerance for risk by pooling those who are willing to take a risk and those who would prefer to shed risk onto others? And can we exchange risk among identical people? To see how, let's look at risk not simply in one period, but in repeated periods.

Let's assume we receive the same income each period to purchase goods and services that yield the same utility each period. Now imagine that we suffer a financial setback every second period, pushing down our income and utility significantly. For instance, consider an income of 20 in the previous example. A risk that reduces our income to zero every second period would result in the same decrement in utility as shown in Figure 6.1. However, if we could spread the loss equally over four periods, our average income each period would be fifteen units, and our utility would drop by much less, as shown in Figure 6.3.

Using this analogy, we would prefer smaller setbacks more often than large setbacks occasionally, even if the average monetary cost would be the same. Those who experience diminishing marginal utility prefer to spread risk over a number of periods. Unfortunately, the nature of risk creates an uncertainty that is difficult to avoid. If we could, we would have the control to avoid the risk in the first place.

There are ways we could instead pool the risk among many and hence manage its cost. We could form an association with others who would also like to spread out similar risk. In the example where we each suffer a ten unit setback every second period, we could each put five units into the pot each period and receive a ten unit pot if the setback occurs. We manage to spread the alternating setback by spreading smaller setbacks over more periods.

Of course, there may be the rare period when the setback does not occur or when the setback occurs simultaneously to both when risk arrives unpredictably.

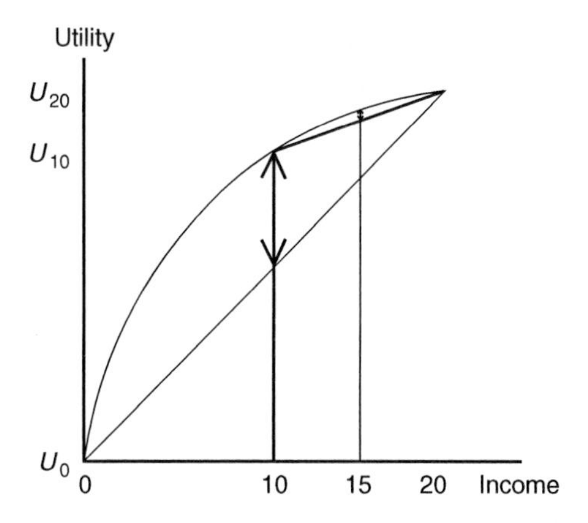

Figure 6.3 Much Smaller Risk Premium if Risk Is Spread over Two Periods

Even so, if enough people join the risk pooling association, the risk of multiple simultaneous calamities is low, and we are effectively indemnified from risk.

A reason for insurance

The mechanism of risk pooling is the basis of the insurance industry. We are willing to pay insurance premiums each month to offset a loss that might be incurred once in a lifetime. We are willing to do this even if the premiums in total exceed our lifetime losses. Professional actuaries, experts who are trained in valuing risk, are able to assess risk and the degree of damage for different individuals and construct optimal pools of the insured and of premiums to indemnify risk. As we find attractive their ability to pool premiums to indemnify us from risk, we are willing to pay insurers premiums to do it. Competition among insurance providers will, in theory, force them to create this service for us at the lowest possible price. We will see in Chapter 10 that such risk pooling and indemnification through insurance can actually create other inadvertent problems.

We will also see in Chapter 8 the effect of changing risk profiles for different periods of our life. Before we conclude though, let me introduce one more concept. Can we avoid insurance, knowing that a little suffering tomorrow is better than paying premiums today? In other words, if we discount the future sufficiently, we may prefer to suffer a setback in the future, and deal with it then, rather than pay for insurance today.

I'll gladly pay you Tuesday for a hamburger today

Discounting the future is entirely human, for many reasons. First, while we know the present, none of us knows the future. This uncertainty means that we can only assess various probabilities to future events, and hence various probabilities to the utility we will derive from these events. Our expected utility is then an average of our possible future events, weighed by the likelihood each will occur.

For instance, in the most extreme and basic sense, none of us is immortal. If the setback is sufficiently distant in time, our probability of suffering its consequences becomes less significant today. Our mortality creates a built-in bias for the present. As John Maynard Keynes is purported to have said, "In the long run, we are all dead."

We may also believe that we will be in a better position in the future to afford the costs of our decisions, today or tomorrow. Borrowing is based on the premise that we prefer current consumption to future consumption. We also discount the future cost of paying for our current consumption.

This model is of course consistent with our observation that interest rates are positive. A loan allows us to consume today but pay for it with larger, but discounted, sacrifices of income and consumption later.

In some sense, the prevailing interest rate is the rate our aggregated society discounts the future. We borrow if we discount the future at a higher rate than the prevailing interest rate, and lend if the interest rate we could earn is greater than our individual discount rate. As a consequence, we are all either potential borrowers, against our future earnings or income, or lenders, willing to lend to somebody today who has a discount rate and a willingness to borrow that exceeds our discount rate and willingness to lend.

It is this tendency of ours to be savers and investors, or borrowers that creates financial markets. Just as any market acts as a forum to pool the fruits of producers and the demands of consumers, financial markets create a pool of willing lenders and investors, collectively constituting the supply of loanable funds, and a pool of willing borrowers, constituting the demand for loanable funds.

Financial markets also segment borrowers and lenders depending on our relative willingness to accept risk. Differences in risk aversion, income, and our individual discount rates, and our tolerance for fear affects whether we are on one side of the market or another. This latter concept, our tolerance for fear, is tied to our perceptions of market volatility. This is the subject of our next topic of discussion.

7
The Fear Premium

We have now assembled the tools that will allow us to see the fear premium explicitly.

Humans are risk-averse, meaning we would prefer a risk-free solution to a solution with the same average value but with variations around the average. The previous chapter demonstrated that we are risk-averse even to uncertainty that can yield an improvement just as likely as an equal sized loss.

Our risk aversion flows from the observation that humans experience diminishing marginal utility from greater income. This implies that we are troubled more by a loss than ecstatic about an equal sized gain.

As we saw earlier, if we were to somehow measure utility, its graph would show that satisfaction or utility rises with income, but at a decreasing rate. In other words, the graph of utility for various levels of income is upward sloping, but flattens after a point.

Let's look at a scenario where the starting income is \$10,000 and it can be invested to either gain \$5,000 or lose \$5,000, with equal probability. This can be represented as in Figure 7.2.

The utility for the sure thing \$10,000 is shown as U (10,000) on the graph, while the utility of a combination of a \$5,000 income or a \$15,000 income is shown as the average $(U[5000] + U[15{,}000])/2$.

Notice that this utility $(U[5000] + U[15{,}000])/2$ is actually no better than a lesser income I^* with certainty.

In other words, the risky proposition gives us a level of utility that would be equivalent to an income of I^* with certainty. The risk has cost us an amount equal to the arrows ←→ in Figure 7.4. Because fear is simply our concern for risk that threatens our happiness and economic security, these arrows also measure our fear premium.

We can see that greater risks induce greater threats to our happiness, even if they do not change our average income. Let us repeat this analysis for three different gain/loss increments. Again, we will assume a \$10,000 starting income, and now risk \$5,000, \$7,500, and \$9,000 in turn.

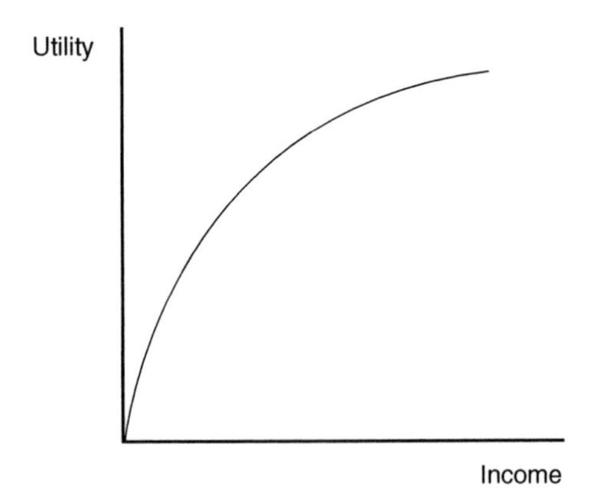

Figure 7.1 Utility Curve with Decreasing Marginal Utility

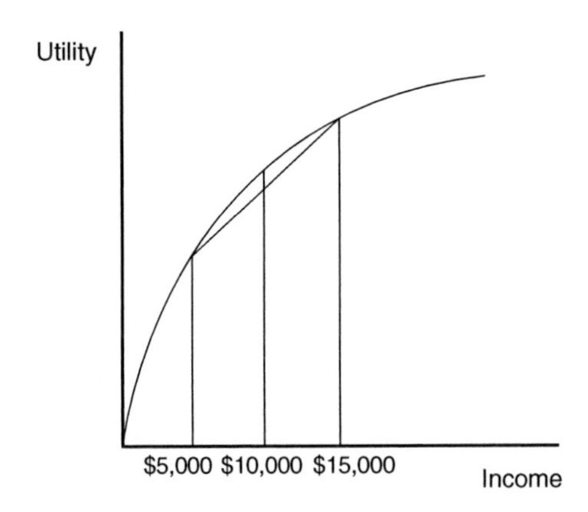

Figure 7.2 Fair Gambles of $5,000 on a $10,000 Income

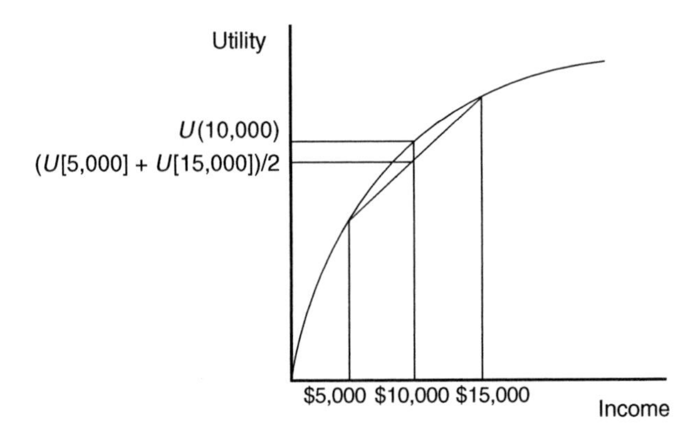

Figure 7.3 Comparison of Gambles with a Certainty Equivalent

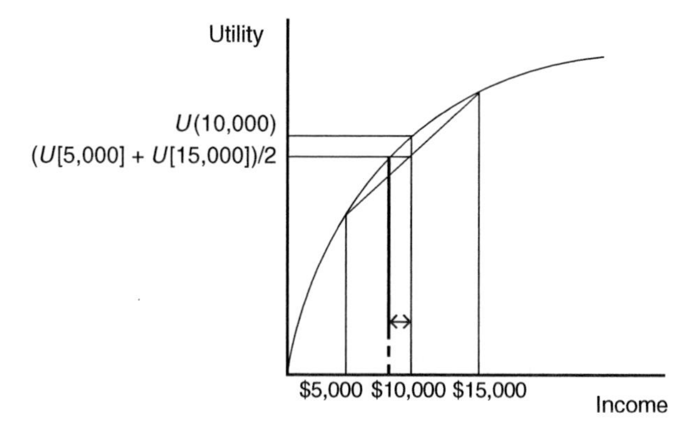

Figure 7.4 Gambles and the Cost of Risk

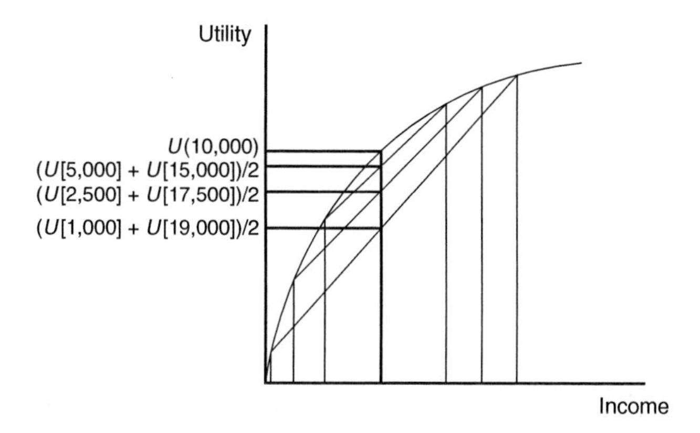

Figure 7.5 Increasing Levels of a Fair Gamble

Each of these increasing risks leaves us with lower and lower overall average utility. Let's recall the risk premium indicated by the arrows in Figure 7.4. We now see this risk premium generating increasing fear as the gains and losses widen.

This ever-widening fear premium as markets become more uncertain is an unavoidable and rational consequence of diminishing marginal utility.

The changing tolerance for risk translates to fear when markets turn sharply downward. These larger gambles show us two things. First, returns are radically diminished. Second, the increasing randomness of our returns generates the fear that can induce huge withdrawals of investment funds from the market place as investors are forced down to an income class that has a greater aversion to risk.

We saw this happen most recently in the Global Financial Meltdown of 2008. From a high of 14,093 less than a year before, the Dow Jones Industrial Average

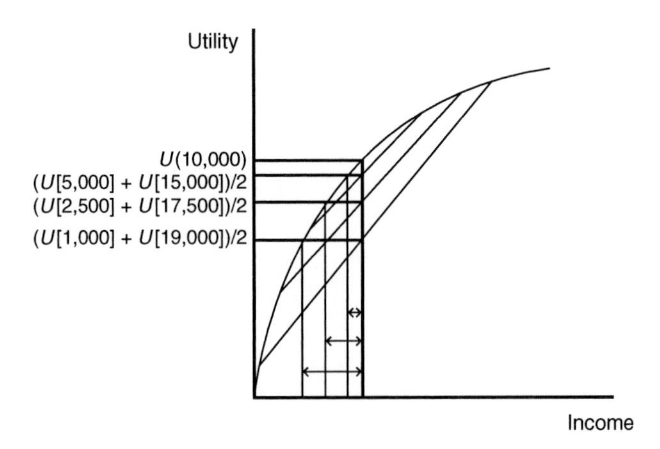

Figure 7.6 Increasing Fear and Risk Premium with Larger Fair Gambles

fell to a low of 7,552 on October 9, 2008. Black October of 2008 saw huge funds withdrawn from global financial markets. These funds remained parked on the sidelines, pushing the yield on cash balances to historically low levels.

As we can see in Figure 7.6, investors moved to the left of their income and utility curves. Their decreased tolerance for risk is a by-product of some observations made by researchers of late.

For instance, a recent body of academic research supports that wealth and risk aversion are related, as the theory suggests. Christian Gollier showed that individual investors indeed develop a greater tolerance for risk with increased wealth.[14] The authors explain this phenomenon based on an individual's access to discretionary investment capital. In the parlance of economists, many potential investors are liquidity constrained. In other words, low-income investors find it difficult to borrow or to generate sufficient savings to invest. It is natural then for high-wealth investors to take greater risks.

Reduced willingness to take risk following market downturns

Our willingness to take risks can change with economic conditions. The newspaper *USA Today* recently reported that the average savings rate in the United States actually became negative in 2006, for the first time since the Great Depression.[15] In 2006, U.S. households spent $41.6 billion more than they earned, representing a negative half percentage point savings rate. There was clearly little capacity for many to save. In the economic environment following the Credit Crisis of 2007, many potential investors simply did not have the capacity to invest that, in normal times, accompanied the capacity to save.

The declining measure of net savings does not necessarily mean that wealth is not expanding. Simply because spending exceeds disposable income, it does not mean existing savings accounts or pension and mutual funds are not increasing in value. However, the article does quote a Federal Reserve survey that shows the number of contributors to savings accounts is dropping significantly, too, from 59.2% of households in 2001 to 56.1% by 2004.

Many of these individuals simply do not have the access to savings or borrowings to invest in the market. However, with greater income and wealth, households, in turn, have more left over after consumption.

As income drops for individuals or in the aggregate, essential consumption, the cost of sending kids to college, and the need to keep some savings liquid and easily accessible for emergencies, begins to impinge on our capacity to invest. Consequently, as income drops, so does investment.

Researchers have verified this tendency to invest less as markets become more volatile. For instance, Nobel Memorial Prize winning economist Kenneth Arrow reasoned that an individual's aversion to risk decreases with accumulation of wealth.[16] Conversely, for our purposes, as major shocks to the stock market decrease wealth substantially, households on average become poorer and hence more averse to risk. As a consequence of such major shocks, fear for financial security forces many out of a market perceived to be too risky relative to our collective capacity to absorb risk.

Leverage risk

There is one additional factor that can force many out of the market. Some are simply forced to liquidate their holdings as a consequence of government regulations or brokerage house rules. These forced liquidations can be the unkindest cut of all.

Leverage risk and regulatory liquidations are not new. The Roaring Twenties was an era of great hope and optimism. So confident were households and banks alike that many dispensed with the usual caution reserved for speculative ventures. While banks were accustomed to lending sixty or eighty cents on the dollar for the purchase of a home, they also became willing to lend sixty cents to eighty cents on the dollar to buy stocks as well.

With stocks climbing by 600% in eight short years, it seemed reasonable for banks to lend for stock purchases. With such almost unbroken market momentum, it was almost unfathomable that stocks would drop by 30% or 40% necessary to jeopardize these loans.

This same optimism fueled the recent subprime crisis. With homes rising consistently for more than a decade, investors and bankers were equally willing to lend upwards of 90%, 100%, or more on homes in 2007. After all, national housing prices had not dropped nationwide ever since the Great Depression.

Bankers were just as comfortable lending on margin for stock purchases in 1927 as Countrywide in the United States and Northern Rock in the United

Kingdom were willing to lend for mortgages in 2007. Just as it was unfathomable to imagine housing prices would drop nationwide in 2008, there was nothing but optimism as late as 1928, on the cusp of the Great Crash.

A margin account is not unlike a mortgage, with stock substituted for the home as the collateral. But while home foreclosure is a relatively lengthy and expensive legal progress, margin accounts are quite a bit easier to liquidate because the brokerage house typically holds the stock on the client's behalf, and has the right to sell the stock if the margin borrowing is insufficiently collateralized.

As an example of the returns and the risk, let's imagine you buy $100 of stock. An investment house would permit an investor to use that $100 of stock as the basis for a margin loan of $100 to purchase another $100 of stock. The investment house holds the stock as collateral, and charges a reasonably affordable interest rate on the loan. This is quite attractive. If the stock quickly rises by 10%, the portfolio is worth $220, $100 is owed, and the investor's equity has risen from $100 to $120. In effect, the one-to-one margining has magnified the 10% return to a 20% return on the initial investment. As long as the interest rate is lower than the rate of appreciation of the stock, the investor will magnify the profit.

While margin borrowing can dramatically enhance returns on one's equity, there are also substantial risks to this leveraged investment strategy. Let's assume the stock we purchased doubles in value. Our $100 investment plus the $100 borrowed allowed the investor to purchase $200 of stock. When it doubled, the portfolio is worth $400, $100 borrowed, and $300 in equity.

If banks and investment houses are willing to lend up to 50% of the stock value, the investor can purchase an additional $200 of stock. The portfolio is now worth $600, with $300 in equity and $300 in loans.

Let us now imagine that the stock simply falls back to its original value. It had doubled in value earlier, so it drops back by one half. If this were to occur, the investor is left with a portfolio worth only $300, but still owes $300. All the equity has been wiped out and the investor, once worth $100, is now penniless, even though the stock has merely returned to its original value.

In other words, the investor has realized the extreme of leverage risk, even under not uncommon circumstances. This example is quite striking, in its realism, its relatively conservative margin borrowing, and the extreme risk that even relatively conservative margining could generate. And it happened to a surprising number of small investors in 1928 and 1929, and again in 2008.

Protecting us from ourselves

Regulators now realize the dangers of even moderate margin borrowing as described in the previous example. As a consequence, the Federal Reserve promulgated Regulation T that prevents an investor from purchasing a stock with more than 50% borrowed from the investment house.

Once purchased however, the portfolio is permitted to fall in value somewhat without violating Regulation T. If this provision were not permitted, there would be forced margin selling even if a stock fell by a small amount after the margin purchase. If the portfolio continues to drop though, brokerage rules kick in to force the investor to sell some of the stock and reestablish an appropriate loan-to-value ratio.

Most treasuries and bourses worldwide have adopted the equivalent of Regulation T to prevent the sometimes complete loss of consumer assets realized in 1929. And all investment houses have other margin requirements that can force an investor to sell if subsequent losses cause the investor to overextend.

Margin borrowing and speculative bubbles

Margin borrowing can also inflate a speculative bubble in stocks. Let's imagine that borrowing is not permitted. The price of stocks depends on the supply of stocks with the existing stockholders, and the demand for stock. If margin borrowing was suddenly permitted, investors would have access to an amount of additional purchasing power equivalent to the level of capitalization of the entire market.

With so much more cash sloshing around, and with no new stock certificates circulating than before, stocks are in very short supply. The extra cash would immediately bid up the price of stocks, conceivably to twice their premargin value, if the market became fully margined. In other words, the relaxation of the regulated margin ceiling can inflate the speculative bubble. Likewise, forced selling of margined stocks can dramatically deflate a market too.

Waves of selling

The phenomenon of the bursting of a speculative bubble through margin calls is not at all uncommon. The frequent corrections over the past two years on foreign exchanges have created significant losses in otherwise nicely increasing global mutual funds. If investors aggressively plowed each gain back into their mutual funds to purchase additional stock on each run up, these same investors are often forced to sell even more dramatically on major market corrections.

Brokers typically offer five days for an investor to voluntarily liquidate some stock to reduce borrowing and increase collateralization. Investors may try to hold off as long as possible before selling, hoping that the market will come back. If the market does not come back quickly, it has become increasingly common for the market to exhibit a second downward correction a week following the first, as secondary forced sales of stock bought on margin further depresses prices.

A perfect storm

Combining this perfect storm of forced selling of margined stocks, the effects of decreased available capital for investment as wealth declines, and a greater aversion to risk with declining wealth, we witnessed a dramatic withdrawal from the market place in both 1929 and 2008. In the recent 2008 panic, these withdrawals forced the market to experience an almost unprecedented drop in value. In addition, the markets moved sideways for months, making little progress in recapturing its historic losses, as it had in the temporary crash of 1987.

Instead, the market remained very volatile, dramatically moving the Dow Jones Industrial Average up and down over a narrow range from 8,000 to 9,000. But with fear gripping the market and so many investors sitting on the sidelines, markets were characterized by fewer traders, either buying or selling. These markets, labeled "thin" by economists, are unable to take advantage of the moderating effect of the law of large numbers and are prone to the volatility described earlier.

We shall see later how the fear generated from this market volatility gripped the wider global economies. Next though, we explore whether our tolerance for risk and market fear has a demographic component.

8
The Demographics of Risk and Fear

Fear, a measure of our tolerance for and reaction to risk or danger, has a demographic dimension as well as a wealth dimension. Our economic security, income, wealth, and human capital all change throughout our lifetimes. In this cycle of life, we also gain knowledge, wisdom, and experiences that can guide us when faced with financial threats. This life cycle has a number of interesting aspects.

Before we embark on a discussion about how risk and fear are correlated with age, education, family status, and wealth, let's be reminded that risk is the objective assessment of the damage from events that cause us harm. This is differentiated from the subjective term uncertainty, which refers to the recognition of decision making when important information is unknown.

The assessment of risk has a cognitive or experiential aspect to it. This is the basis of our first observation. Risk is related to experience.

We all have experienced the fearlessness of youth. It is common knowledge among ski instructors that children are the easiest to teach because, despite their reduced ability to process rational explanations of the dynamics involved in skiing, they have no fear of falling. Children are not overly cerebral about this physical activity and hence their processing does not get in the way of learning. On the other hand, adult students have experienced a lifetime of the pain of falls, and tend to overanalyze their style to a point that they cannot react quickly or intuitively enough.

Certainly increased cognitive power comes with age, and with the ability to calculate risk comes a greater appreciation of risk. With the greater appreciation for the cost if the dangerous event occurs, and the greater ability to estimate its probability, we would expect age to increase fearfulness.

There is an implicit assumption we have made, though. For this conclusion to be true, we must assume that youth have no fear because they have reduced appreciation for the probabilities of harm, or the costs if damage occurs. Let's explore each of these in turn.

The first factor is exposure to risk. Children live in a protected environment. Their caregivers prohibit them from participating in risky situations and protect them when there is some risk. Institutions and society too insulate children from risk. As a consequence, to children, the world is a relatively low-risk place. This should naturally engender some fearlessness.

Let's model how our perceptions about probabilistic events can affect our expectations. I look at three sets of perceptions – those who believe they live a charmed existence, those that perceive a doomed existence, and those that are entirely rational about the future.

Past observations affect future expectations

To better understand why a protected upbringing could give rise to a sense of a charmed life, let's assume that events happen at a random rate. For instance, let's consider a once-in-a-decade event. As an example, barring for now any ability to influence its probability, let's assume a once-in-a-decade event has a 10% probability of occurring in a given year.

Such random events that occur at a given rate are described as a Poisson process, named after Siméon-Denis Poisson, a French physicist and mathematician who discovered the method of calculating the probability of occurrences of such random events. Using his formula, we can calculate the probability that an event will not occur, given it has a 10% chance of occurring in any year. This is given by:

$$p(0) = \exp(-10\% \times 10) = 36.8\%.$$

Contrary to the common view that a once-in-a-decade event has a 100% chance of occurring in a given decade, there is a 37% chance that it will not, and a 63% chance that it will occur at least once in the decade. This rational probability that an event will occur at least once in the next ten years is affected if something shielded us from risk and distorted our risk perceptions.

A charmed existence

What is the probability something will not happen in the immediate future given our good fortune to not have experienced it in the past? In other words, do those living a charmed existence have a distorted sense of risk?

Let's assume we have been fortunate enough to avoid the once-in-a-decade calamity for ten years. Those who believe in divine intervention or a charmed existence may use the observation that the event has not occurred to reassess its future probability. If an event has not occurred yet, they may reason that perhaps it is a once-in-two-decades event rather than a once-in-a-decade event. If those charmed revise downward their assessment of risk because of the luck they have experienced, or the magical thinking that permits them to believe they are less prone to the risk, the new assessment that a once-in-two decades event will not occur in the next decade becomes:

$$p(0) = \exp(-5\% \times 10) = 60.7\%.$$

In other words, those who believe they are charmed because they have had the good luck and divine intervention to have skirted the risk for a decade may conclude they have a 61% chance of skirting it for another decade. With each year gone by, the charmed individual will reassess their risk downward, even though the basic probability of the event has not changed. To those living the charmed existence, the perceived probability of avoiding the calamity has risen to 61% from 37%.

A doomed existence

Alternately, others could calculate a completely different probability of risk. Given that something has not occurred in the past, some may mistakenly believe that there is an increased probability it will happen in the future. Adherents to this philosophy might believe there is such a thing as a doomed existence. For instance, they may assess the probability of a once-in-a-decade event that has not occurred yet to have the following probability of occurring at least once in the next decade:

$$1 - p(0) = 1 - \exp(-.1 \times 20) = 86.5\%.$$

Those living the doomed existence may conclude that an event that occurs once in a decade but has not occurred for ten years is almost certainly going to occur in the next ten years.

As an example of three different world views, I recall a scene in John Irving's book, *The World According to Garp*. An airplane loses control and crashes onto a property. A rational observer might conclude that this is an appropriate event that occurs once in a while, right on schedule. While a pessimist might conclude that the world is a dangerous place, and will constantly be wary of future crashes. Garp, the eternal optimist, concluded that the property is now disaster-proofed. The chance of something bad happening again is now infinitesimally small. In fact, the probability of occurrence of the event has not changed at all, though one's perspective of risk has been forever influenced.

A rational existence

Not surprisingly, the actual risk falls between that surmised by the charmed and the doomed. Events that occur at random are no more likely to occur in the near future simply because they have not occurred in the recent past. Random events are random and are not correlated with a past occurrence. However, our assessment of risk changes as our perceptions change.

Rationally, the probability of the event occurring in the next decade is the same 63% probability that it should have occurred within the past ten years.

Those believing in a charmed existence underestimate this probability as only 39%, while those believing they are doomed anticipate an 87% chance that the risk will be realized. One underestimates the risk by almost half, while the other overestimates the risk by almost a half.

An assessment of damage

Given the cocoon we create for our youth, young people who experience low risk in their formative years may also associate a lower than rational risk going forward. This creates a certain immortality of youth, something that evidently is amplified by the testosterone coursing through the veins of adolescent males.

Risk has two components. One is the assessment of the probability of an unfortunate event and the other is the damage that would occur as a consequence. Here too, the exuberance of youth may underestimate sacrifices. We likely underestimate the pain of a broken leg until we experience it. Experience certainly focuses and intensifies anticipation of pain.

However, those that have not experienced pain must instead take their cues from others. While few who relate stories of accidents underestimate the pain, a listener strongly influenced by the tales of others may actually exaggerate their estimation of damage, should the risky event occur to them. Living in an environment that reinforces such fears may create in a young person an overly acute sense of fear.

To now, we have been concentrating on the assessment of the probability of a risky occurrence. Let us next explore why our risk profile may change over our life cycle, even without such distortions in our assessment of the probability or consequences of a risky event that may occur if we are charmed or doomed, rather than rational.

Freedom's just another word for nothing left to lose

Our risk profile over our life cycle depends on two other important factors: what we have to lose and how long we must live with the consequences or, alternatively, how long we have to recover.

Households follow what economists call a life cycle of savings, investment, and consumption. Such a life cycle model tracks the pattern of spending, investment in goods, services, and a household's human capital over a lifetime.

For instance, a college graduate enters the workforce having borrowed to invest in her own human capital. She begins human capital rich but asset poor with financial liabilities in the form of student loans that exceed any financial assets. She may even go further into debt by purchasing a home. However, the home will offer her a corresponding, and appreciating asset for her life cycle balance sheet.

Such young investors will also rent out their stock of human capital, acquired through their investment in their education, to consume and begin to repay their liabilities. Meanwhile, they augment their human capital through work experience, which further adds to their appreciation of the value of their home. Both effects further increase their asset base.

Unfortunately, these young investors are unable to mortgage their stock of human capital as they can a home. For a moment, let's imagine that young professionals could mortgage their future in even a modest way. Let's assume an employer could front to the employees their salary from year forty to year one as an early purchase of some subsequent human capital.

Neglecting inflation, such an advance that must be repaid in 40 years could be invested to earn, let's say, a real return of 7% per annum. By the time that mortgage in human capital would have to be repaid, it would have increased 700%. The advance from year forty to year one could allow the professional to retire seven years earlier.

Young people are typically barred from this opportunity to mortgage their stock of human capital. The life cycle of earnings observes that income and asset accumulation is slowest precisely when young investors most benefit from savings over their subsequent career. Instead, young investors only slowly move from the net borrowing they incurred early in their career, to a maximum asset accumulation rate at middle age, and a maximum asset value, in their home and retirement fund, just before retirement.

Diversification

There is one additional benefit that can accrue as a consequence of a long life cycle. Financial planners recommend that an investment strategy should change over the investor's life cycle. The investment strategy should be relatively aggressive at first and become increasingly cautious as the investor nears retirement. Financial planners often employ Rule 110 that recommends that the investor's stock portfolio should be divided up between stocks and less risky assets based on the investor's age. The percentage of the portfolio held in stock should equal 110 minus the investor's age at any point in time. A 30-year-old investor would then maintain a portfolio that is 80% stock and 20% bonds or money market investments. Alternately, a 60-year-old investor should hold 50% stock and 50% less risky assets.

The reason for this rule is that young investors have a greater length of time to recover from a risky investment gone bad. One way to demonstrate this is to imagine what would happen with the average return of an uncertain portfolio over time.

Let's assume that the return from the uncertain portfolio can fluctuate with equal probability. Over one period an investor has an equal probability of gaining or losing. Over two periods, the investor would have a one in four probability of gaining in both periods, one in four of losing in both periods, and two in four chance of holding steady. This is because, over time, gains have time to moderate losses. A greater number of periods create a more diversified portfolio.

Financial planners use this to conclude that a long planning horizon reduces risk and acts as the basis for Rule 110. The simple reasoning is that investors have more time to overcome financial calamity if it occurs early in their career rather than later.

For instance, if there is one major setback for every ten successes, those with a longer time horizon can have the confidence that they will recover from such one in ten events a number of times over their lifetime or career. However, near the end of the time horizon, those who suffer a major setback may not have sufficient time to recover through ten subsequent successes. Reliable averages arising from the levelling effect of the law of large numbers is lost when the planning horizon is short.

The recent Global Financial Meltdown demonstrated the precariousness of those nearing the end of their careers. In a year's time, global wealth fell from over $60 trillion to about $35 trillion. Many investors lost 40% of their wealth. Some who may have been more highly leveraged lost much more.

A setback of such a magnitude at the sunset of one's career is almost catastrophic. If one intended to retire in the following five years, there is little chance the setback will be fully reversed. For instance, a fall of 50% in asset value would require more than seven years of 10% real annual returns to attain the former asset value. Tens of millions of individuals are instead forced to significantly revise their retirement plans, extending retirement perhaps by a decade or more. Certainly a setback of that magnitude can be a life-changing event, and rightly invokes fear in those that must somehow come to terms with the meltdown.

Young people also have a huge lifelong asset that rises as they gain experience and drops off as they near retirement. Their human capital can represent the safe asset portion of their portfolio and allow them to round off their investment portfolio with riskier assets like stocks.

However, those nearing retirement no longer have the safe asset of human capital for the long-term, and must instead balance their portfolio between safe assets such as bonds and some riskier assets such as stocks.

The rate of time preference

There is a factor that prevents young people from developing the forward looking investment strategy just suggested. Individuals shift their consideration for the future as they age. For instance, young people have less experience in surviving on their own or planning for their future. They also have experienced fewer of life's challenges that may induce them to plan more carefully. These brushes with calamity and mortality shape their outlook as they age, and create a greater willingness to plan for the future and to exercise more caution today.

Young people also have fewer needs that depend on their immediate wealth. They often haven't yet had children to support or significant housing debt to maintain. Fluctuations in their income or economic security carry with them neither the penalties nor the fears that increase with age.

Economists summarize this effect as a changing rate of time preference. These observations would predict that young people discount the future at a greater rate and thus save at a lower rate. Their high discount rate makes the prevailing interest rate more attractive to borrow, inducing them to incur debt rather than invest. Interestingly, the elderly also do this, not because of a lack of experience, but because of a shortened time horizon as they near the end of their life.

Those between youth and old age would then be expected to be the most forward planning and would maintain the highest savings rate accordingly. We can summarize this effect in Figure 8.1.

This graph shows the savings rate over time. The savings rate can actually begin at a negative amount as young people borrow to invest in their education and human capital. They devote the most to savings and the creation of equity in their middle years as they contribute more to growing retirement funds and as their homes appreciate in value. In retirement, they will spend the earnings from their retirement accounts and may even sell their home in a reverse mortgage. If they plan well, they would time it so most of their savings and equity is consumed when they pass away. Since that date is not known with certainty, the elderly may not use up all their savings capital and can bequeath any remainder.

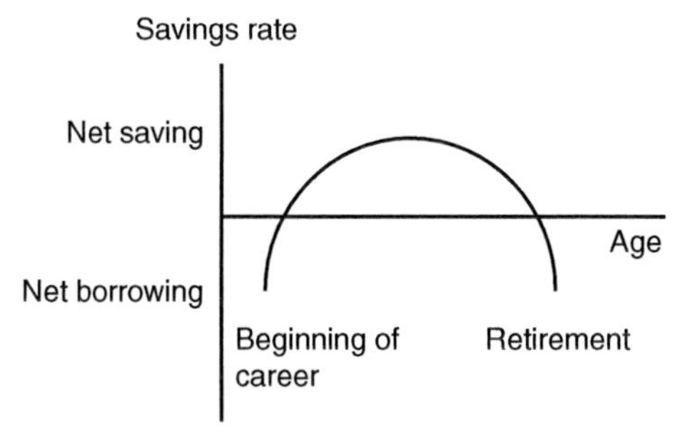

Figure 8.1 The Pattern of Savings over a Life Cycle

Gender and risk aversion

Researchers have even discovered a gender component to risk aversion. For instance, a researcher shows that risk aversion extends to various risky activities. Margaret Brinig reports that women are less willing to risk being charged with speeding than men.[17] More recently, Joni Hersch discovered that women made less risky choices than men in such decisions as smoking, wearing seat belts, dental care, and medical examinations.[18]

Nancy Ammon Jianakoplos and Alexandra Bernasek of Colorado State University draw similar parallels to financial decisions. They recently discovered that investment in risky assets increases more slowly with increased wealth for single women than with single men.[19]

For instance, in their study they report that single women surveyed indicated they held 40% of their investment wealth in risky assets, while their male counterparts held 46% in risky assets. By comparison, wealthier married couples hold 50% of their wealth in risky assets. Interestingly, they report studies by other authors that show risky behavior in lifestyle decisions also have a gender bias.

Jianakoplos and Bernasek conclude, based on their surveys and their econometric analysis of data, that women are more cautious than men. They note that women too become less risk-averse as income rises. However, their risk aversion falls from a higher base and at a lower rate than their male counterparts. This leaves an even wider gap in risk aversion between women and men as wealth rises.

Women also hold fewer risky assets as their number of children increase. Interestingly, they find that single black women tolerate risk better on average than single white women, single men, and married couples. This result adds interesting dimensions of culture and race to global investment as the financial world becomes much more diverse in the coming decades.

As women invest less in risky assets than their male counterparts, they do not incur as much risk, and therefore their returns too are commensurately lower. This means that single women will accumulate wealth slower than their male counterparts, all else being equal.

These results have important implications on how the population will tolerate risky financial markets in the future. It also shows us that the fear premium can be expected to change as world demographics change. For instance, we see the population aging in the developed and developing nations. With an increased proportion of our population having a shorter time horizon, we may see increasing risk aversion and more fearful reactions to market volatility.

The share of unmarried women in the population is also growing. If the various cultures that make up our rapidly expanding world of developed nations also follow the path of the developed world in delaying marriage, it may also be the case that overall risk aversion increases.

While Jianakoplos and Bernasek found that black women have a greater tolerance to risk than their white female and male counterparts, their study was confined only to the United States. They agree though, it is an interesting and open question as to how tolerance toward risk will change across cultures and in the future.

However, as emerging countries increasingly participate in global finances, they join at a lower wealth base than their counterparts in the developed countries. If they, too, experience the decreasing tolerance for risk at low wealth levels as we find in the developed countries, we may find overall that markets become increasingly fearful and risk-averse with the convergence of the First and Second Economic Worlds.

Our next concern is how increased fear will affect market volatility. Let's now look at how the fear premium and volatility affects market valuations.

9
The Microeconomics of Risk Aversion

Before I describe the economic approach to decision making in risky circumstances, let me offer some truth in advertising. It would not be unfair to conclude by now that most individuals do not behave as homo economicus, that uber-rational decision making fiction employed by economists to permit us to use the tools of rationality to analyze markets and human behavior. A simple example will demonstrate this.

Let's consider the classic *Let's Make a Deal* dilemma. In this popular game show that ran on U.S. television from 1963 to 1978, contestants were asked to choose a prize to be found behind one of three doors. Two of the doors hid booby prizes while one door might have hid an all-expenses-paid trip to Hawaii or a new car. Contestants chose their door, but before the door was opened, the host Monty Hall would open another door. He would then ask whether the contestant would like to switch their choice of doors to the one unchosen and unopened instead.

Most contestants would not switch, believing that there are equal odds the prize is behind either of the two remaining doors. This is an erroneous assumption. Let's see why.

Mr. Hall, of course, knew that the door he revealed contained one of the two booby prizes. In other words, by displaying what was behind door number two, he was providing more information about where the good prize is not hidden.

However, humans tend to attribute equal probabilities to various uncertain events. In other words, the contestants initially assigned probability of one in three that the good prize can be found behind one of the three doors, and then a probability of one in two that the good prize is found behind the remaining two doors.

To see the error in our ways, consider the consequence of Bayesian probability analysis. Named after Thomas Bayes, an eighteenth century Protestant minister and mathematician, the statistical theorem states:

> The probability of any event is the ratio between the value at which an expectation depending on the happening of the event ought to be computed, and the value of the thing expected upon its happening.[20]

In plain English, this means that the probability of an event must be modified by what we have since discovered. In this case, we knew from the beginning that there was a one in three probability that the great prize was behind the door we initially chose, and a two in three probability that it was behind one of the other two doors. Nothing changes that. Once Mr. Hall showed us the prize was not behind one of the two other doors, the entire remaining two in three probability must now rest with the other door we did not choose. Nothing has been learned about our first choice.

In effect, we are left with two choices – our original choice with a probability of one in three, and an offer to choose a new door with a probability of two in three. We doubled our odds by switching doors. Yet few contestants switched. They were bitten with the common human assumption of placing equal probabilities across the range of unknown events.

Are we smarter than bees?

This departure from rational thought is relatively universal in humans and animals alike. For instance, in a set of experiments, Shafir et al. showed that humans and bees alike perform differently to payoffs based on expected returns if the ambiguity of their environment is changed.[21]

In one part of the experiment, students were asked to choose between earning three credits with certainty or four credits with 80% probability. The expected return from the risky strategy is $.8 \times 4$ credits, or 3.2 credits, which exceeds their certainty equivalent of 3 credits.

When the students could clearly discern this, they chose the risky alternative most times. The researchers then made it a bit more difficult to discern between the certain and the risky alternative, but without changing the actual probabilities or reward. In the more ambiguous environment, students veered toward less risk.

Bees, too, were subjected to risky and safe alternatives, with a greater reward but at a lower probability in one alternative, and a lesser reward with certainty. Again, as the environment becomes more ambiguous, but without changing the average rewards in each scenario, the bees tended to become more cautious.

Both these experiments suggest that we are hardwired to be unwilling to take as much risk when the environment becomes more uncertain or volatile. In other words, fear of risk increases with ambiguity or volatility.

Fear and investment in volatile markets

This empirical result has obvious implications on our finances when markets become volatile. We have a choice to hold our savings in cash or receive, on average, a higher but riskier reward by investing in equity markets. In times that are less volatile or are moving in more distinct directions, we tend to be willing to invest in the market. However, when times seem more random or volatile, we have seen large-scale withdrawals from more speculative markets, even against the prognostications of commentators that very weak markets bode well for future returns.

How do we determine the appropriate trade-off between returns with certainty and higher, but risky returns? While we treated earlier the theoretical underpinnings of the risk premium and our preference for certainty, economists are not able to directly measure an individual's willingness to take on risk for greater return. We see from the experiment above that our willingness is situational.

We can nonetheless observe how the collection of individuals trade risk and return by observing the return commanded of risky assets compared with the lower return yielded on more certain assets. In this case, we can benchmark risk and return compared with the return on U.S. treasury bonds, an asset generally agreed to be risk free.

The Capital Asset Pricing Model (CAPM, pronounced cap-em) does just that. Flowing from the work of, then PhD candidate, William Sharpe, it eventually earned the Nobel Memorial Prize in Economics for Prof. Harry Markowitz, William Sharpe, and Merton Miller. The CAPM is a natural extension of early work on risk and return in financial markets.

CAPM is a ground-breaking work built upon Prof. Markowitz's research on risk and return. Markowitz was the first to describe what is called the efficient frontier of optimal investment. This frontier acted as the basis of a description of the market trade-off between high risk with low return, and low risk with high return.

While there are various ways to measure risk, the most common and easy to calculate a measure of uncertainty is the standard deviation of the returns of an asset. If we graph the return of a stock over time, the relationship can be characterized by two parameters. One is the average or mean return; the other is the amount the return varies around its mean. A stock, for instance, with an average return of 10% per year, but with wide swings up and down, would be considered more risky than another stock with a 10% return consistently from period to period.

Common statistical tools can extract from stock data a mean return and one measure of its variations, called the standard deviation. This calculation of a mean and standard deviation assumes that stock returns are normally distributed, based on the observation that many physical phenomena follow this sort of distribution. While subsequent refinements of this approach improve upon these assumptions, the approach to measure return and risk based on means and standard deviations remain the simplest, easiest to calculate, and most widely applied technique.

If we measure the return and risk for the wide variety of stocks, indexes, and portfolios, we can graph the combination of return and risk according to the following graph.

The various points represent the return and risk combination for various stocks and portfolios, while the solid line represents the outer boundary of the best return and risk combinations. By constructing a portfolio representing a combination of assets found on the upper boundary, an individual can obtain the best possible return for a given amount of risk, or alternately, the lowest risk for a given return.

If only the leftmost point on the horizontal axis represents the zero risk point, note that none of these investments is risk free. We do know that some assets have almost no risk, though. To recall, Rule 110 suggests we divide our investment portfolio between stocks and low-risk or risk-free bonds, depending on investor's age. An asset such as U.S. treasury bonds and its commensurate return, give one more point for our own investment portfolio – the return for a risk-free asset, as shown in Figure 9.2.

The financial portfolio does not have to contain only the highest return assets along the efficient portfolio frontier, nor only the risk-free asset. A portfolio can also own a combination of the two.

Let's assume an investor would like to obtain some combination of a risk-free asset and the best the market can offer. We know one point on that combination

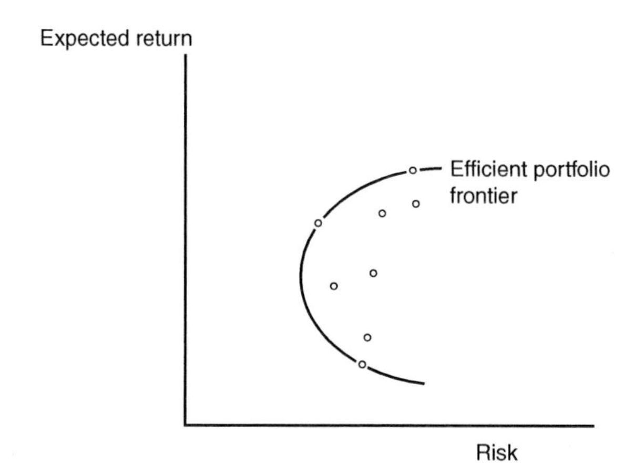

Figure 9.1 The Portfolio of Possible Returns and Risk

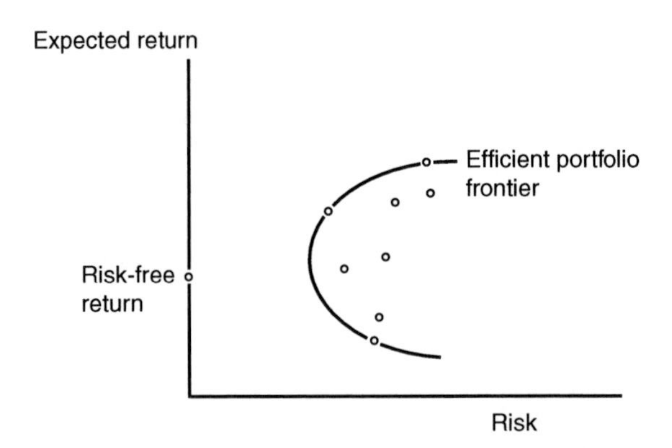

Figure 9.2 The Efficient Portfolio Frontier and the Risk-Free Return

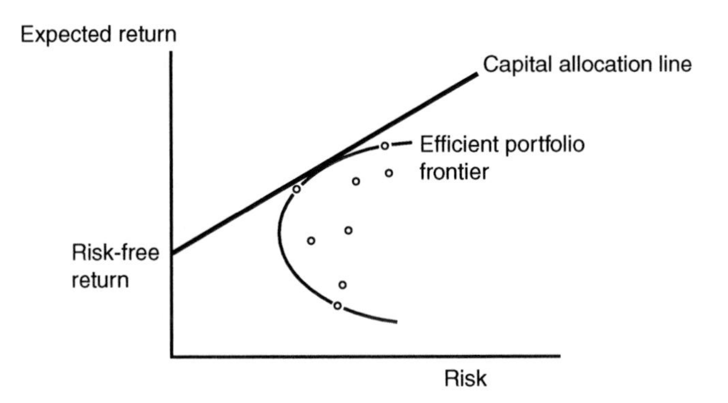

Figure 9.3 The Capital Allocation Line

would be the risk-free point in the diagram. Let us draw a line from that point which is positively sloped, representing the willingness of an investor to absorb some risk for a greater return. In Figure 9.3 is such a line.

We have constructed this line in a unique way. The line starts at the risk-free point and rises as steeply as it can while not exceeding the range of possibilities given by the boundary along the efficient portfolio frontier. A line any steeper would not be able to meet the combination of any possible asset portfolio; and a line any shallower would not allow the maximum feasible return for any given amount of risk.

An investor can then construct a portfolio anywhere along this line, between the risk-free return and the efficient portfolio frontier. An investor can even reach beyond the points on a ray beyond the efficient portfolio frontier. For instance, to move twice as far out on this line as the point it touches the efficient portfolio frontier, the investor would have to somehow purchase twice the return, but also absorb twice the risk.

Extreme leverage once again

Investors can do just that by using cash to purchase the optimal portfolio where it just touches the capital allocation line, and then borrowing an equal amount of cash to double the size of their portfolio. If they can purchase these additional securities "on margin" at an interest rate equivalent to the risk-free return, they can actually attain any point on the capital allocation line.

Highly leveraged investors can even choose a point significantly well beyond the efficient portfolio frontier. Hedge funds and investment banks have been able to leverage their equity purchases upwards of 30 to one or more. This permits them to earn a return far beyond the points that constrain small investors.

Of course, the point investors actually choose also depends on their own personal preference for risk. As we discovered in the previous chapter, individuals differ in their preference for risk, based on many factors – their assessment of risk, their capacity to absorb risk, their inherent level of risk aversion, their age and financial security, their planning horizon, and such.

The final issue, then, is to resolve where an individual investor will choose to locate on the capital allocation line. Starting from the risk-free point, those with low risk tolerance would require a significant increase in expected returns for a given increase in risk. In other words, they would be equally satisfied with points along the low risk tolerance line as in Figure 9.4.

However, those with high risk tolerance would be willing to take on more risk for a given increase in the return. These individuals would be indifferent to points on the high risk tolerance line as in Figure 9.4 .

Actually, there are an infinite number of such lines that we could draw for low risk, medium risk, and high risk tolerance individuals, alike. We could use any risk-return starting point, as shown below for an investor with a high risk tolerance.

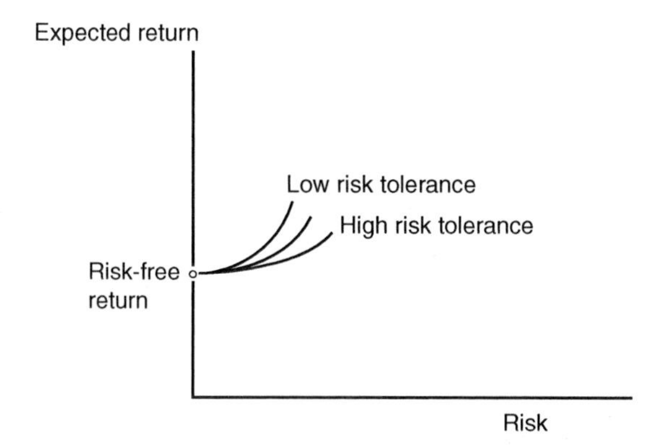

Figure 9.4 Varying Return/Risk Trade-offs for Different Individuals

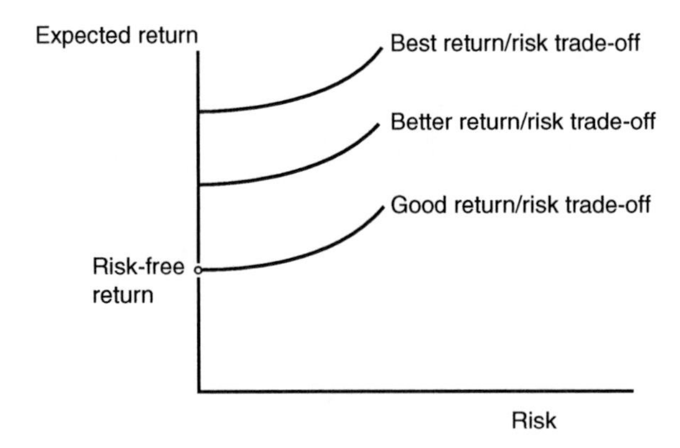

Figure 9.5 Different Return/Risk Trade-off Points for the Same Individual Facing Different Investment Opportunities

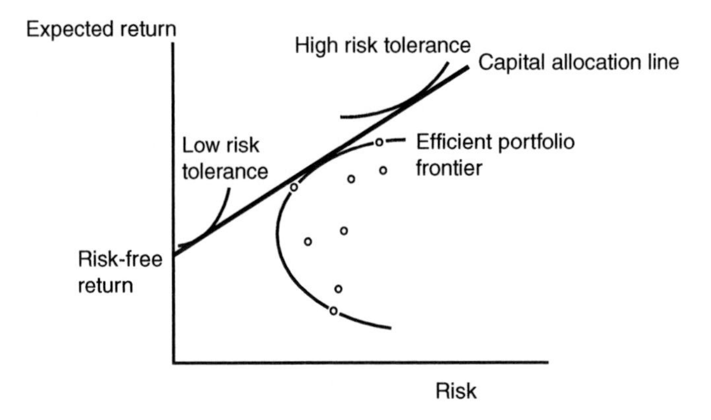

Figure 9.6 Different Portfolio Choices for Low and High Risk Tolerance Investors

Each investor will move along the market's capital allocation line to reach one's most preferred return/risk trade-off represented by the highest attainable curve. We see from the next diagram that low risk tolerance individuals will find a point near the risk-free return point on the capital allocation line, while those with high risk tolerance may actually find a point on the capital allocation line beyond its intersection with the efficient portfolio frontier through margining.

This analysis shows how different individuals will choose combinations of risk and returns. Later we explore how fear affects the efficient portfolio frontier and the capital allocation line. We also explore how financial collapse moves some high risk tolerance individuals down the risk line.

Next, we explore how various incentive schemes affect the risk of some and often leave the rest of us footing the bill.

Part IV
The Problems with Risk

Each of us is willing to take on some calculated risk under some circumstances. Unfortunately, sometimes we get more than we bargained for. Risk can be distorted by the actions or inactions of some. And risk can be shirked from those who ought to absorb it, often to the rest of us. This part describes some economic phenomena that distort risk.

We look first at the problem of moral hazard. When this phenomenon arises, decision makers commit to strategies that offer them some sort of a return, but impose the risk of their actions on others. Chapter 11 demonstrates that it is often the taxpayer of the long-term shareholder who is left with additional risk they had not bargained for.

Shareholders must also be concerned about adverse selection. Investors rely on the responsibility of others to make decisions that maximize shareholder value. However, there is no perfect compensation scheme that ensures our representatives will always make the best decisions on our behalf.

Finally, we must differentiate between gambling, investment, and speculation. While both investment and speculation try to manage risk, gambling is often close to a zero sum game. Winnings are approximately equal to losses, but for a house take that goes to the operator of the game. While investment is hopefully a positive sum game that profits from the march of innovation and technology, speculation and insider trading may extract some of these profits and reduce the process of investment to little more than gambling.

10
Moral Hazard

One might surmise that, like matter, risk is inherent and cannot be created or destroyed. However, the choices of our corporate decision makers can actually amplify risk, while shareholders, as the residual claimant, are often left holding the bag.

To better understand this, we must define some terms. Economists label decision makers "agents," acting on behalf of those they represent, their "principals." For publicly traded companies, these principals are the shareholders, sometimes called the residual claimants because they receive any profits left after all factors and accounts payable are paid, and debt-holders are paid off, too. Any residual that is left goes to shareholders. If there is nothing left, a corporation is declared insolvent and prone to reorganization or liquidation in bankruptcy court. In that case, the residual claimant receives any remaining assets once everyone else is paid.

The principal-agent problem sets us up for some serious problems that no economic theory has successfully solved completely. To give us a sense of these principal-agent problems, let me relate to you a story told to me by a former Fortune 500 chief executive officer who is now an ethics professor at a business school.

In his chief executive officer days, he received a presentation from his finance department regarding a new investment strategy. It depended crucially on housing prices. The young finance stars told him how much money the company would make if housing prices went up by 5%. They also calculated what would happen if housing prices went up by 10% or even 15%.

Frustrated, the CEO asked them what would happen if housing prices went down. They said the model does not include that scenario because housing prices never go down. Within their realm of experience, they were correct. Until 2007, housing prices at the national level rose consistently every year.

Incredulous, the CEO asked them why they would propose a plan that, if successful, could earn these young bucks millions of dollars in bonuses, but if it failed, could destroy the company and the investment of thousands of shareholders. Of course, if the firm went bankrupt, all that would happen to the finance whizzes is they'd have to find a new job.

This story, in a nutshell, describes the moral hazard problem. When decision makers do not face the brunt of the risk they generate, there is a serious, and sometimes tragic, misconnect.

Unfortunately, the term moral hazard has entered the vernacular all too often of late. A term that, until now, was almost entirely confined to discussions between economists and policy wonks, it has emerged as one of the most common expressions among financial commentators.

Moral hazard and insurance

The term was originally coined to describe a special class of problems arising from insurance. In the case of insurance, the mere indemnification of loss can induce some to make decisions that they would not normally make.

For instance, those who insure their car for theft are less likely to lock their doors. Or, those with collision insurance may drive with less care than those without. Each of these problems causes concern for insurance providers. The providers are forced to jack up premiums to the pool of insurees who exhibit such adverse behavior. But because the entire pool of insurees bears the brunt of a single insuree's moral hazard decisions, there is little the insurer can do.

This does not stop the insurer from trying to properly apportion risk, though. They can require cost sharing through deductibles, up the premiums of customers who file insurance claims, use proxies of the care exercised by customers such as their driving record or age, or refuse to insure some customers altogether. Each of these policies is designed to force the insured to bear some of the risk and adjust behavior accordingly.

Health insurance, too, can induce patients to subscribe to more doctors' visits than they might if they were not insured. Interestingly, the problem of moral hazard in this case actually may reduce risk overall.

However, those purchasing health care already suffer from another problem. Their diligence in remaining healthy provides a return to their employer and family, maintains the value of their productivity and education that was subsidized by society, and ensures they do not infect others.

Economists label each of these factors external to the decision of the patient. The resulting "externalities" are the consequences of decisions we make from which we either do not benefit or suffer. In this example of diligent health care, it is a positive externality, imposing a positive benefit on a number of associated individuals that do not have to pay for this benefit. As a consequence, because individuals do not receive the full benefit of their health care choices, they refuse to purchase enough health care. In the case of some health insurance, they would then commission more health care. If health care is optimally provided, one problem – the externality – may remedy the other problem of moral hazard.

We are not typically so fortunate, though. While we can try to create incentives that properly apportion risk, such incentives are frustratingly elusive.

Principal-agent problems

To see this, consider the subset of principal-agent problems that exhibit moral hazard. If we want to ensure the corporation and its shareholders, the principals, assume the proper amount of risk commensurate with reward, how can we induce the executives and managers, the agents, to make decisions that are in the best interest of the principals?

Part of the problem lies in the very nature of corporations. Considered legal persons, a corporation can assume debt and obligation, earn profits, and contract with others. Similar to individuals who declare personal bankruptcy, a corporation can declare it has more obligations than assets and walk away from its obligations, and much of its assets. A publicly traded corporation can issue shares that distribute ownership among shareholders. And a publicly traded limited liability company protects these shareholders should obligations exceed assets.

Unlike the case of the sole proprietor, or the producer that also owns the company, a publicly traded company suffers from the principal-agent problem. It is necessary for shareholders, and the board of directors that represent them, to entrust the day-to-day operation of the corporation to others who may not have the same stake in the enterprise's success.

Differences between the interests of the principal and its agents cause problems that must be balanced against the advantages of the publicly traded corporation. Corporations can more easily raise investment funds if the equity ownership of the corporation can be traded on mature financial markets. Shareholders are more willing to buy these stocks because they know their shares are relatively liquid and can be converted back to cash with relative ease and low cost. This detachment of ownership from management not only creates certain advantages but also creates new and difficult challenges.

Corporate disconnects – short-term profitability

The first challenge is on the emphasis of short-term earnings. Shareholders value both the return and liquidity. Some stocks turn over upwards of 25 times each year, creating a preference for stocks that are most marketable. On a recent day, one in eight shares of Bank of America changed hands. This marketability is enhanced if the company can pay dividends more frequently, issue reports quarterly, and articulate an ambitious agenda of short-term strategies that can be more immediately and easily reflected in the share price.

Boards of directors respond to this mandate by creating a sense of immediacy among the executives of the company. The chief executives likewise respond by demonstrating financial progress each quarter. In essence, the corporation acts as if it faces a short life cycle and time horizon, biasing its decisions toward those who can produce immediate gains, even if it is at the expense of long-term profits. Acting as if the corporation discounts the future, this strategy is much like those of the young and the less risk averse.

This creation of a sense of immediacy for publicly traded firms is at odds with the decisions of closely held companies. A closely held company often has owners that are intimately involved with the operation of the company. There is more immediate alignment of owners' and managers' interests and planning horizons, with the principal-agent problem at least partially solved.

These owners and managers are more likely to promote strategies that emphasize long-term profitability. Freed from the constraint that they must produce short-term profits to satisfy financial markets and maintain liquidity, these firms have at their disposal a vast array of possible strategies, some of which may also be the short-term strategies employed by the publicly traded companies. Reduced constraints, though, must translate into greater profitability and a better alignment between shareholder value and corporate strategy.

The second principal-agent problem is in executive and employee compensation. The art of a well-designed compensation plan will be in its correlation between pay and performance.

Executive compensation

It is common to read in the press these days about executive compensation. Chief executive officers and their executive team must be compensated in proportion to the generic and unique skills and abilities that they bring to the corporation. The generic skills of running an efficient office should command a competitive wage. However, the unique skills a particularly effective manager can command compensation in proportion to the unique profits that are produced by these idiosyncratic skills.

This combination of generic and unique skills then elicits a competitive executive-level salary in combination with additional pay for performance. This pay for performance is typically linked to the degree to which the executive can raise the share price of the corporation.

Such compensation is offered usually in the form of corporate stock. As the stock price rises, so does the value of the compensation plan. This may produce some undesirable tax consequences for an individual that takes all his or her compensation in this form. Executives may be forced to sell some of the stock to generate income for their household. This creates a double tax liability though, on the income taxes for the stock received and for the capital gains that must be paid of the stock sold that has risen in value. As a consequence, executives are also given a comfortable salary with the option of redeeming stocks, purchased at a fixed price but redeemable at a market price. Of course, executives would only accept this option if the redemption price exceeds the fixed price, as we see next.

An unfortunate asymmetry

Executives would prefer to be given a premium if the value of the stock of their employer rises, but not pay a penalty if the stock falls. This may be under the questionable premise that they are fully responsible for spectacular gains of the company, but not at all responsible for losses that are, of course, beyond their control. The sometimes too cozy relationship that can exist between the executive suite and the board room may allow these executives to be partially compensated in options to buy stocks at a predetermined, favorable price.

In such cases, they can reap the reward of a stock that has risen by exercising their option by buying the stock at the predetermined price and immediately selling the stock at a higher price. However, if the price of the stock instead falls, the executive merely chooses not to exercise the option. Consequently, the executive bears little downside risk of a job poorly done or a plan poorly executed, beyond the risk of being fired, a risk they ought to bear no matter what the compensation scheme.

Bonuses, too, have this feature of rewarding upside profit without forcing employees to face downside risk. For instance, the U.S. megabank, the Bank of America was bailed out to the tune of $10 billion in the aftermath of the Global Financial Meltdown in 2008, yet offered upwards of $10.9 billion in bonuses to senior management in the same year. Morgan Stanley was bailed out with $10 billion as well, and yet paid out $2 billion in bonuses shortly thereafter.

After the extensive bailouts in 2008 of a banking industry that contributed to a global financial meltdown and a $25 trillion decline of wealth from a $60 trillion global economy, banks enraged regulators, legislators, and taxpayers alike through the issuance of sizeable bonuses. Like no other time in history, executive compensation appears to have been paid by funds provided by taxpayers, rather than from rewards bestowed on banks by competitive financial markets.

Surely the recipients of these bonuses and executive compensation see things differently. However, there must be some constraints on self-interested interpretations when taxpayers are left holding the bag for decisions not their own.

A responsible compensation plan

Some banks have offered solutions to this dilemma that better align reward with responsibility. Fear has gripped the marketplace and caused wholesale reduction in wealth because of an almost complete disintegration of some critical credit markets. Investment banks and hedge funds were central to the design of new and questionable financial instruments that gave rise to the financial meltdown. Such mortgage-backed securities and credit default swaps are the infamous toxic assets that crippled global financial markets and forced a number of the world's largest investment banks to their knees.

While it outraged the taxpayers who had to indemnify these banks for their antics and the damage they have done to themselves and to the global economy, there is no small measure of poetic justice from the solution to the downside risk chosen by Credit Suisse.

This global investment bank, with a market capitalization of $27 billion at the time of writing, had on their books approximately $5 billion in the toxic assets that the U.S. government's Troubled Asset Relief Program (TARP) were expected to buy up, before it decided not to. Credit Suisse set a model program to avoid future moral hazard and align both risk and reward by offering these assets for senior management bonuses. In essence, the cooks must eat their own meal.

Corporations, or their employees, shed their downside risk to others in additional ways. For instance, jobs protected with tenure or sinecure remain reasonably invulnerable to performance accountability. Employees afforded extensive union protections that may, in effect, remain unaccountable for all but the most serious failures.

Corporations may also perform many of their most important contracts under provisions that enable them to shed almost all their performance risk to others. For instance, it is not unusual for defense and public works contractors to perform under a cost-plus provision. While they must prepare a budget and win the successful bid for the project, any cost overruns are borne by the taxpayer rather than the contractor. Often, only those actions of such irresponsibility that rise to negligence or criminality can force these contractors to assume the downside risk they create.

Subprime problems

These problems of moral hazard are not confined to executive compensation alone. Commissioned mortgage salesmen share a certain responsibility to the meltdown of credit markets and the risk and fear the resulting global financial meltdown created.

In the 2000s, mortgage company agents became increasingly aggressive in selling a new product, now known as subprime loans. These mortgage brokers were permitted to process local mortgages and earn a commission, free of any risk whether the mortgage remained solvent. As the housing and mortgage market heated up still further, they were even encouraged to broker NINJA (no income, no job or assets) loans of up to 100% of the assessed value of the home, or more. In some cases, they even maintained cozy relationships with local real-estate appraisers to be sure that appraisals could come in high to permit a larger mortgage.

These loans were then assembled in pools, packaged, and sold in financial markets, again for a fee and no risk. To add some credibility to these packages, middlemen asked bond ratings agencies to rate these mortgage-backed collateralized debt instruments. The packagers even had ratings agencies compete with each other in favorably rating the pools. Once these highly rated products were sold in the market, they ended up in the portfolios of mutual funds, investment banks, and commercial banks.

We now know these mortgages as subprime loans, and these collateralized debt instruments as toxic assets. Ultimately, it is these toxic assets, laden with risk that brought down world credit markets and plunged us into the worst global financial meltdown since the Great Depression.

These toxic assets were the product of an era of profound financial irresponsibility. Mortgage brokers offered whatever they could to entice new homebuyers into mortgages they could not afford. By offering attractive "teaser" rates that would allow those with low income to at least temporarily make the payments, brokers could expand to markets that were previously untapped. Because buyers were not from a group that typically had experience with homeownership, brokers and lenders have stood accused of manipulation or exploitation in their contracting for these subprime mortgages.

There certainly were informational asymmetries between sophisticated brokers and brand new buyers that had never before existed to the same degree. Buyers and brokers alike rationalized that they could always sell the property at a profit once the teaser rate expired and could walk away from the transaction with a small profit. As long as housing prices continued to climb, there would be no harm and hence no foul. Lucky first-time buyers and commissioned brokers committed a conspiracy of silence – for a while. And nobody was willing to ask what might happen if this scam became oversold.

Handsome rewards

The perpetrators of this risk shirking that has cost us all so dearly and plunged markets into fear and disarray actually profited quite handsomely. Certainly, the brokers who asked few questions and even helped their borrowers' forms received their no risk commission. The former chief executive officer of one of the most notorious of these originators, Angelo Mozilo of Countrywide Home Loans, left the company disgraced but with a $24 million pension, $20 million in a deferred compensation plan, and stock then valued at approximately $6 million. The bond rating companies, too, received their commissions and ultimately the taxpayers, homeowners, and banks left holding all the risk.

Bailouts du jour

Even the biggest banks in the world were suffering from moral hazard. As the current Global Financial Meltdown unfolds, we have made an effort to bailout the banks, under the argument that the biggest banks are too big to fail. Smaller banks were encouraged to be absorbed by the bigger banks. Most of the first half of the $700 billion U.S. TARP bailout package was lent to the megabanks most exposed to this scheme, under the best possible terms at the time. These banks were able to keep record profits earned in 2005 and 2006, and received government bailouts for record losses in 2007 and 2008. Moral hazard reared its ugly head once again.

These losses were nothing compared to the real losses in depressed housing prices as the mortgage market came to a grinding halt. After being burned, banks simply refused to underwrite mortgages to any, but the very best customers.

Unfortunately, in the housing market, it does not take much of an imbalance between the supply of available homes and the number of buyers that can be mortgage qualified to buy these homes. Sellers of homes often do not have the luxury to wait until the market excess supply clears up. Their homes are often vacant, they have moved onto jobs elsewhere, and the tax, heating, and mortgage payments continue. These sellers must sell, even at a considerable loss, forcing housing prices nationwide down by an average of 20% to 30%.

At this point, we have all assumed the risk of these follies. Our home prices have fallen, too, and many are now underwater in their mortgages, meaning the remaining mortgage principal is larger than what their houses are worth. More people are now seriously considering simply walking away from their now undervalued and overmortgaged homes. When they do, the banks, the customers of those banks, the taxpayers, and even the homeowner next door assume the risk shed by others.

These examples show that risk is often magnified as it is shirked. By imposing risk on those unprepared to assume the risk, the consequences are more severe and the additional risk created is more problematic. This risk without commensurate control has driven the fear factor in the marketplace. It also requires us to address how markets can fail to operate efficiently and in the overall interest of the economy.

11
Privatized Gains and Socialized Losses

Before the subprime crisis, mortgage markets had been operating efficiently for generations. Originally facilitated by local banks, mortgage societies, and savings and loans, these markets matched long-term and nicely collateralized borrowers with lenders that were equally interested in long-term lending. Risk was low because the approximately 60% of households who purchased homes strived toward and prized this American dream. Times have changed.

Risk is not entirely new, though. Let's recall the scene with George Bailey in Frank Capra's classic movie *It's a Wonderful Life*. Bailey, played by actor James Stewart, was experiencing a classic run on the bank as word got out that the local savings and loan association was under investigation. As fearful savers clamored to withdraw their savings, Bailey explained to his customers that their short-term cash was bound up in lending on long-term mortgages that could not be easily called in.

This mismatch between long-term mortgage assets and short-term deposit liabilities is one risk that banks must always manage. Their ability to manage this sort of risk has been facilitated by the innovation of mortgage packaging. These instruments are subsequently sold on national and even international markets, freeing local banks from the asset and liability mismatch risk.

The innovation of packaging these mortgages into larger mortgage-backed securities was a relatively safe proposition. In the process though, lost was the first of the three Cs of Character, Credit, and Collateral that was the underpinning of the local banking industry. No longer would character mean much because character is traditionally in the eyes of the beholder. With mortgages collected and packaged from all around a state or region and assembled into a much larger debt instrument, there is no way to reflect the individual character of a particular borrower.

In essence, commoditization replaced character. Two government-sponsored enterprises, the Federal National Mortgage Association, nicknamed Fannie Mae, and the Federal Home Mortgage Corporation, also known as Freddie Mac, were formed in 1938 and 1968 respectively to help standardize and market mortgages. By designing a set of lending criteria, and ensuring the mortgages were offered to credit-worthy households purchasing sound, marketable, and insurable homes, these institutions helped reduce the risk of funding mortgages. In doing so, they promoted a national market for mortgages and helped convert much of the local banking business to a mortgage brokerage business rather than a frontline lender.

This innovation was not necessarily a bad one. Properties were standardized, and there were now well developed credit worthiness criteria. Mortgage syndication also allowed markets to pool risk much better, too. Before pooling, a small lender might be reticent to lend because of the calamitous downside risk of a default. While the odds of a default might be a one in a hundred event, the consequences of a default are dire for a small lender extending a single mortgage. Given the natural risk aversion discussed earlier, such a lender may be unwilling to take on a risk that presents as little as a one in a hundred chance of ruin.

With pooling, however, the downside risk is very small. A pool of 100 mortgages, each with a 1% chance of default, can offer a return of 99% of the interest payments and principal with near certainty. This is because the variation of a large pool of random events is equal to the variation of one of the events divided by the number in the pool. Risk falls very rapidly with pooling, and hence the law of large numbers works in favor of the lenders.

This positive aspect of pooling even works if 100 investors provide capital to the pool. Each of 100 investors in a 100 mortgage pool has the same financial interest as the model where one investor underwrites a single mortgage, but with a hundredth of the risk.

Of course, while such pooling can reduce the nonsystemic or individual risk inherent in each of the underlying mortgages, it cannot reduce the systemic risk that might simultaneously affect all mortgages and broader markets at the same time – for instance, the risk of an economic downturn. However, nor were markets immune to such risk in the days before the syndication and commoditization of mortgages.

This system worked relatively well for decades. However, in the decade before the Credit Crisis of 2007, the United States adopted a national goal to expand homeownership. Those that could not previously afford to own a home had been shut out of traditional mortgage markets for a number of reasons. They may have been nontraditional borrowers, or perhaps they could not easily conform to the strict and mainstream requirements for mortgage qualification that federalized mortgages required.

Banks were encouraged, perhaps even pressured, to lend to nontraditional borrowers. Even Fannie Mae got into the business of insuring the repayments of some of these mortgages. Because these new borrowers were not the traditional prime borrowers, the term subprime mortgage was applied to these easier-to-attain mortgages.

And because of the strength of the economy in the 1990s and the observation that nationwide home prices had never fallen since the Great Depression, these NINJA (No Income, No Job or Assets) loans opened up a whole new market of potential home purchasers.

Underwriters of such mortgages were assured that the risk was low. It was argued that, because home prices were rising so rapidly, if worse came to worse, an unfortunate homebuyer could always sell, reap a handsome profit, and repay the mortgage.

Subprime meltdown

Few foresaw the collapse of a housing bubble that would bring the subprime market to a grinding halt. Actually, some saw the warning signs, most notably Dean Baker of the Center for Economic and Policy Research in Washington, D.C., and Edward Gramlich, then a member of the Board of Directors of the Federal Reserve. After all, regional pockets of the national housing market, most notably Massachusetts in the late 1980s and bubbles in California, Florida, and the Southwest demonstrated that there can be irrational exuberance in housing markets, followed by steep declines that could represent 30% or more of housing values. Critics were not heeded though, perhaps because no one wanted the party to end as everyone is having the time of their economic lives.

What these soothsayers saw that others did not was that even if markets could diversify away the significant nonsystemic risk of pools of these mortgages issued in oversold markets, there was a significant amount of systemic risk that was not accurately priced or diversified. After all, the ability to make the mortgage payments, or the ability to sell a home if the borrower becomes financially distressed, depends on the overall health of the economy. If an economic downturn is broad based, it will most surely affect first those individuals who were not eligible for traditional mortgages and had, by necessity, resorted to the subprime instruments.

To be fair, there was some due diligence on the part of those who packaged, sold, and bought these subprime mortgage pools. They asked ratings agencies to give their stamp of approval on these instruments. Later, we discuss in detail the failure of these raters to adequately price the inherent risk in subprime mortgages. Suffice to say for now that investors were either mislead or did not appreciate the inherent risk of the mortgages they underwrote.

The common themes of mispriced risk, moral hazard, and adverse selection of borrowers unable to repay the mortgages conspired to bring about the subprime crisis. At times there was even blatant incompetence. And at other times, there was genuine criminality. However, rarely did these failures rise to the level of bringing whole institutions to its knees. And never before has significant market failures brought whole economies to their knees.

These mortgage instruments became the notorious toxic assets that paralyzed credit markets worldwide. No longer could we easily and transparently judge the soundness of a collateralized debt instrument. As a consequence, lenders fled. And legitimate borrowers who would have, at one time, been considered the bread and butter of the credit industry were characterized alongside the NINJA borrowers.

Panic on Main Street

How could nonsystemic risk from one market become systemic risk that pollutes all markets and brings down global markets like nothing else since the Great Depression? In a word – fear.

We shall explore later the role of market psychology in amplifying market fear. Let us first explore the domino effect of how failures in one market affect others. While each of these failures may have begun with some poor decisions in one industry, ultimately the risk that was generated would be absorbed elsewhere. Let us track the ultimate destiny of risk from some notorious recent failures.

The recent history of colossal failures began with a spectacular loss by Long Term Capital Management (LTCM) in 1998. While considered mammoth among failures at the time, it seems relatively insignificant today. However, it did produce a blueprint for how we have handled large failures since.

LTCM was the poster child of, and one of the first big players in, the modern hedge fund industry. Ironically, it began with a strategy to extract profits with no risk to itself. Of course, their gain was another's loss – as we shall see.

Founded on a new concept, but born out of scandal, LTCM was formed in 1993 by former Salomon Brothers head bond trader John Meriwether. He had resigned in the wake of a scandal in which Salomon Brothers was accused of manipulating bond trading. The strategy developed in his bond department was designed to circumvent a policy the Treasury had developed to prevent dominant bond bidders from manipulating prices at the Treasury auction.

It was discovered that Saloman Brothers, at that time the single largest auction bidder, had been misrepresenting its identity to bid beyond the 35% market share limit imposed by government policy. As the scandal broke, large shareholder Warren Buffett insisted on executive reforms that resulted in Meriwether's resignation.

Meriwether was not unemployed for long, though. Using his connections with financial whizzes, mathematicians, and two Nobel Memorial Prize in Economics winners, Myron Scholes and Robert Merton, he formed Long Term Capital Management, a company registered in Delaware, operating in Connecticut, trading through a partnership in the Cayman Islands, the home to many hedge funds because of its lax regulatory scrutiny of their operations.

LTCM was successful from the start. Raising over a billion dollars before it began trading in 1994, its trade strategy was to hunt out small price differences in long-term bonds trading in different markets or with slightly different redemption dates. By making a fraction of a penny on the dollar but repeating millions or billions of dollars of trades, the company was able to profit handsomely from others' imperfect information or imperfect access to markets.

Because these trades created such a reliable return with almost no risk, LTCM was able to secure loans from its investment bank associates that represented almost thirty dollars for each dollar of their equity invested. That, in essence, magnified its reward by 30 times, before making interest payments to the banks. To ensure the principal equity investors could keep as much of these returns as possible, they even tried to construct trades that could avoid long-term capital taxation, a strategy that ultimately netted them fines from the United States Internal Revenue Service.

The spectacular profits earned by LTCM strategies ratcheted up expectations of the original investors and attracted new investors that demanded the firm develop new opportunities to earn similar profits in new ways. The basis of their returns was to seek out schemes to profit from nonsystemic risk. However, they were ill-prepared for the losses that can occur across the board when a major financial meltdown occurs.

LTCM first fell victim to the mounting global losses accruing from the 1997 Asian Contagion. The contagion began with a dramatic devaluation of the Thai currency, the Baht, which resulted in a ballooning of its foreign debt. This debt, mostly denominated in U.S. dollars, became much more costly, in terms of the Thai Baht, after the devaluation. Thailand was technically bankrupt following years of spectacular financial growth.

Many began to wonder if the Thai economic miracle was merely financial rather than real. This also cast doubt on similar financial miracles in Korea, Japan, and China, among others, and cast a multitude of Asian markets in financial disarray. Those who invested in the instruments of these markets paid dearly, including LTCM.

On the heels of LTCM losses from the Asian Contagion were losses generated from Russia's threatened default on billions of dollars of bonds issued by its treasury. This further meltdown in 1998 infected the world market for bonds, good or bad alike.

After years of spectacular growth and profits, LTCM amassed an unprecedented loss of more than $4 billion in a few short months.

Of course, the LTCM strategy in itself did not create value. Its financial brilliance was its ability to usurp the profit that would ultimately have been earned by other slightly slower moving bondholders. Then again, LTCM did not incur significant losses either. Like many too clever by one half strategies, they were ultimately engaged in elaborate games of financial poker, a constant sum game with winners and losers, but with no product to show. This was true at least until it failed spectacularly, leaving others to pick up the downside losses.

Once these mounting and spectacular risks came home to roost, Warren Buffett, one of the world's richest people, also known as the financial Oracle of Omaha, offered to personally bail out LTCM. However, the principals of LTCM resisted, believing that they could broker a better deal elsewhere. They knew that they were so large, and their failure so spectacular and demoralizing for already jittery financial markets that they were ultimately too big to allow to fail, at least in a disorganized and ruthless form of economic Darwinism.

Ultimately, the Federal Reserve Bank of New York, a regional branch of the U.S. Federal Reserve system, brokered a bailout of almost $4 billion assembled from a veritable who's who of global investment banks. While the financial system dodged that bullet in 1998, it set the scene of a new strategy that we still live with today.

We have since come to approach potential major financial collapses as an opportunity to share the mistakes that led to their demise with the taxpayers and investors that played no part in their failures but would ultimately pay if global financial markets failed. We opened a Pandora's box and we have not been able to close it since. In doing so, we have proven that spectacular profits are privatized but spectacular losses are socialized and the term moral hazard entered the popular lexicon.

Global Meltdown of 2008

The next financial crises arose from the poisoned assets debacle following the subprime mortgage problem. Let's recall the rapid wealth creation of the 1990s and 2000s that inevitably found its way into rising housing values. At the same time, a push to increase the rate of home ownership in the United States and elsewhere added fuel to the fire. There were exorbitant profits to be had by all and, in such an economic culture, no one asked questions that would bring the party to an end.

And party we did. Mortgage companies such as Countrywide in the United States and Northern Rock in the United Kingdom made it too easy for anyone to realize the dream of home ownership. Many who could not afford home ownership were lulled into the home buying contagion, with the confidence that they could always sell for a handsome profit if they ever found themselves on the ropes. But once the bubble popped, the home ownership dream became a nightmare. It is this nightmare that still haunts us and brought on a severe global recession.

The first victim was Bear Stearns. Long one of the stalwart global investment houses, it found itself more vulnerable than most to the government-encouraged repackaging of bad subprime debt into novel mortgage-backed securities, and their derivatives, that had never before existed.

Relatively early on the watch of the new Federal Reserve Board Chairman Ben Bernanke, there was a mounting expectation that global finances could not afford to let these toxic assets force Bear Stearns under. Until then, the Fed had been engaged in a wait-and-see strategy toward what many believed had the potential to develop into an unprecedented financial collapse, not just for a single firm but for a whole industry. And despite equally strident concerns about encouraging moral hazard by proving those that profit will keep their profits but those that fail will be bailed out, the Fed could not resist acting. It first lent to Bear Stearns and eventually brokered a buyout of Bear Stearns with J. P. Morgan in March of 2008.

Why would the U.S. Fed go beyond coordinating a bailout to actually pump taxpayer money into reorganizing one of the top five investment banks to prevent its failure? After all, Bear Stearns was overexposed in the mortgage-backed securities that arose from the subprime mortgage debacle. However, the investment banking industry is notoriously incestuous.

It became quickly apparent that if Bear Stearns fell, it would also jeopardize many other investors and investment banks. Despite the calls to let those who invested poorly fail, and not create another problem of moral hazard, the Fed felt this situation was just potentially too damaging to financial markets. They forced a merger, and the Fed in turn assured an anxious investing public that it would more fully regulate this previously less scrutinized sector.

Close our eyes and see no evil

Up to this point, the Fed and governments worldwide were reticent to bailout this and similar firms. Memories of Long Term Capital Management had faded, and the affluence of the 1990s and the Bush free marketeering of the 2000s had engendered a fair amount of trust in the marketplace. Much of the regulatory structure had not necessarily been dismantled, but it had been disenfranchised. The pragmatism that typically governs business and government agencies alike had been replaced by free enterprise zealotry and faith in free markets.

As a consequence, the signs of an imminent collapse of global financial markets were ignored, and the responses to the failures, once recognition was impossible to avoid, were weak. The United States, still in 2007 and early 2008 the leading financial force in the world, relied early in this meltdown on two quite traditional and inadequate mechanisms.

The Bush administration offered an anemic response of its own, perhaps more as an effort to appear on top of the situation, but without truly intervening to fix the cascading problems. The Economic Stimulus Act of 2008 offered a tax rebate, deemed by many as too little and too late from the start, and distributed less than $100 billion to U.S. taxpayers beginning May of 2008.

Just four months later, Congress debated and ultimately approved seven times this amount in the Emergency Economic Stabilization Act of 2008. Even this massive sum of $700 billion was, by then, too little and too late. Even a subsequent $825 billion bailout package less than six months later is still regarded by many as coming up short.

Almost $2 trillion had been spent in the United States, and trillions more worldwide in the wake of the Global Financial Meltdown of 2008. But these acts telegraph to us a dramatic shift in the level of fear within Congress in a short period of time; they seem destined to be unable to avert a long and deep economic recession unparalleled since the Great Depression 75 years earlier.

European leadership

At the same time as banks were failing in the United States, European governments became increasingly alarmed. While the Fed was expressing concern about hedge funds and market volatility, the Securities and Exchange Commission was offering the appearance that they were at least running fast, and not getting too far behind. In the leadership vacuum, European central banks began to offer the leadership lacking on the U.S. side of the Atlantic. European clarion calls, at a time when worldwide central banks and finance ministers were still not cooperating closely, may have helped spur the Fed, the U.S. Treasury, and the U.S. Congress along to deal more directly with rapidly worsening problems.

As major investment banks began to write off their investments gone bad in hedge funds and mortgage-backed securities, the Fed also began to step in with injections of tens of billions of dollars to prevent wholesale market collapse. The Fed even began to play an important role in coordinating bailouts and underwriting loans to prevent failures of investment banks.

Meanwhile, Gordon Brown, the prime minister of Great Britain, and its former finance minister, became the de facto global leader in his attempts to get out in front of the rapidly deteriorating market. Brown had recognized that need for coordination of banks' lending to ward off the rapidly growing credit crisis. This also points to very different regulatory responses on each side of the Atlantic.

Countrywide Homes and Northern Rock Mortgages were mortgage companies in the United States and the United Kingdom that grew rapidly with the homeownership run up in the 1990s and 2000s, and were most skewered in the subprime meltdown.

Both were imperiled by both moral hazard and adverse selection problems when the market provided mortgages to those who could not afford the payments and were willing to walk away from their obligations. There was also the moral hazard problem when brokers were allowed to peddle these mortgages without absorbing some of their risk.

The U.S. regulatory response to this dilemma was to encourage Countrywide to be absorbed by the Bank of America. A similar looming failure of U.K.'s Bradford and Bingley's subprime business likewise induced a buyout by Spain's Grupo Santander bank for less than 10% of its previous value.

The United Kingdom instead realized that this could be an opportunity to solve the growing unwillingness of banks to extend new credit. The British government, in a stroke of pragmatism, nationalized the Northern Rock Building Society through the creation of a new quasi-public corporation, U.K. Financial Investments Limited.

In doing so, the government stamped as solvent and credible some leading banking entities, and was able to prop up the U.K. credit market to some extent.

In stark contrast, the U.S. monetary authorities took a more laissez-faire approach. Their neglect could not prevent further deteriorations of credit markets in the United States. It facilitated a forced marriage for the major brokerage firm Bear Stearns and permitted the bankruptcy of Lehman Brothers, which was subsequently bought up by U.K. megabank Barclays. And it agreed to bailout American International Group (AIG), a mammoth company that had on its books large liabilities from its bets in the notorious credit default swaps that grew out of the deteriorating subprime mortgage crisis. The U.S. regulatory approach seemed as varied as there were major shoes to drop.

Ultimately, the United States was forced to adopt a strategy that was more consistent, more interventionist, and more like Gordon Brown's strategy in the United Kingdom. Congress heard terrifying testimonies about an almost complete freezing of global credit markets and were driven, by fear, to pass a sweeping $700 billion Troubled Assets Relief Program. Its stated intention was to use the money to buy up these troubled assets that polluted the balance sheets of U.S. investment banks.

U.S. response

U.S. interventions following the Bear Stearns collapse in March of 2008 came well after the first European responses, and were considered too little and too late. It also required a significant expansion of the Fed's traditional role, limited to acting as the lender of last resort to commercial banks but not investment banks. The Fed had decreased its interest rate on short-term loans to banks from 2 to 1/4%, but its actions were ineffective to stem the growing problems. And this inaction was wreaking havoc on world financial markets which became incredibly volatile and fear began to overtake rationality.

With each announcement of intervention by the Fed, the Dow Jones Industrial Average would soar by perhaps 300 points, only to fall back the next day if not followed up with equally dramatic interventions the next day. The markets became addicted to good news and immediately went into withdrawal symptoms if calming words and credible actions were not forthcoming on a daily basis. Meanwhile, world stock markets oscillated even more wildly.

By October 2008, 300 point daily drops in the Dow Jones Industrial Average seemed like good news. The Federal Funds rate had effectively dropped to 0%, with additional statements that the Fed stood by to do even more. Unfortunately, benign neglect of the looming disaster forced the Fed to become relatively ineffective as households became perilously close to the Keynesian liquidity trap that induces households to pull out of financial markets altogether when interest rates become so low it is not worth our bother to participate in the financial system.

The trouble with the Troubled Assets Relief Program

With the approval of the Emergency Economic Stabilization Act in 2008 and the creation of the Troubled Asset Relief Program, there was recognition that the once almighty investment banks and mortgage houses were a mere shell of their former existence. Lehman Brothers, Merrill Lynch, Bear Stearns, Citigroup, Bank of America, Carlisle Group, Northern Rock, Morgan Stanley, Union Bank of Switzerland (UBS), Nationwide Financial, and Goldman Sachs are no longer the major funds and sources of capital that swept up smaller competitors to create mammoth stores of wealth and capital. Indeed, almost half of these historic investment banks and mortgage giants no longer exist in their previous form.

As these banks were regularly being bailed out by governments, government and central bank funds, and other banks and financial houses, this veritable who's who of finances were just some of the latest too big to fail. Half of the $700 billion fund created by the Emergency Economic Stabilization Act has been spent to reestablish integrity and confidence in U.S. financial markets, in return for government ownership of newly issued preferred shares in U.S. banks.

The problem with the Troubled Assets Relief Program is that it was never really used to purge troubled assets. The banks remain sufficiently unrelieved and are still unwilling to lend. The U.S. Treasury has jumped from one strategy to another, but while some of these actions have arguably prevented things from getting worse, none have made them better. Even the likes of former Fed Chairman Alan Greenspan now recognize that interventionist policy is necessary.

A new export industry

Financial mayhem is the new export industry. Countries the world over depended on U.S. consumerism. With global wealth dropping by nearly $30 trillion, or almost one half, and with tens of trillions of dollars of drops in housing and stock wealth translating into hundreds of billions of dollars of decreased consumption, the U.S. financial meltdown went global. Markets in China, India, and elsewhere dropped precipitously, while Japan's Nikkei dropped to its lowest level in the history of the index. U.S. indices also dropped by the largest sustained amount since the Great Depression.

Most economists acknowledge that by late 2008, the United States had been in a deep recession for more than a year. Most agreed that the recession would likely be long and deep. Some even feared a full blown depression, popularly defined as a drop in gross domestic product of 10%, along with price deflation.

The most significant casualty is the rapid deterioration of consumer confidence. This sentiment, calculated monthly by The Conference Board in the United States, has hit a record low in November 2008, and continued to drop. This index, began in 1967 as a survey meant to capture consumer optimism, is an important measure because it captures the willingness of consumers to spend. But like the announcement that the United States was officially in a recession, it merely confirmed what consumers had known for some time, and had been responding to by keeping their wallets in their pockets.

When will fear abate?

By early 2009, the most helpful sign was the articulation by a newly elected economic commander in chief who acknowledges the extent of the problem and articulates a plan to augment the decrease in private spending with significant government stimuli. We saw some optimism returning. While we were still met with more bankruptcies, financial scandals, layoffs, and declining wealth, there emerged a recognition of the seriousness of the problem, and elected leaders began to show resolve to do something about it. The attention began to have some positive effects.

This recognition is important. Without willing consumers ready to reinvest in the economy, we cannot move forward. While most economists expected considerable pain to linger, and nations were braced for another tough year or two, there was finally some glimmer of light at the end of the tunnel. And that makes all the difference.

The challenge will be in creating a real reform. The problem with merely indemnifying risk is that it does not dissolve risk. It simply takes risk from decision makers and places it on shareholders or taxpayers who have little control in executive decision making. It is this downside risk without a modicum of individual control that is our definition of fear. Rather, there is growing sense that we must get back to the basics of production.

Ultimately, it is not necessarily that we now mistrust capitalism. All the more power to entrepreneurs like Steve Jobs and Steve Wozniak that sit in a garage and invent the Apple computer. They deserve all they receive, as long as they play fair. And all the more power to the banker who produces a better financial instrument that does not impose risk on others but makes the market more efficient and even perhaps homeownership more affordable.

But do business school graduates leave their programs hoping to do well by doing good, or do they simply clamor for their piece of a fixed economic pie? We entrust our managers and executives to make decisions on our behalf. Yet do we provide them the education and tools to do so, and the better incentives that prevent the missteps we have seen increasingly of late? The financial crises give us pause to wonder if we have truly created an efficient set of incentives for our principals to manage in the best interest of shareholders, corporations, and the economic system that offers them such rewards.

12

Adverse Selection and Imperfect Information

We entrust to others the task of ensuring that our corporations are well run, our markets well regulated, and our assets kept safe. We cannot always ensure that the agents we hire will actually perform this duty. In an environment with imperfect information, many problems can arise that will confound our trust.

Trust is important for certain types of transactions. Every day, we exchange cash that is nothing but pieces of paper backed by the "full faith and credit in the U.S. government," or other monetary authorities. We trust that banks keep our money safe, our insurance agent keeps our home and automobile covered, and our doctors and teachers keep us healthy and informed. How do we then ensure that our leaders, managers, agents, brokers, chairmen, and chief executive officers put our collective interests before their personal interests? Can we trust them to maximize our returns while minimizing our risk? In a world with hidden agendas and incomplete information, can we ensure those we select to represent us do not treat us adversely and the value of our dollar remains true to faith? Probably not.

Problems abound in maintaining a viable financial system with the integrity we need to justify our trust. Like few other times in history, we have recently seen this trust violated.

We have known trust to be an issue for centuries, indeed for almost as long as there have been financial markets. Gresham's Law, named after Thomas Gresham, a sixteenth-century British financier under the rein of King Edward VI, demonstrated the costs of violated trust.

Gresham came from a family of forefathers who had been knighted by various kings. He became Sir Thomas by the sword of King Henry VIII, partly as a reward for his uncanny knack for management, at times mismanagement, and practices we would no doubt consider shady today. Ironically enough, he garnered favor from the royalty when he concocted a scheme to revalue a British pound sterling that had been beaten down in value because the policies of Henry VIII drove foreign-held interest on the debt to almost intolerable levels.

Bankers in Antwerp feared default on this debt. Sir Thomas came to the rescue by surreptitiously purchasing the sterling each week at the foreign exchange market in Antwerp. At the same time, he advised the King to set a policy that would force merchant ships that carried British credit secured in Antwerp at one exchange rate to be repaid in London at a lower rate, with the King pocketing the arbitrage profits.

Sir Thomas was also known for founding the Royal Exchange in London, a central forum for trade in stocks and for commerce. With this transaction, too, we question whom Sir Thomas was representing. He stood accused of building the exchange with money from the City of London, but would profit himself from rents paid by some of its occupants.

His law in economics, while not actually developed by him, is inspired by his efforts to improve the quality of the coinage used as a medium of exchange. The law now known as Gresham's Law states in its simplest form that bad money drives out good. It also indicates that violations of trust make it difficult to trust in any regard.

Specifically, the law tells us that money that is easily counterfeited or otherwise debased could pollute the marketplace and force good and valuable coinage to withdraw from the market. For instance, it is fair to deduce that the holders of counterfeit currency would like to exchange this currency for legitimate money. If those trading on this exchange profit, legitimate money must lose. The holders of legitimate money would then prefer to literally take their money and run, at least until confidence is restored. Until it does though, it will soon be the case that the only money left for trade is the bad money, thereby casting into question its use as a medium of exchange.

The concept of Gresham's Law is relevant to modern financial markets in a number of ways. For instance, we see that traditionally stable and useful markets can also become polluted by toxic assets that cast doubt on the value of all assets, good and bad alike.

Subprime mistrusts

As an example, the subprime mortgage crisis invoked a series of Gresham's Law failures. If real-estate markets had traditionally been a bastion for long-term investors and agents, each rewarded by the strength of their reputation, it recently became a haven for fly-by-night speculators hoping to make a quick buck by "flipping that house." No longer could we easily ensure value in a home well built and well maintained, casting doubt not just on those real-estate transactions, but also real estate as a whole. And so goes the market – no longer could we rely on real estate as an excellent medium-term investment.

Similarly, the pools of mortgages called mortgage-backed securities surely contained some mortgages that were good and trustworthy. However, they also contained NINJA loans that were much riskier. Just as it was difficult to see the quality of construction behind the walls of a house, it was also difficult to see the quality of a complicated pool of mortgages.

In these pools, good mortgages were put at a disadvantage because the interest rate that must be paid to investors to market the questionable pools rose for good and bad mortgages alike. In the end, even potential mortgagees that were good risks could not be financed as the subprime mortgage problem polluted mortgage markets of all sorts and gave rise to a complete freezing of credit markets.

As a consequence of Gresham's Law in financial markets, we see risk and fear increase, volatility rise, and net returns fall. While the subprime mortgages were only a small minority of all collateralized debt pools, all securities in the same family became suspect, market prices were depressed, and the ability to raise capital curtailed.

A market for lemons

A more recent corollary of Gresham's Law can be attributed to George Akerlof in his Nobel Memorial Prize winning concept embodied in the paper "The Market for Lemons."[22] In this seminal paper, Akerlof notes that certain types of transactions are more dependent on trust than others.

While it may be easy to deduce if an apple is damaged or overripe, it is not easy to determine if a used car is reliable or is a problematic "lemon." As a consequence, there is a greater incentive for the unscrupulous to peddle these lemons, cars of inferior quality or reliability. This raises the probability that a used car you might buy is a lemon, thereby causing the price of these used cars to fall.

At the same time, if you own a used car that you know is not a lemon, you realize the depressed price afforded used cars discourages you from selling, even if you would have been happy to sell at a price that reflects your known valuation of the car. In the end, only lemons are sold, with no ready market for high quality cars of the same type.

This pollution of a market also causes a general breakdown of market confidence. However, a cowinner of the Nobel Memorial Prize in Economics, Michael Spence, offers a possible solution. If items in such markets can somehow signal to buyers that they are of high quality, in a way that lemons credibly cannot, market confidence can be restored. Such signaling could come from regulators who can punish those that sell inferior products, warranties offered by sellers, or agencies that can somehow inspect and rate the quality of items brought to market.

We discuss a little later the role of ratings agencies in their failure to adequately weed out toxic assets. For now, let us further explore how these toxic assets can infect even unrelated markets.

Market pollution

Many people still living today recall the Great Depression, the last time that fear and cynicism gripped financial markets on a grand scale. The common memory of those who had to endure that ordeal is a general mistrust for institutions. These unfortunates learned to keep their money in their mattress. They avoided borrowing for fear of the ruthlessness of lenders should an economic calamity befall them, and learned to do without the risks and advantages of financial markets.

We learned earlier that financial markets serve some essential roles in reducing risk and increasing returns, when they function properly. However, when the greed of some creates toxic markets for many, the greedy negatively affect even those external to their decisions. This negative externality, defined as when a transaction negatively affects other nonparticipants, creates fundamental market inefficiencies. These inefficiencies ultimately decrease the returns and increase the risk and fear of others.

Policy makers recognize the toll on us all when some try to take advantage of markets for their own greed that is ultimately unaligned with the public interest. We have, in fact, passed antitrust, financial conspiracy, money laundering, insider trading, and other such laws to prevent this toxic behavior. We are also willing to impose treble damages on those successfully prosecuted, forcing them to pay three times the damage we can prove they caused.

We prosecute because we recognize these illegal acts tear at the integrity and trust of our financial markets and institutions. We impose treble damages not only to deter their acts and to force them to pay for the provable damages but also the harm they inflict on market integrity. The penalty may also reflect the fact that so few are ever caught and prosecuted.

Even tripling the damages would be inadequate if we only caught one in four shady dealers. In reality, we probably catch far fewer. As a consequence, we sometimes make great public spectacle out of those we do catch, hoping the modern equivalent of a tar and feathering in the town square will deter others.

An environmental protection agency for financial markets

We cannot expect prosecutors alone to police markets and renew our trust in financial institutions. What else can we do to reestablish market confidence and our trust in institutions? The fear and breakdown in trust ultimately arises from other's greed and fantastic rewards, with the rest of us assuming much of the risk. If this premise was not understood by all before, there is almost a universal understanding following the Credit Crisis and the Global Financial Meltdown. Even Alan Greenspan, the Pharaoh of Free Markets, recently became the Apologist of the Financial Apocalypse. While he maintained a lifelong love affair with free markets, he recently discovered that they are an attractive but illusory ideal.

In his testimony on Thursday, October 23, 2008, before Henry Waxman's Congressional House Committee on Oversight and Government Reform, Greenspan stated, "Those of us who have looked to the self-interest of lending institutions to protect shareholders' equity, myself included, are in a state of shocked disbelief..." When asked whether he still believed that markets are self-correcting and self-regulating, he stated, "The whole intellectual edifice, however, collapsed in the summer of last year." He then went on to admit the role of greed over good public policy:

> The evidence now suggests, but only in retrospect, that this market evolved in a manner which if there were no securitization, it would have been a much smaller problem and, indeed, very unlikely to have taken on the dimensions that it did. It wasn't until the securitization became a significant factor, which doesn't occur until 2005, that you got this huge increase in demand for subprime loans, because remember that without securitization, there would not have been a single subprime mortgage held outside of the United States, that it's the opening up of this market which created a huge demand from abroad for subprime mortgages as embodied in mortgage-backed securities.[23]

The market took at face value the grossly erroneous assumption that complex financial markets could peddle ever more complicated financial instruments just as we might peddle apples in the local farmers market. While perfect competition relies on the inviolate assumption of perfect information for all parties, it is impossible to have such perfect information when the transacted instruments are so complicated and opaque that almost no one can truly assess their risk. If transparency is the necessary criterion for perfect competition, financial markets are anything but competitive today.

Just as the former CEO recently explained to us that the financial whizzes under his employ did not include in their models the prospect that critical markets like housing could fall in price, Greenspan reflected that his assumptions on market valuation too were tragically mistaken. The cleverest people in the financial rooms in the 1990s and 2000s convinced themselves that only the recent past was the best predictor of risk and returns for the new financial instruments they were developing. They sold their ideas to their supervisors, who probably did not fully understand the models either, under the premise that prices have risen in the past and any blips that defy this trend are simply anomalies to be discarded. Ultimately, the market bought it as well – at least until it was too late.

Renewed confidence

Our first step to renew trust and market confidence and to weed out the cynicism that has brought markets to their knees is to understand what caused the market breakdown in the first place. We must better ensure those who generate the risk must also absorb the commensurate risk rather than shirking it onto others. We must repeal the notion of privatized gains and socialized losses, and we must ensure that executives are paid for performance but also somehow penalized for mediocrity or worse.

Economists sum up the various ways in which the actions of those we select to represent us are adverse to our interests. We must redesign reward systems so that our agents are paid based on the performance of their team in meeting our goals. For instance, bonuses on Wall Street were the sixth highest on record in 2008, the very year that saw more than $25 trillion of global wealth wiped out. Unless we defined the goal for our agents to plunge us into a global financial meltdown, their near record bonuses were misplaced.

At the same time, we must ensure they direct their efforts in ways that actually move the team forward, rather than merely giving the illusion of team play. Shirking must be discouraged, and such individual actions as networking must be designed to improve team performance rather than the advancement of an individual's marketability.

As appealing as they may seem, we have come to realize that performance standards and quotas that are too blunt may force our managers to cherry-pick, avoiding riskier projects with higher returns for the projects that will safely allow them to meet the objectives imposed upon them.

On the contrary, our best intentions may even make managers too willing to take risks. If there is no downside for failure and if there is great reward for hitting the home run, our agents may be induced to go for the long ball and take on too much risk in the process. And if middle managers view promotions as a tournament that rewards those who perform relative to others in the company, we may inadvertently be encouraging one employee to sabotage another. Middle managers may even become fearful of up-and-comers, and may even repress or fire whistle blowers that are, in their eyes, too eager to point out the shenanigans or perverse acts of compensation schemes gone wild.

If it is difficult to design employee compensation that correctly balances risk and reward in the interest of the shareholders, it is equally dangerous to avoid the issue of performance-linked compensation altogether. Fixed salaries within a firm encourage the mediocre to stay and the meritorious to seek better compensated rewards elsewhere. Fixed salaries also engender individuals to seek additional ways to be compensated. Patronage, corruption, acceptance of perks bestowed by suppliers, and the other nonpecuniary benefits that occur when employment markets do not reward excellence, are all the costs of a poorly designed principal-agent solution.

Every possible solution to such adverse selection problems seems to impose new pitfalls and costs. Agency costs, defined as the costs and risk of optimally motivating our agents and the costs of mitigating the principal-agent problem, have a whole slew of additional fees that ultimately are borne by stockholders. These include the share dilution that occurs when executives are offered stock in return for their performance, and the fees associated with regular financial reporting designed to inform the shareholders of the success of their agents.

The recent granddaddy of all costs borne to try to get managers to do the right thing, in the interest of shareholders and society alike, is Sarbanes-Oxley. This act of Congress, also known as the Public Company Accounting Reform and Investor Protection Act of 2002, came in the wake of a series of corporate scandals over the late 1990s in the United States. Ethical meltdowns at Enron, WorldCom, Adelphi, Tyco International, and others cost shareholders, employees, and their pension funds billions, while leaving the company managers grossly undeterred. We will return to the ethical breaches that gave rise to, and the costs that flowed from, the Sarbanes-Oxley Act in Chapter 24.

For now, let us note that this act, which is estimated to have cost U.S. corporations approximately $200 billion, as reported in the December 21, 2008 *Wall Street Journal* editorial, has helped to renew some trust, but at tremendous cost. We will return to the effects of ethical breaches on trust and fear in later chapters. Suffice to say for now, such breakdowns occur because of a surprising level and number of failures along the way. It should not be surprising then that the costs of fixing these problems will be large. However, we can afford nothing less.

Ultimately, we must ensure that those who act in the best interest of shareholders and the public, alike, do so with the proper incentives. The sustainability of the free market depends on it. And the failure of well functioning financial markets makes a gamble of what should be a prudent and rational long-term investment.

13
Risk, Uncertainty, Fear, and Gambling

We all aspire to "invest" our hard earned savings into financial markets that offer a return in excess of the small but risk-free return on Treasury bonds. With a typical inflation rate of 3%, bonds earning less than 3% do not even keep pace with inflation. They certainly do not build the nest egg we all require for a comfortable and, hopefully, extended retirement. What portion of our savings is truly invested, though, and what is merely rolling the dice?

To make our investment experience less like gambling and more like an opportunity for clever capital formation, we must assume a fair amount of risk. First, we must ensure that we have done what we can to minimize risk by constructing a well-balanced and diversified portfolio. Second, we must ensure that our investment strategy is well informed and responsive to market signals that are difficult to detect. We must also ensure that we have the market information insiders have. Finally, investment must be a positive sum game. Let me describe these in turn.

Market gambling

While it might be most entertaining and exciting to invest heavily in just one or two individual stocks, such a nondiversified investment strategy probably is more like following your favorite football team than true investment. A lot of emotional energy is devoted to that game, but the returns on average would be unlikely to beat a well-diversified portfolio, or even an index fund, over the long run. Of course, we can get lucky and realize higher returns, and much higher risk. But our gains are more likened to the wins of our favorite football team rather than the product of a well-designed investment strategy.

The game analogy is not a bad one, for a number of reasons. First, there are three types of games. Most games of entertainment are zero sum games. Nothing is produced, and one has, on average, a 50/50 chance of winning if playing against another similarly skilled individual.

If it is a game of chance at a casino, the odds might be a bit lower because the house has to always take its cut. And if it is a lottery, the odds are significantly worse because 40% or so of the proceeds are normally directed to various worthy social causes. These are negative sum games as losers must lose by more than winners gain.

Economists also study another type of game labeled positive sum. This game describes a competition in which the sheer act of competition produces some benefit. We can still lose in a positive sum game, but the overall winnings will exceed the losses.

We must decide whether stock market investing is a positive sum, zero sum, or negative sum game. To better understand the subtleties of game theory, let's continue with the poker analogy. Let us also assume that there is no "house take" as in casino card games. In other words, we ignore the small house take in the form of stock markets' commissions to brokers and other transaction costs. These transaction costs are ever decreasing, especially given the electronic trading technologies that have brought down the cost of matching buyers and sellers of stock. Even the rich commissions usurped by market makers and floor traders do not impose the same imbalances they once did. In other words, all bets come from and go to the players.

Hold their cards close

Few games provide full information to all participants. If there is a strategic element, the players do not reveal their strategies to others. Players also know their own cards, or the common cards on the table, but do not know the cards in the hand of others. The strategies players develop are then a measure of their skill and experience, and the ability of each player to surmise the strategy and information of others. Typically in these games, the more experienced or skillful player takes home a bigger share of the bets.

If all players are of equal skill and experience, no player has an informational advantage over the other and each is able to develop equally effective strategies, we would expect players to neither consistently come out ahead nor behind. In such a well-balanced zero sum game, there is really no point in playing unless one simply enjoys the entertainment value of the game or harbors a belief they have some sort of advantage.

Zero sum game

Before we go much further, we must still decide whether stock-market trading is a positive or a zero sum game.

Let us ignore information asymmetries for a moment. Is there something by the very nature of trading stocks that adds value to industry?

Many note that the value of stocks do rise over time. Technology marches forward, creating new value all the time. The size of the markets for individual industries may rise as the population rises. Some industries may fall in value if producing an obsolete product, once it is understood there is a better product in a competing industry. Stocks in firms from the innovative market will then rise in value and the stocks of obsolete firms will fall.

Industries can create true innovations that enhance the efficiency of production, our ability to use resources better, or can simply produce a better mousetrap. These innovations, increases in population, and increases in overall global demand will increase the value of these stocks and of the overall market over time.

Returning to our earlier analysis of loanable funds, some of the capacity that allows a firm to meet the expansion in demand for its goods is funded by taking on debt. If a firm believes that it can reliably earn a 10% return by expanding its capacity to produce a new product, but must only pay the banker 5%, the firm would choose that avenue. By doing so, the additional profit goes to stockholders, the residual claimant that receives whatever is left over once all the other factors are paid.

Because stockholders, as the residual claimant, can capture the value of all the growth in markets once borrowed debt is paid; they essentially capture the value of all growth of publicly traded companies in the economy.

To the degree that growth and innovation are unexpected and unknowable, stocks rise in value. However, the growth that can reasonably be predicted should be, it is argued, factored into the value of a stock very early on. This is at least true if we subscribe to the theory of arbitrage and if there is sufficient investment capital floating around to purchase today the right to profit tomorrow.

Positive sum game

Innovations aside, financial markets do create value in another important way. By having tens or hundreds of people individually and frequently research the outlook for a stock and its industry, a new marketplace for information is created that did not previously exist. We also benefit by the fact that they put their money where their mouths are, by investing in promising stocks and withdrawing their capital when the collective and best insights suggest the industry or stock is on the decline.

This information is most valuable in directing funds to their best returns. It also allows those companies with promising products and valuable stocks to more easily borrow based on the capitalization of their firm by the market. And it hastens the demise of firms whose stocks no longer curry favor because of weak underlying fundamentals.

These thousand points of light that pour over financial statements, shine on every recess of a corporation, and expose the potential of the industry also create a certain corporate transparency that uncovers shenanigans, questionable practices, and principal-agent problems.

Finally, these markets allow investors who no longer desire the mix of return and risk for a particular firm to easily liquidate their holdings without harming the company or themselves. Such an assurance of liquidity makes it easier for firms to raise new money from initial public offerings to fund new enterprises.

Negative sum game

We have seen of late, though, that the market may sometimes provide a small fortune for a few while costing the many a much larger fortune. To catch as catch can, even if it brings about the demise of the wealth of so many others, can only be rationalized by those holding the most warped view of free enterprise. Actions that undermine free enterprise itself cannot, in any stretch, be justified. Unfortunately, we now see we cannot always rely on individual unregulated actors to do the right thing.

A horse race

To now, the discussion has taken a leap of faith that investment serves a purpose beyond shear gambling. Let us now consider the words of John Maynard Keynes in his classic treatise The General Theory of Employment, Interest, and Money:

> It is said that, when Wall Street is active, at least a half of the purchases or sales of investments are entered upon with an intention on the part of the speculator to reverse them the same day. This is often true of the commodity exchanges also.[24]

More than 70 years ago, Keynes was concerned about the level of trading in stocks and commodities, absent any new information, simply for the sake of quick profits by the end of the day. This phenomenon of active and speculative floor trading is even more common today, with day traders around the world sitting at home and using the Internet to trade all day but liquidate their holdings before they close at the end of the day. While these activities of traders may have a marginal side-benefit of providing liquidity to the market, their effort, and the scale of their transactions, is disproportionate to the benefits that increased liquidity may provide to the financial marketplace.

Such trading may also be harmful. Implicit in the actions of the traders is the presumption that they can profit from such speculation. But without an activity that truly expands the size of the economic pie, in the sense of a positive sum game, their activities must deflate the earnings of longer term investors. Not only are they engaging in an activity that requires effort which could be directed toward something that could actually expand the pie – but they also devote this energy simply to diminish the return of long-term traders. As a consequence, they actually may be making the zero sum game of trading during the day into a negative sum game for the long-term equity market.

Let us now turn to the characteristic of asymmetric information. If the masses simply trust that the game is not fixed and all necessary information has been fully reflected in the price of the stock, then it may be the case that those with superior and inside information are investing, while the rest of us may simply be gambling or speculating.

Speculators or investors?

Keynes also suggested that we must make a distinction between speculation, the pursuit of profiting from our collective psychology, and the more economically useful concept of investment:

> If I may be allowed to appropriate the term speculation for the activity of forecasting the psychology at the market, and the term enterprise for the activity of forecasting the prospective yield of assets over their whole life, it is by no means always the case that speculation predominates over enterprise. As the organization of investment markets improves, the risk of the predominance of speculation does, however, increase. In one of the greatest investment markets in the world, namely, New York, the influence of speculation (in the above sense) is enormous. Even outside the field of finance, Americans are apt to be unduly interested in discovering what average opinion believes average opinion to be; and this national weakness finds its nemesis in the stock market.[25]

Clearly, Keynes was concerned even 70 years ago about the predominance of speculation at best, or gambling at worse, over the creation of profitable and useful enterprises. He also seemed to harbor a certain resentment for American-style capitalism, even then.

It is important for each of us to make this distinction. If we are truly investors, with the singular goal of creating long-term value by producing a better mousetrap or using our factors and resources more efficiently, then we should do as we must to invest in the time and research necessary to succeed in the long-term. Alternately, we can hire others who are better able to research on our behalf, assuming we can remedy some of the principal-agent problems described earlier.

However, if we are speculators hoping to pick the next winning horse, we may share more with gamblers than we might like to think. We may also be prone to the maladies that inflict gamblers of all sorts. If we know our limits, are confident that rationality can trump emotion, and can view any losses as the cost of this particular form of entertainment, then labeling the acts of some as speculation may not be important. On the contrary, if such day-trading and speculation is profitable, and if it does not improve the long-run information, while depressing the long-run returns of others, speculation may depress the returns and incentives for long-term investors.

However, to differentiate between poker players and speculators may be a distinction without a difference. We next explore the nature of an economy which is increasingly speculative and volatile.

Part V
Risk and the Market

Consumers are by nature risk-averse. However, we all are willing to take on some calculated risk if the compensating returns are sufficient. We next explore how we formulate our willingness to trade-off risk and return, and show how market volatility fuels our risk aversion.

We begin by outlining our changing willingness to absorb increased risk for a greater return as market conditions change. We find that market volatility indeed affects our willingness to invest.

We then construct a New York Times Panic Index, and show that this panic index is correlated not to returns but to market jitters. We extend this result to Chapter 16 by demonstrating that our fear factor can eventually affect market returns and plunge us into cycles of market fear and loathing, we experienced in the Great Crash of 1929 or the Global Financial Meltdown of 2008. We conclude from this part that the emotion of fear can be a significant factor in market performance, and may even be the predominant factor at times like that experienced in the aftermath of the Global Financial Meltdown in 2008.

14
Market Volatility and Returns

We can use the results gleaned from the capital allocation line developed earlier to explore what happens as general market risk increases. To recall, the capital allocation line is a line drawn from the risk-free interest rate to a point on the frontier of the best combinations of return and risk in the marketplace, as shown in Figure 14.1.

The efficient portfolio frontier combines the best trade-offs of return and risk that can be found in the marketplace. Some of the assets in the mix have high return and risk inherent in their industry or enterprises. Others have lower return but lower industry risk. We can diversify away the nonsystemic risk that is found in each of these sectors. However, we can do little about the systemic risk that affects all risky assets.

For illustrative purposes, let us assume that market fundamentals are unchanged, but the inherent overall market risk rises. Actually, this scenario is quite unlikely because increased risk will also increase the cost of borrowing, as some lenders in the loanable funds markets will choose not to participate. We see in the next chapter how yields fall if risk increases. For the moment, though, to better understand the dynamics, let's consider what would happen as the efficient portfolio frontier shifts out to the left, commensurate with greater systemic risk and volatility across the entire market.

If this rightward shift in the efficient portfolio frontier were to occur, the capital allocation line would necessarily have to pivot down.

This outward movement of the risk-return frontier and the resulting downward pivot of the capital allocation line necessarily forces investors to lower indifference curves along the new lines. Both high risk and low risk tolerance investors will face lower returns at their new equilibrium. Some may subsequently choose lower risk, while others may actually take on higher risk.

If we can demonstrate that higher levels of risk will reduce investors' yields, the converse actually points to a potential advantage of high finance. If

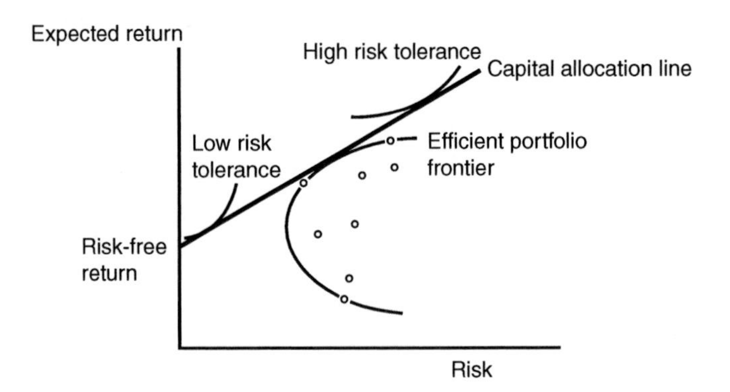

Figure 14.1 Different Portfolio Choices for Low and High Risk Tolerance Investors

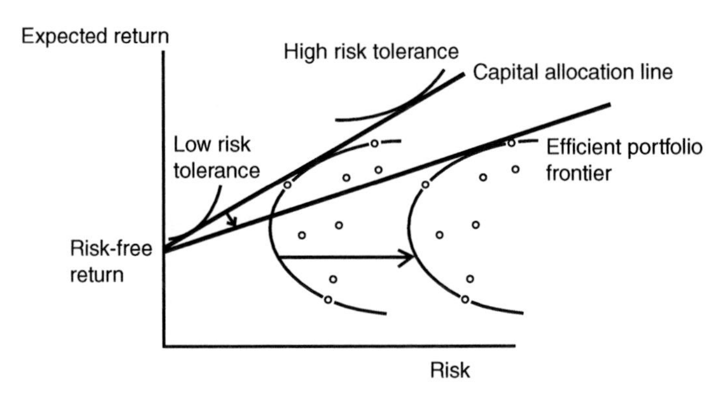

Figure 14.2 The Effects of an Increasingly Risky Market

financial models can indeed figure out ways to reduce risk, the efficient portfolio frontier can move inward, and returns can rise for all.

While reducing risk without reducing returns is the holy grail of finance theory, its pursuit also sets us up for some financial alchemy. Increasingly and incredibly complex financial theories and models designed to reduce risk without reducing returns probably do not work as designed. There is a certain amount of inherent risk that cannot be diversified away. And so much of the risk can be reduced with just a little diversification. Increasingly sophisticated financial models are likely to be increasingly ineffective, experiencing diminishing returns in their efforts to decrease risk without a commensurate decrease in returns. Rather, their sophistication may even create a new form of risk – a complexity risk that occurs when models are not transparent or easy to understand.

Too clever by one half

Brilliant investors like George Soros and Warren Buffett alike have become suspicious of models too complex. Many blame these models, at least in part, for the subprime mortgage crisis, the resulting Credit Crunch, and the Global Financial Meltdown we are all experiencing. If a financial model is so complex that only its designer, with a PhD in physics or mathematics, can understand, the model perhaps should not be trusted. This is especially so if we must now rely on these same developers to explain the model to the rest of us and, especially, to tell us when they think the model will not perform well.

We cannot expect these financial scientists to objectively discard their own models, even when the models fail to perform well. Rather, it is natural for scientists to focus only on the data that support their world view. Because science could not move forward limited by such a failure of objectivity, the scientific ethic demands that sciences adhere to the scientific method.

In the scientific method, no theory can ever absolutely be proven true. Instead, theories are considered to be a temporary resting stop toward a greater truth. Competing researchers use experiments to offer a successful theory a temporary reprieve from its repeal, or use the results to reject a theory. This active, competitive, transparent, and sometimes adversarial process is at the heart of successful science.

The financial theories developed in-house by top researchers employed by top investment banks do not face this same scientific scrutiny, however. An investment bank hires these financial scientists to produce secret and proprietary models that will yield proprietary profits for only that firm. It is then no exaggeration that some theories are understood only by a single person. And while we might hope that these researchers in each firm could be objective and critical of their own life's work, this hope is not a reasonable reflection of human nature.

There is probably little that can truly be done to substantially reduce the systemic risk of the marketplace any further, at least at the finance level. There are likely social, political, and economic policies that may have this desired effect. And there may be some financial models that can give an investment bank a temporary advantage over its competitors, and hence earn extraordinary profits for a while. The wholesale investment in the industry of increasingly complex financial models now seems a fool's path, especially when we factor in the tens of trillions of dollars lost when these black boxes explode on us.

A shifting return/risk trade-off

Referring to Figure 14.2, if markets become more risky, the efficient portfolio frontier moves to the right. This translates to lower returns for the same level of risk. For instance, if population growth begins to falter, the growth in demand will fall too, bringing down profits and returns to shareholders. The net effect is similar to the rightward movement of the efficient portfolio frontier. The risk/return trade-off point for both high and low risk tolerance investors will drop, resulting in lower returns, with the same amount of risk, more or less.

Similarly, if the risk-free interest rate falls, the pivot point for the capital allocation line will likewise fall. This steepens the capital allocation line and may even raise the efficient portfolio frontier as firms have access to less expensive borrowing and can take on additional profitable projects.

The resulting steepening of the capital allocation line reduces returns for those with the lowest risk tolerance, but may actually increase the return and risk for those with a higher tolerance for risk. The fall in interest rates allows less expensive access to money to purchase additional stocks on margin.

Those of moderate risk tolerance may benefit, too, if the resulting boon to returns is sufficiently substantial as a consequence of lowered interest rates. These investors of moderate risk tolerance may find themselves taking on more risk for greater return, while the high risk tolerance investors may take on substantially more risk, and receive a significantly higher return if there is a fall in the risk-free interest rate.

Too loose monetary policy

Some argue that the policies of former Federal Research Chairman Alan Greenspan may have had this effect. By keeping interest rates artificially low following the terrorism acts of September 11, 2001, he is now blamed for encouraging too much risk taking and for artificially inflating the housing and speculative bubbles. By maintaining low interest rates not consistently seen since the Eisenhower era in the 1950s, the loose monetary policy provided plenty of liquidity to allow hedge funds and small investors alike to borrow and invest in financial markets.

Corporate lending, too, is often linked to the federal funds rate. With corporate borrowing rates also very low, corporations are able to take on additional projects that may not have been economically viable at more traditional interest rates. This further increases corporate earnings and the price of stocks.

Consumers also had access to lower borrowing and mortgage rates because of the loose monetary policy and its effect in keeping interest rates low. The low borrowing costs stimulated consumption as it meant a smaller sacrifice in future consumption for more consumption today. Lower mortgage rates on second mortgages and home equity loans allowed households to borrow still more and consume still further. The interest payments on these home equity loans were even deductable from their income taxes.

Finally, the low interest rates reduced the payments on new mortgages and permitted households to purchase more expensive homes than they could otherwise afford. The shortage of upscale homes allowed prices and average housing quality to rise, and precipitated a boom in upscale housing construction. Meanwhile, recipients of subprime mortgages could purchase the modest homes vacated by those moving to the upscale homes.

Blowing up the bubble

The net effect was a speculative bubble in prices of new homes, existing homes, stocks, and new financial instruments that were derived from stocks and subprime mortgages. The Dow Jones Industrial Average rose from 7,701 on September 27, 2002, to 14,093 on October 12, 2008. This represented a solid 10% return in an era that will be remembered for relatively stagnant economic progress.

This trend continued until it failed more spectacularly than any failure in most people's memory. The Dow Jones Industrial Average fell from a high of 14,093 on October 12, 2007 to a low of 6,547 on March 8, 2009. The market stayed within the range of 7,500 to 9,000 for months. The month of October, 2008 saw huge withdrawals of capital from stock markets worldwide as investors, large and small alike, saw their investments drop by almost one half. Investors are yet to return.

Falling prices resulted in dramatically declining yields to stockholders. The efficient portfolio frontier fell, and investors collectively lost almost $30 trillion of wealth worldwide. In doing so, investors became much more risk-averse. Many investors could not tolerate the upward and downward gyrations of the market that was essentially moving sideways – realizing no great gains or losses overall, but with considerable volatility.

When the fear premium becomes large and many participants remain parked on the sidelines, it becomes incredibly difficult for the market to mount a comeback. We see later how this fear, which grips the marketplace perhaps but once in a generation or two, and not to this degree since the Great Crash I in 1929, puts in play a whole series of economic events that only confirm the market's fear instincts.

The theory tells us that increased market volatility should depress returns, even for the most rational investor. We next explore the relationship between return and volatility in markets gripped with risk and fear.

15
Fear, Panic, and Market Returns

We recognize that markets have two personalities. One is of the rational and careful analyst, researching the fundamental ability of a firm to generate future earnings, and establishing a best match between risk and return in the marketplace and their own tolerance for risk. The other personality is bipolar, carried to new emotional heights when the market is optimistic, and sinking to deep emotional lows when the market mood turns ugly.

As a consequence, emotional terms are often attached to the market mood. One day it can be characterized as exuberant, while the next day it is in a funk or a panic. Financial commentators make much of attaching overall market moods to the day's activities. Commentaries like "markets turned bearish today as the fear of an interest rate increase grips traders," or "the market becomes euphoric over earnings reports" are typical of this personification of market mood.

When there is market euphoria, we see the main stock market indexes rise, individual investors revel in their mutual fund earnings, and new investors move some cash into stocks. Champagne corks pop and people walk with a lighter step. With each additional day of improvements in the indexes, more and more jump on the party wagon, pushing stock market earnings to new heights.

However, when markets fall for any extended period, it can result in bedlam. The market mood turns ugly, individual investors become fearful and may sell some of their stocks to convert to cash, and some pull out of the stock market altogether. Any discretionary money on the sidelines and in the pockets of the rational investor may use this opportunity to snap up some good values. But if there is not enough new money coming into the market to compensate for the money leaving, we begin to characterize the market with one word – panic.

The New York Times Panic Index

The word panic is not frequently invoked in commentaries on the stock market. It is used more than one might think, though. To test this relationship,

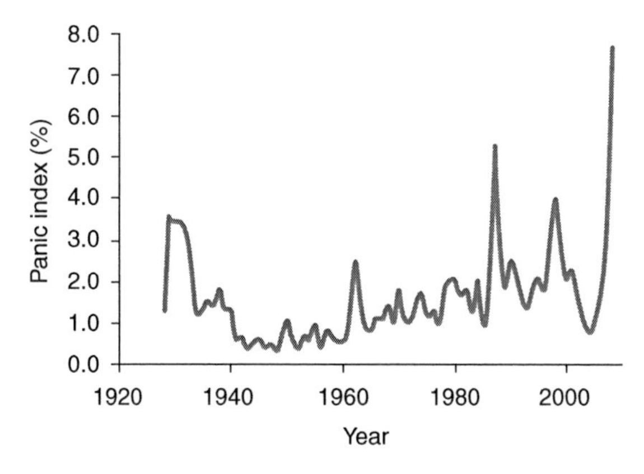

Figure 15.1 The New York Times Panic Index 1928–2008

I searched articles in the *New York Times* since 1928 and found there were 213,603 articles referring to the stock market over the 81 years from the beginning of 1928 to the end of 2008. The average number of citations was 2,637 per year, or 7.2 articles per day.

The analysis was then repeated for each year between 1928 and 2008 for the combination of the words "stock market" and "panic." There were 3,796 such references, averaging almost 47 per year, or less than one reference per week. Such references occurred in only 1.8% of the articles.

This pattern is not at all consistent over time. The fourth highest panic index was over the Crash of 1929 and its aftermath. The third highest panic index was in 1987 when the market fell by almost 25% in a single day on October 19. The Crash of 1987 stood as the single biggest crash in market history. "Panic" was also used as the bubble from the 1990s began to pop in 1998 and as a wave of corporate scandals hit the headlines.

By far, the highest panic index occurred in 2008. With 7.7% of stock market articles invoking the word panic, the index was more than twice as high as the panic that began in 1929. Figure 15.1 maps the panic index since 1928.

The lows are lower than the highs are high

Why does the term panic focus our attention to such a degree? What is it about such an unfortunate market accident that causes us to turn our heads, when euphoria or irrational exuberance does not capture the same attention? In other words, why do market lows extract such emotional gut-wrenching while market highs merely generate a broad grin?

Humans are by nature conservative with our own resources. We work a lifetime to create economic security. When we have temporary windfalls, we may put some of our bounty away for a rainy day, or we may splurge for a while. If we experience what we believe to be a permanent increase in wealth or income, we will adjust our consumption and savings upward.

But when we experience a setback, permanent or not, our entire economic security is cast into doubt. We reflect on our hard work to get to this point, and we lament our losses. If the losses are substantial enough, we may even go through the five stages of economic grief discussed earlier. Some of these

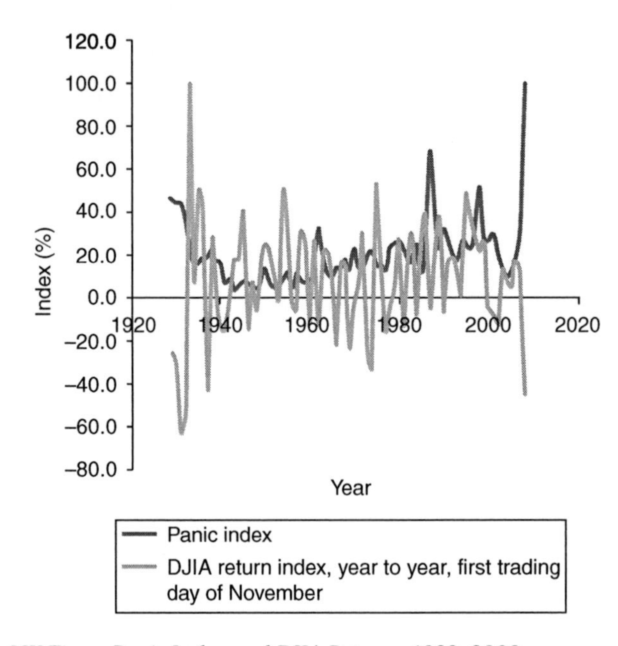

Figure 15.2 NY Times Panic Index and DJIA Returns 1929–2008

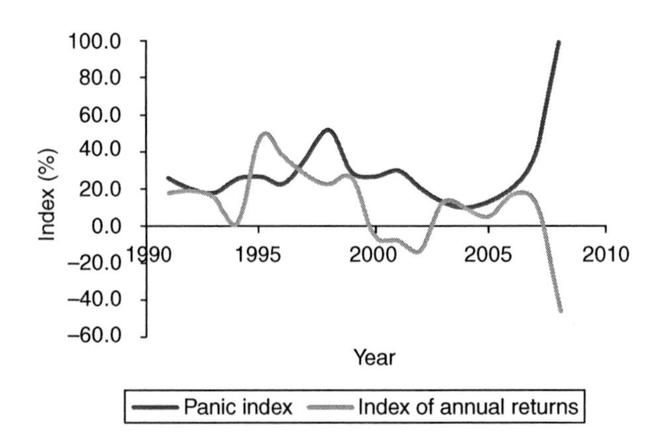

Figure 15.3 NY Times Panic Index and DJIA Returns 1991–2008

setbacks may be only fleeting. For instance, the market recovered from the Crash of 1987, leaving the index higher overall for the year by the end of 1987. Nonetheless, our fear of loss induces us to panic and the financial commentators reflect this panic in their articles.

Are these panics about loss of returns or are they about fear of the uncertain? For instance, if we woke up one day and discovered that we should expect lower returns from here on, would we panic? Not likely. Rather, we panic when we are faced with such uncertainty that we cannot divine which way the market will go. In such an environment, we reasonably attribute a certain probability that the market could drop substantially, and really threaten our economic security.

Graphing the panic index on market returns from 1929 to 2008 shows no definitive pattern.

Even if we confine ourselves to the narrower range of 1991 to 2008, we see surprisingly little correlation between returns and the panic index.

Rather, it appears that the panic index may instead be correlated with the degree the stock market fluctuates.

The Panic Index and the Fear Index

Many have argued that it is market volatility that induces panic. When the market swings dramatically, it is difficult for us to determine where it may come to rest. The much larger potential for a large downward movement when the market is very jittery invokes our greatest fear of economic security.

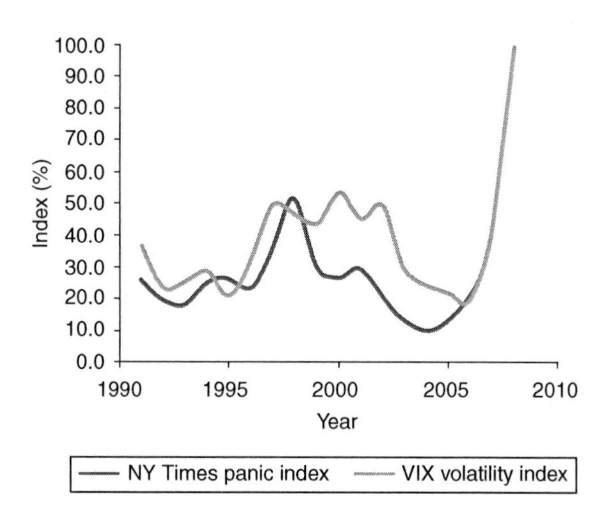

Figure 15.4 NY Times Panic Index and the VIX Fear Index 1990–2008 (set to maximum=100)

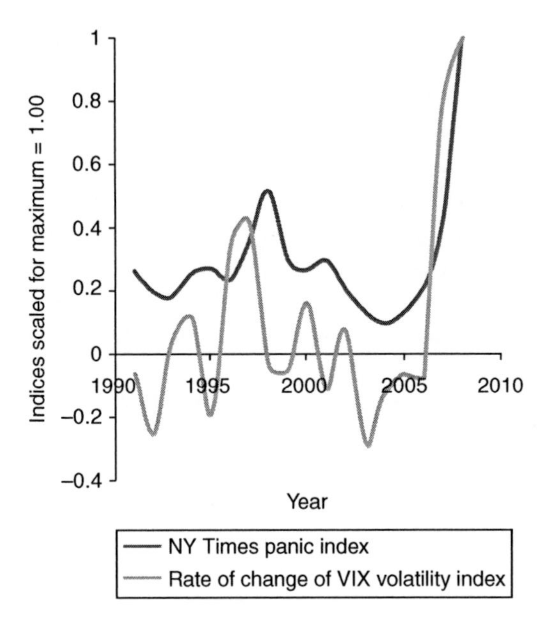

Figure 15.5 NY Times Panic Index and Changes in the VIX Fear Index 1991–2008

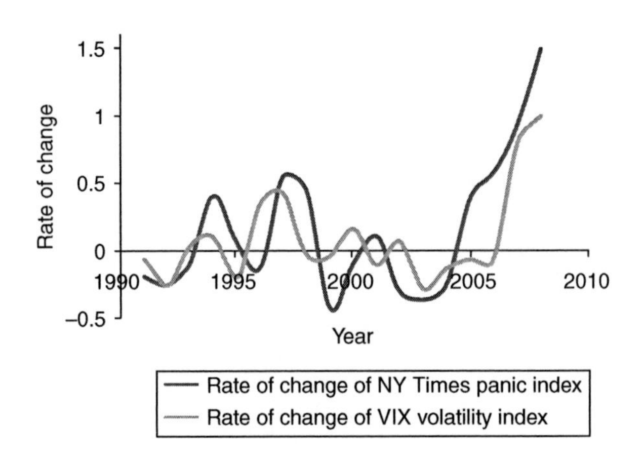

Figure 15.6 Changes in the NY Times Panic Index and the VIX Fear Index 1991–2008

In 1991, a new volatility index was formulated called the VIX index. This index is calculated in real time based on prices of options on the Chicago Board of Trade. Often labeled the fear index, this measure yields a high value if the market is considered more volatile.

Using this fear index, we see from Figure 15.4 that the NY Times panic index moves with the fear index.

We can also explore whether the panic index is responding to the fear index, or whether it is responding more closely to how much the fear index is changing.

There are of course many social, political, and global issues that can invoke panic. To separate these issues from the market forces, let us next graph how much the NY Times panic index changes with changes in the fear index.

Figures 15.5 and 15.6 suggest that the panic index and the fear index move with each other, with market panic sentiment lagging the VIX fear index by between six months and a year. We observe that the fear index is a leading indicator of subsequent market panic. We next explore the extent to which fear and volatility translate into reduced market returns. It is this cost to portfolio returns, as measured by the drops on our pension and mutual funds statements, that is the human and economic cost of fear.

16
The Fear Factor

There is a clear link between fear, panic, and economic crises, as subsequent chapters will document. But what is the true cost of fear?

We can actually calculate a quantitative measure of the cost of fear, in market returns, and in the diversion of profits from production to financiers. We shall see that financial profits rise in times of fear and volatility, while at the same time, our individual stock and mutual fund returns fall.

We can correlate measures of volatility and market returns more directly. Ultimately, the market is concerned about producing strong returns at low risk. We see that returns are harmed by volatility. This is partially because of the effect of market volatility on traders' decisions, based on their natural aversion to risk. However, we also see that market volatility induces fear and panic, and this panic can translate into dramatic declines in market returns.

I have created an index of the Dow Jones Industrial Average so that the largest value from 1997 to 2008 corresponds to 100. I compare that to the VXD, a volatility index on the Chicago Board of Options Exchanges that measures expected volatility in the Dow, which has also been normalized to a maximum of 100. The correlations almost precisely mirror each other.

Figure 16.1 shows that when the volatility index is low, the Dow is rising. Alternately, the Dow declines as volatility increases and fear sets in.

A regression analysis

We can also perform a statistical regression on the relationship between market volatility and market returns. A regression is a common economic tool to show how one variable changes with another. It produces both a coefficient that measures the interrelationship between the fear index and the market index, in this case, and a measure of the reliability of the relationship. By taking the logarithm of these variables before I perform the regression, I am able to directly calculate the percentage drop in market returns for a 1% rise in the fear index.

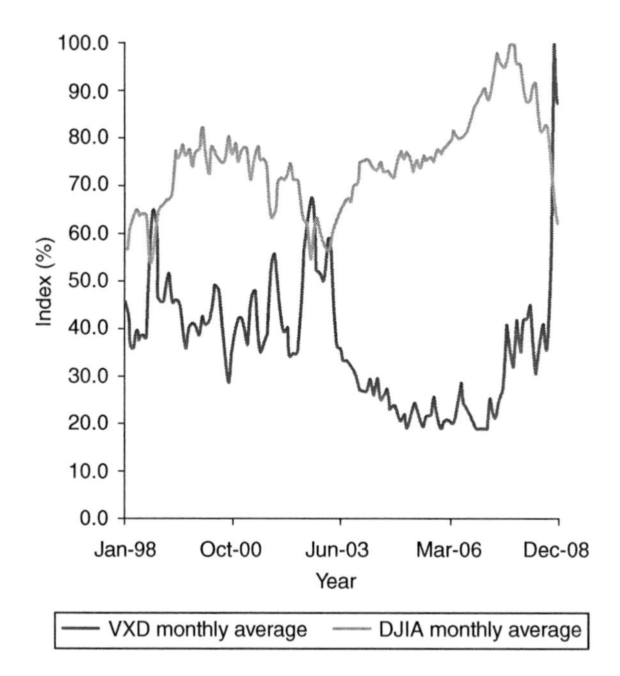

Figure 16.1 The Fear Index and DJIA Returns 1997–2008 (normalized to 100)

Performing the regression of the logarithm of the monthly VXD index between 1997 and 2008 on the logarithm of the monthly Dow Jones Industrial Average, we find a coefficient of –0.2084. This is interpreted to tell us that a 1% rise in market volatility results in a 0.2084% fall in market returns. In other words, market returns fall by about 1% for every 5% rise in volatility. This is a measure of the cost of fear that is seen in declines in our pensions and financial statements when times are volatile.

We can also see that this relationship is reasonably strong. While the R-squared for the variation overall is a relatively low 0.294, implying there are also other factors that obviously affect market returns, the t-statistic measures the strength of the relationship between volatility and market returns directly. In this case, the t-statistic is –7.44, which tells economists and statisticians that there is a strong and significant negative relationship between fear and market returns.

An industry of volatility

It may be argued that the financial sector has become an industry that thrives on volatility. Let us compare changes in the earnings in the securities and trusts industry with changes in market volatility. The graph is normalized so the maximum of each curve equals one.

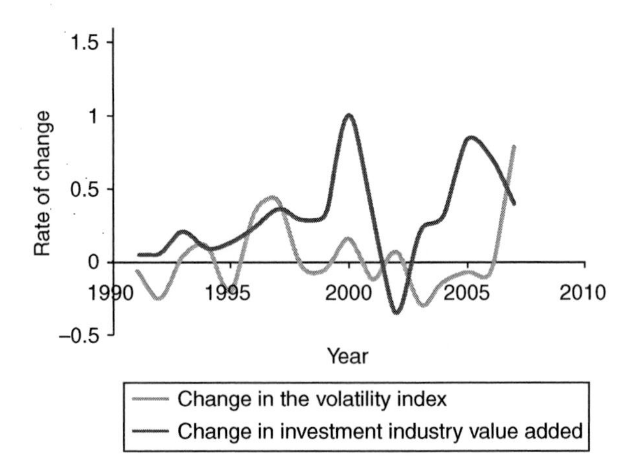

Figure 16.2 Changes in Volatility (VIX) Index and Financial Profits 1991–2008

We see that when volatility is rising rapidly (the volatility index graph is positive and large), financial profits are also rising quickly. Declining volatility after 2001 reduced profits, while financial industry earnings rose with increased volatility after 2005. The industry is in the volatility business, profiting when markets are jittery, and risk and uncertainty are high. While household investors may be losing money in volatile times, the financial capital industry appears amazingly robust and has grown and profited consistently in recent volatile years.

An interpretation of the fear premium

With profits in the financial industry in these most volatile of times exceeding $400 billion annually in the United States, the profits accruing to those that produce the goods and services has declined. One out of every three dollars of profit in the United States recently accrued to the financial industry rather than to the industries that make the products we buy. Greater volatility means greater redirection from production to finances. In other words, the price that producers of goods and services pay to the financial industry increases with increased volatility and fear. This fear diverts resources from production and toward increasingly complex financial instruments and derivatives that increasingly place us in even more fear.

The duration of the panic depends on a variety of issues which we turn to next. These issues can range from the extent to which the factors creating the panic go unaddressed, a failure of economic leadership to guide us away from our natural emotional intuition, or even the ability of media to amplify our panic.

If we acknowledge that volatility can give rise to panic, and panic to significant declines in market value, which in turn breeds more panic and greater aversion to risk, is there anything we can do to remedy this nasty feedback mechanism? This remains an open question. History seems to repeat itself, time and time again, sometimes with tragic consequences.

Part VI
A History of Panics

Theory tells us that panics are the product of increasing market volatility and our human response to threats to our economic security. With any downturn, our risk aversion increases, forcing us to retrench and often sell. This feedback mechanism often brings the market to its knees. With this dynamic in mind, we next look at past crashes and notice some distinct patterns.

We begin with a discussion of a series of market panics. We see that these panics share certain characteristics that are epitomized by the Great Crash of 1929 and the ensuing Great Depression through the 1930s. We end with the insights of John Maynard Keynes, the depression-era economist that have returned to the vogue with the Global Financial Meltdown of 2008.

17
A Brief History of the Fear-Gripped Market

Panics seem as old as markets themselves. Over the last 200 years, the United States and Great Britain experienced a dozen severe panics: in 1819, 1825, 1837, 1857, 1873, 1893, 1901, 1907, 1929, 1987, the Asian Contagion of 1997, and 2007–2008. While each of these arose from a different calamity, they share some important characteristics. Each provoked a fear that brought the market to its knees. It is instructive to understand the common dynamics of each of these crises. Clearly, our economic leaders are now doing just that. Perhaps so should we.

Before the Great Crash of 1929, the common element of earlier crashes was the dogmatic unwillingness of a credible coordinating authority to intervene to prevent calamity. The prevailing economic theory at the time was that free markets got into the mess, and free markets must work their way out. These crashes, perhaps, tell us as much about our failure to recognize coordination failures as it does the way individuals panic and markets crash.

Crash of 1819

We begin with the U.S. crash of 1819.

The United States was still in its infancy. Coming off the War of 1812 with Britain, panic was an inevitable result of rapid post-war movement to a more complex and unwieldy economy. Heavy borrowing to fund the war had left bank reserves strained. At the same time, some banks, most notably the Second Bank of the United States, had been expanding rapidly and without the sophistication in banking tools that a more mature banking industry might demonstrate. Overextension ultimately forced banks, large and small, to limit credit and withdrawals and call in loans that had been extended to fund American rural expansion.

Unaccustomed to busts at the scale then gripping the young country, President Monroe gave in to pressures to intervene. His intervention was, in retrospect, inadequate, as it was essentially limited to a moratorium on conversion of soft money to gold and silver, the hard cash of its day. However, banks eager to expand had done so through extension of credit notes. The federal government, and some states, also began to issue notes (greenbacks) backed only by the full faith in government rather than by the intrinsic internationally recognized by hard, precious metal-backed currencies.

While this expansion based on credit was useful to fund the war and rural expansion, it was only as sound as the banks backing these policies were liquid. As banks began to fail, backing of notes began to disappear, creating panic on the part of those holding such soft money. While the rapid expansion of the use of such soft money had created the purchasing power that pushed prices for commodities and land up very rapidly, the scarcity of hard money and the inability to convert notes to hard money created a deflation.

It is this deflationary effect, in combination with insolvency of banks or moratoria on withdrawals, that is a common theme on subsequent panics. The deflationary factor meant that those incurring debt on their land found that the mortgages were underwater, in common parlance. One holding a $1,000 mortgage on an asset valued at only $100 had little reason, beyond a moral imperative, to continue to bear the burden of their mortgage. By walking away from such obligations, individuals, too, were declaring the equivalent of bankruptcy, placing banks that owned the notes in ever more precarious circumstances.

As now, there was a clamor for two responses. One was to forgive borrowers, at least partially and temporarily. The other was for a reinflation of the money supply to reflate assets to their previous levels. Both policies had severe consequences for one or another group. And both policies could have been avoided had there been a monetary authority that was on watch to keep the banking industry away from the precipice. The consequences of a central monetary authority would not be appreciated for nearly another 100 years. Over time, though, the debilitating effects of the crash dissipated, only to return less than a generation later.

Crash of 1825

While Britain had a much more sophisticated monetary system than yet existed in United States, it was not immune to problems of its own.

The Crash of 1825 shared many of the causes of the U.S. crash just a few years earlier. Britain, too, was financially overextended, having also fought the War of 1812 and the Napoleonic Wars. Following these wars, Britain expanded rapidly, also through the creation of soft money. But while the nation was already well-developed, the empire was continuing to expand to Latin America and beyond.

The London stock market had also been exhibiting a speculative bubble. The Bank of England, as the monetary authority of the empire, was concerned about the inflationary effect of such broad-based expansion of credit. It called for tighter money, and did just as we do today to tighten the money supply. By selling a large number of Treasury notes, the central bank essentially sopped up cash from the private sectors and contracted the money supply. This contraction forced banks to contract too, and to call loans, which increased the default rate of their customers.

The specter of bank failures induced a bank panic, with customers clamoring to convert their deposits to cash. The central bank recognized the recessionary effects of its policy, but only too late. The crisis spread first through Europe and then to the United Kingdom's new colonies in Latin America.

The banking crisis and credit crunch also caused the deflation of a speculative bubble on the London Stock Exchange. The Bank of England stood accused of carelessly fueling and failing to adequately monitor the money supply expansion and credit creation on the run up, and then failing to act quickly enough to reverse its contractionary policy on the way down. It is striking that, 184 years later, our financial systems remain seemingly as vulnerable as they were in 1825.

The central bank was also accused of the creation of an atmosphere of inflation and deflation that made it difficult to properly assess the risk and return of financial instruments. Finally, the bank failed to act as the lender of last resort, supporting the banking industry on the brink of insolvency. This failing ultimately led to the bank panic and is a lesson that has certainly caught the attention of central banks worldwide that must deal with the current Global Financial Meltdown.

The Panic of 1837

This U.S. panic was severe enough to plunge the country into a five-year depression of a severity comparable to the Great Depression of 1931–1937. And while the makings of the crisis predated the new president, Van Buren was held responsible for the calamity, in no small part because of his refusal to allow the government to intervene in a meaningful way.

While the earlier U.S. panic in 1819, and the British panic in 1825 should have offered a good understanding for the need of a monetary authority to act as a lender of last resort, the United States remained reluctant to intervene at such a scale. Indeed, it would not be until the aftermath of the panic of 1907 that the U.S. government would sponsor the formation of a central bank or monetary authority through the creation of its Federal Reserve System.

Another aspect shared with depressions before and since was a huge run up in asset values, followed by a significant deflation. President Van Buren, and the presidents before him – John Quincy Adams and Andrew Jackson felt that they presided over a nation bestowed with a divine providence of wealth and growth. This arrogance of entitlement, along with a peculiarly zealous faith in free markets, despite some significant convulsions, created an atmosphere of economic disengagement on the part of Van Buren.

The markets gave every reassurance of such bounty. Asset values tripled from the years 1831 to 1834. The spending that this paper wealth created also forced an inflation of nonasset goods such as food and cloth. And this wealth was not sufficiently spread out to appease the workers who were most hurt by the ensuing inflation that often accompanies speculative bubbles. They were angry, and riots resulted in New York City.

The seeds for the demise were actually sown by Van Buren's predecessor, President Andrew Jackson. He authorized the withdrawal of government funds from the Second Bank of the United States, and ultimately forced the bank to lose its charter. Problematically, the Second Bank had been acting as a de facto lender of last resort to other New York banks, in the absence of a central bank in the United States. The closing of the Second Bank of the United States created a domino effect that forced the closure or partial failure of almost half the nation's banks, wiping out hundreds of millions in bank capital in the process.

Soon after the bank failure, there was rioting in the streets of New York City over the subsequent wrath of smaller bank failures. Soon the companies depending on these banks began to fail as well. The dramatic deflation in prices that results when there are mass layoffs and fire sale prices for assets caused a deflation that threatened the remaining banks and borrowers alike. Because of President Jackson's failure to recognize the consequences of a broken banking system, and Van Buren's unwillingness to create institutions for lending of last resort, the deflation and the resulting depression held the nation down for another five years.

The Panic of 1857

While not quite as severe as the Crash of 1837, the Crash of 1857 nonetheless managed to become the first global financial contagion.

As with all other panics, it began with the dramatic failure of some bank and created a domino effect that could not be contained. As with past U.S. panics, the federal government still lacked the sophistication and the lender of last resort to prevent a small problem from becoming a big one.

This crash was initiated by a spectacular case of embezzlement at the Ohio Life Insurance and Trust Company. The crisis of confidence in this major company and shifting patterns in world trade induced some large international accounts to repatriate their funds away from the United States. These shifting trade patterns deflated commodity prices in the United States. Finally, the loss of hard money in the coffers of the U.S. Treasury created additional lack of confidence in the U.S. currency.

While each of these instances should not have, in themselves, caused a crisis in confidence that forces a major recession that persisted until the U.S. Civil War in 1861, it was the inability of the emergence of economic leadership to avert a crisis that was ultimately to blame.

Certainly, the roots of the 1837 crash were more severe and shifting trade patterns had been common in the nation's infancy. Government tried to respond to the ensuing recession by offering land grants in the West and by lowering tariffs. However, these antirecessionary policies only divided a nation at quarrel even further. Southerners feared that the policy of westward expansion was designed to create more antislave states, while Easterners found the reduction in import tariffs weakened their ability to sell their crops at sufficiently high prices. The country was divided economically, and would soon attempt to divide physically.

Panic of 1873

The Crash of 1873 was the first U.S. crash that began abroad and was transmitted to the United States. At that time, both the United States and Germany were experiencing dramatic growth, on the heels of the end of a civil war in the United States and following a military victory over France by Germany. Both countries were rapidly expanding their railroad networks in a wild era that included some malfeasance and fraud.

In May of 1873, the Vienna Stock Exchange failed, precipitating a series of bank failures. A railroad speculative bubble burst in Berlin, and a major railway concern in the United States, financed by Jay Cooke and company, also went into bankruptcy.

Meanwhile, the United States decided unilaterally to move off the dual gold and silver monetary standard, in favor of a sole gold standard. This caused silver prices to drop, damaging the fledgling silver industry in the Western United States. The sudden shortage of precious metal backing at the Treasury, in effect, reduced the size of the money supply, again causing deflation and placing borrowers in peril.

In the end, a subsequent presidential election would be fought primarily over the appropriate precious metal standard for the U.S. currency. While election battles over a currency standard may seem quaint today, the issue was most intense then.

Following the failure of the Vienna Stock Exchange, the New York Stock Exchanges too succumbed to a collapse in asset prices. The market was actually forced to close for ten days in September of 1873 as a quarter of the nation's railroads collapsed and a great expansion came to an end. Soon, the unemployment rate reached double digit proportions, labor strife hit the nation, and there was a prolonging depression until 1879.

It would still be 30 years before the United States saw the need for swift action to maintain financial liquidity in the immediate wake of bank crises. And the United States would have to endure yet another more railroad-led crash and one more monetary standard crash in the meantime.

Panic of 1893

In some ways, the Panic of 1893 was an echo of the panic 20 years earlier. The country had yet to put institutions in place that prevented the fundamental causes from reoccurring.

As with the crashes of the past, the panic of 1893 was preceded by a dramatic period of growth on the coattails of railroad expansion and the wonder technology of the nineteenth century. The Chicago World's Fair in 1893 celebrated 400 years since the arrival of Christopher Columbus, and was a showcase to modern advances such as fluorescent lighting, moving pictures, power generation, and Cracker Jack, the Hershey Bar, the Ferris Wheel, Juicy Fruit gum, and the hamburger. Just as we saw a century later in the dot-com bubble, hundreds of railroad companies began with waves of mergers, acquisitions, and overbuilding opening up the market and the nation. These expansions were made primarily on debt, making the propositions highly levered for equity holders, but also highly vulnerable to the slightest misstep.

And misstep it did. The Philadelphia and Reading Railroad was bankrupted early in 1893, followed by the Northern Pacific Railroad (which also played an important role in the previous panic of 1873), the Union Pacific Railroad, and others. Banks began to fail, European capital was repatriated, and bond markets dried up.

The financial meltdown especially hit small mill towns in Eastern United States. High unemployment forced millions west, further fueled by a gold rush in British Columbia and growing urban centers in the western territories. The displacements of that depression forever changed the complexion and economic geography of the young nation.

Panic of 1901

While the previous crashes were primarily fueled by overexpansion and a failure of the federal government to coordinate policy, the Panic of 1901 was rooted in financial near-monopolies and manipulated by financial magnates. And once again, Northern Pacific Railroad was in the middle of the crisis, for the third crash in a row.

But while past crashes had swung the economy into a depression, this crash was limited primarily to financial markets.

This crash of the New York Stock Exchange resulted from a battle of titans over financial control of the Northern Pacific. Rockefeller money, from William Rockefeller's First National City Bank and Standard Oil, and the wealth of New York financier and banker James Stillman were used to orchestrate a cornering of the market for Northern Pacific. On the other side was J. P. Morgan and Jacob Schiff money backing E. H. Harriman's misguided attempt to monopolize all rail coming in to and going out of Chicago.

Harriman's attempt to augment his holding of Union Pacific Railroad by buying up Northern Pacific stock began to bring down the entire railroad sector. Sharp declines in railroads created a herd mentality of selling everything in sight. Once the dust had settled, Harriman did end up adding to his railroad empire. His victory was short-lived though, as his holding company was busted up by the Sherman Antitrust Act, a piece of legislation passed in 1890 to prevent just such an eventuality.

The Dow Jones Industrial Average would go on to lose some of the luster it had gained in the run up of the previous few years. Those financiers who began to view the stock market as little more substantial than a boxing match had their entertainment. And many had their comeuppance. But unlike previous crashes, much of the damage was confined to those who made artificial fortunes in a few short years, some whom subsequently lost them. It taught the largest of the financiers, too, that they must police their own. If government would not step in to preserve order, the likes of J. P. Morgan would. It was not for the last time.

The Panic in 1907

This panic was the panic of all time, if we view panics as a spectator sport. It came about once more from an effort to corner the market in a particular stock. When the ploy came to rest, the New York Stock Exchange had given up half the gains it had made over the previous year.

Even though the stock at the center of this meltdown was no longer Northern Pacific Railroad, the railroad industry nonetheless played a role here too.

As a consequence of the battle of titans over Northern Pacific in 1901, and the subsequent near monopolization of Chicago rail lines, the Interstate Commerce Commission was given power by Congress in 1906 to regulate railroad tariffs. A century ago, the regulation of the railroad industry, which was the equivalent to the dot-com industry today, caused across-the-board price declines in the railroad sector. These declines had collateral effects, too. Bonds issued by railroads had represented large shares of the loan collateral of some of the nation's leading banks. In the early 1900s, as goes the railroads, so goes the market.

In addition, New York City had failed in a bond issue of its own. And on Monday, October 14, 1907, financier Otto Heinze tried unsuccessfully to corner the copper market in the United States.

Heinze's brother F. Augustus Heinze, a copper magnate himself who made a fortune from mining in Butte, Montana, was believed by his brother to control a large majority of the shares of the United Copper Company. Otto believed these shares were being sold short. This process of short selling requires traders to borrow the stock from a long-term holder, who Otto presumed to be his brother F. Augustus. The short sellers would then sell the stock, forcing the price lower, and then sweep in to buy the stock back, at a lower price later, to return to the rightful owner, and in turn make a quick profit.

Otto's ploy was then to buy the stock aggressively. Otto surmised that if he could move the stock up instead of down, the short sellers would be forced to buy the borrowed stock back at a much higher price to return to the original owner. They would experience an extortionary financial calamity. Otto figured this would put him in the catbird seat and allow him to extract some extraordinary profits.

Otto, F. Augustus, and an investor named Charles Morse, who had earlier done a similar bear squeeze in the ice market, had borrowed heavily to finance their buying scheme. But when the short sellers were actually able to buy the stocks elsewhere, the ploy failed, forcing Otto and the gang to sell, sell, sell to recover what was left of their investment. Prices of United Copper toppled, and so did the Knickerbocker Trust Company that lent them much of the money.

In turn, Otto's broker also toppled, as did the savings bank owned by his brother. F. Augustus also had convinced one of the major New York banks over which he presided to hold a sizeable portfolio in United Copper. It, too, failed after customers who heard about these dealings began a classic run on the bank, just as Knickerbocker Trust was simultaneously experiencing.

The failure of a large bank, a large trust company, and a brokerage induced banks to stop lending to each other, at least until the dust settled. This practice of banks lending to banks to maintain solvency of the entire banking system had essentially created a privatized bank of last resort, in the absence of a central bank to serve that necessary function. With the private central bank equivalent to taking a holiday, a chain of bank failures spread across New York City and beyond.

J. P. Morgan, then one of the world's richest men, and a stalwart of the New York banking and finance scene, called an emergency meeting of all the available bankers who could fit into his library. He had worked out a plan in advance to add liquidity in the markets with the secretary of the Treasury, George Cortelyou, the president of First National Bank, George Baker, and the president of the National City Bank of New York, James Stillman. You may remember Stillman as one of the principals in the battle of the titans over Northern Pacific Railroad that brought about the Panic of 1901.

Morgan quite literally had the door of his library locked from outside, and insisted that none of the assembled bankers could leave the room until they had raised the funds necessary to avert an even greater disaster.

These bankers eventually collectively pledged sufficient funds to keep the banks afloat and keep the stock exchange open. Morgan even lent money to New York City to keep it afloat. They also formed two committees, one to convince the press that order had been restored, and another to implore the clergy to tell their flocks on Sunday morning to have faith in the financial system.

Trouble still loomed, though, and Morgan and his band wheeled and dealt with every turn. They eventually had to force some marriages of convenience of weak firms that could only survive in combination. At one point they had to steal down to Washington, D.C., for a secret meeting to implore President Theodore Roosevelt to suspend by executive order the antitrust rules for one particular merger that was critical to the survival of the exchange. Teddy Roosevelt would later comment that he believed this single act may have saved the market from complete ruin.

While complete disaster was averted, the Dow Jones Industrial Average dropped from a high of over 100 in 1906 to 53 by November of 1907. In turn, the country experienced a wave of bankruptcies and unemployment doubled over the next year. And the realization that it was only through the intervention of private citizens that prevented a complete meltdown led to the creation, for the first time, of a federal lender of last resort. Congress passed, and on December 22, 1913, President Woodrow Wilson signed into law the Federal Reserve Act that finally created the Federal Reserve System.

Unfortunately, the Federal Reserve Bank was not sufficiently sophisticated or proactive enough to deal effectively with the next major panic and threat to a national banking system, beginning in 1929. As we have treated the Great Crash and the Great Depression elsewhere, we next see that there are equally ineffective institutions for coordinated monetary policy once panics go global.

Panic goes global – the Asian Contagion

Until recently, international trade was the primary link between national markets. Crashes tended to be localized because of these weak global links. All that changed in the 1990s with large-scale global trading in securities and foreign exchange.

The first financial contagion to strike the global economy occurred in 1997. Now called the Asian Contagion, the financial market panic started typically enough. A dramatic run up in asset prices accompanied a period of sustained growth in Thailand and other South East Asian countries.

Much of the development growth in Thailand had been fueled by foreign borrowing, mostly denominated in U.S. dollars, through traditional channels and through international agencies such as the International Monetary Fund and the World Bank. Thailand, in particular, became burdened by this debt. When the United States began to raise interest rates in the late 1990s to slowdown its overheated economy, capital was instead diverted to the United States, raising demand and the value of its dollar. This in turn harmed Thai exports worldwide because the Thai currency, the Baht, had been pegged at a fixed value to the U.S. dollar.

In an effort to stem a decline in exports and in the realization by the Thai government that they could not afford to support the Baht any further, it announced it would allow its currency to fluctuate with foreign exchange market forces. This caused an immediate devaluation of the Baht and effectively raised the value of its foreign debt denominated in U.S. dollars. In effect, Thailand became insolvent.

The diversion of funds away from investment in South East Asia, and the rising dollar likewise increasing the debt of nations that had lent in U.S. dollars caused massive job losses in the Thai export sector. This in turn created a severe deflation in housing and real estate assets. As is typical in these deflations, banks failed and assets were lost.

As a consequence of a run on the Baht, other South East Asian countries, most notably Malaysia, the Philippines, Singapore, South Korea, and Indonesia, and also China and Hong Kong to a lesser degree, experienced difficulty maintaining their own currency values. As investors fled investment in these stock markets, they converted from the South East Asian currencies into other currencies, driving down still further the demand and the price of the South East Asian currencies. The devalued Asian currencies caused their dollar denominated national debt to rise, causing stock markets across Asia to plunge further. A broad Asian recession set in.

The Asian downturn affected other parts of the world as well. The decreased demand for resources in these slumping economies forced oil prices down, precipitating dramatic declines in Russian securities, which in turn led to the collapse of Long Term Capital Management in the United States.

A global lender of last resort

We cannot expect any one national monetary authority to redress the problems that led to an international financial meltdown. Once panics cross borders, the global economy needs a much larger lender of last resort and some entity to coordinate the policy responses in the various nations. Many have argued that the World Bank and the International Monetary Fund had to bear some responsibility for the run ups in Asia, and should also have been more proactive once the panic hit.

In particular, Nobel Memorial Prize winning economist Joseph Stiglitz was critical of the response by the IMF, deemed by many to be too little, too late.

His insights are quite valid, given that he was for years the chief economist at the World Bank. Interestingly, he has also been a vocal critic of an equally slow and anemic response (at first) to the next economic crisis to hit the global economy, the Credit Crunch of 2007, followed by the Global Financial Meltdown of 2008.

Global Financial Meltdown of 2008

Not unlike other crises, the Credit Crunch of 2007 came about because of a crisis of confidence in the U.S. financial system. The innovation of the subprime mortgage made homeownership temporarily affordable to an entirely new cohort of the public who, until then, considered homeownership beyond their reach. In the midst of a strong and almost unprecedented housing price run up nationwide, there was much concern that the price rises would not be sustained unless we created more potential home owners. At the same time, investors were hungry for new financial products that would offer a better interest rate than the paltry amount U.S. treasury bonds were offering.

Some too-clever financiers came up with a new instrument, the mortgage-backed security, that would allow them to market packages of these questionable loans to an unwitting public. The marketers even had these new securities rated by agencies that were unaccustomed to rating such instruments, and were appreciative of the significant increment this new business would add to their bottom line. The risk-distorted instruments were sold to banks, mutual funds, and investment houses.

However, once the market realized the true risk of these liabilities, it was too late. The value of the assets plunged, banks were forced to write off significant parts of their investment portfolio, and the freezing up of mortgage markets because of banks' increased risk aversion reduced effective demand for homes. Housing prices fell, and we once again found ourselves in an asset deflation led downturn.

The downturn had significant effects on the entire investment industry. Layers and layers of dangerous speculation, incompetence, and fraud were discovered at a massive level never before contemplated. In the end, major investment houses were forced to merge or were permitted to go belly up, financial scandals ensued, and governments worldwide had to pledge trillions of dollars to prop up global financial markets that lost almost half their value.

Common elements – inaction and fear

The most profound aspect of this series of crashes is a common pattern among them. They invariably began after a long and sustained asset run up. They were precipitated by some minor crisis. The crisis, while too small to create a wholesale crisis in consumer confidence, did not attract the full-blown attention of the economic leadership. As the ensuing deflation placed consumers in such jeopardy in wealth destruction, debt to asset value inflation, or employment uncertainty, they were gripped in fear and did what they do every time when fear replaces rationality – they curtailed their spending.

We next look at the granddaddy of all crashes, until lately – the Great Crash of 1929 and the ensuing Great Depression.

18
The Roaring Twenties and the Great Crash

Art Deco, construction of the Empire State Building, F. Scott Fitzgerald, Jazz, Babe Ruth, Ernest Hemingway, Charles Lindbergh, women's suffrage, speakeasies, and the lost generation – these are things that defined the 1920s. A huge financial capital appreciation, popularization of the automobile, movies and radio, design of the DC-3 aircraft, and the wholesale creation of retail investment by the masses also characterized what we affectionately call the Roaring Twenties. This wild and revolutionary era came to a grinding halt on Black Tuesday, October 29, 1929.

Over a decade following the Great War, anything seemed possible. The population in the United States and the developed countries were rapidly urbanizing and industrializing. After overcoming a brief recession, the U.S. population first, and Europe five years later, began spending their peace dividend following the end of the Great War. Presidents Harding, Coolidge and Hoover became the first supply side presidents. The age of consumerism and "buying on margin" began, fueled by a cutback of taxes to the wealthy, which in turn fueled the greatest speculative bubble to that time. Parallels between then and the recent era could not be more profound.

The level of economic growth may have given rise to some of the excesses of the Roaring Twenties. Rising from 63.90 on August 24, 1921, to 381.17 eight years later on September 3, 1929, the Dow Jones Industrial Average rose by a factor of six, at a rate of more than 22% per annum. Over the same period, inflation was almost nonexistent, and labor productivity rose by more than 5% per annum. The Fed's discount rate averaged about 4.5% over the same era.

By all measures, the cost of capital and margin borrowing was low, growth was strong, and the return to risky assets was spectacular. It would have been hard to be an investor and not make out brilliantly. And given banks' willingness to lend to small investors on margin at most affordable rates, it would not be difficult to earn a consistent 50% annually on invested equity in the stock market.

Let it ride

When markets climbed consistently for almost an entire decade, it would also be quite compelling to "let it ride." Investors would plough their gains each year right back into the market, and even expand their borrowing as their assets afforded them. Fortunes were amassed, even by small-time investors. Everybody wanted to get in on the action, and millions did so. With so much capital piling into the market, a speculative bubble could almost not be avoided.

One measure of the size of the speculative bubble is the Price/Earnings ratio. A measure of the price of the stock compared to the profits it earns each year, the P/E ratio hit an historic low of around six in 1921. This measure means that a stock will return its price in dividends and other earnings in just six years. However, the P/E ratio reached an historic high of about 32 only eight years later, just before the crash. At the height of the speculative bubble, a stock would take thirty two years of earnings to recover the stock purchase price. As measured by the price earnings ratio, this bubble was large indeed, and has only been exceeded once since, in the year 2000.

While it is commonly assumed that the piercing of the speculative bubble in the Great Crash of 1929 led to the Great Depression, the situation is quite a bit more complex than that. While the stock market crash was severe, it was not as dramatic as the percentage drop experienced in 2008. And the one day drop was not as large as the Crash of 1987.

The speculative bubble was not without foundation, based on the dramatic technology boom of the 1920s and its concomitant effect on increased productivity and efficiency. And the bubble started from an artificially low P/E ratio of only six in 1921, less than half the traditional P/E ratio in the United States.

The beginning of the end

While the wealth effects of the Crash of 1929 were disturbing, factories were still producing the week after the Great Crash, and unemployment rates continued to hover around 6%. Firms found themselves overproducing in the latter half of the Roaring Twenties, perhaps preparing themselves for what they thought would be the Terrific Thirties. They began to contract somewhat in the latter half of 1929, just before the Great Crash occurred.

If the Great Crash did not dramatically precipitate a market consolidation that had already begun in the latter half of 1929, it is true that it was but one of a series of events that culminated in a perfect storm. Mounting inventories led to layoffs as industry became jittery. Banks were overextended following an era of rapid expansion and their newly acquired role as the bankroller of small investors everywhere. In that era, lenders had been willing to front investors two thirds of the cost of stocks, a level of margining that is now illegal by federal regulations.

Some began to comment more stridently about the growing speculative bubble well before the Great Crash. The Fed already began raising the discount rate to slowdown the economy by discouraging lending and new investment, and banks and investment houses were increasing margin requirements. The Fed was also participating in a great internal debate whether to use even more dramatic increases in interest rates to slowdown the rapid advance of financial markets. However, it was decided that more subtle forms of persuasion, more carefully aimed at financial rather than all markets, was appropriate.

Finally, some attributed the passing of the Smoot-Hawley Tariff Act as a contributing factor to this perfect storm. Designed to sustain domestic growth in the wake of flagging production beginning in 1928, this antitrade tariff bill was an attempt to discourage imports from Europe, just at a time when Europe was trying to create wealth to pay back its wartime debt.

Flagging production always seems to bring about our worst fears on the evil trade intentions of others. Then, as now, our fear causes some of us to argue for a "beggar thy neighbor" policy and raise the fences to curtail imports.

Fear, protectionism, and panic

Despite protests from prominent U.S. economists and prime ministers worldwide, the antitrade Smoot-Hawley Tariff Act passed. In just three short years, imports from Europe declined by more than two thirds. Because of international retaliation, U.S. exports declined by a similar amount, and trade worldwide also fell by two thirds over five years.

The actual magnitude of the tariff increases were relatively small, especially when compared to the dramatic effect the act and its aftermath had on worldwide trade. The Act remains distasteful to this day, though, because of the symbolism of its stated purpose. At a time when the developed countries could most benefit from coordination to avoid a possible recession, one country instead chose an isolationist policy, worried about its domestic position at the expense of its partners. Time and time again, we see this pattern of inward looking proposals each time our market becomes fearful.

These various forces, in trade policy, mounting inventories and layoffs, concern about the speculative bubble, and tightening credit, gave the market pause for concern. Failure of a credible voice to lend calm to the marketplace allowed the market to panic. And panic it did.

On October 14, 1929, the Dow Jones Industrial Average remained above 350, and very near its record high. Ten days later, on the close of Black Thursday, October 24, 1929, it had broken the 300-point barrier on a slow downward spiral and on a huge trading volume. After this decline of almost 15% over ten days, it rebounded above 300 briefly that Friday, but continued to plunge, falling to 260.64 by Monday, and a 230.07 by Black Tuesday, October 29, 1929, a further 23% decline.

The market continued to move sideways for the next year, and had even managed to claw its way back to 294.07 by April 17, 1930. It finally gave up the ghost, though, falling below 230 once and for all on September 19, 1930, almost a year after Black Tuesday.

The market then continued to worsen for two more years, reaching a floor of 41.22 on July 8, 1932. Adults in their forties that somehow managed to hold on to their stock would not see it fully recover in value in their lifetime. It took 25 years for the market to again surpass 350, on August 24, 1954, in the midst of the affluence of an Eisenhower era built on promises of a chicken in every pot and a car in every garage.

A generation of suffering

This dramatic 25-year ride, spanning a great boom, a Great Crash, a Great Depression, a successor to the Great War, and a build up to a Cold War, is more likely a consequence of a variety of factors. However, perhaps the greatest precipitating factor in the obliteration of consumer confidence may have been in the decimation of the banking industry in the wake of the Great Crash.

There is no doubt that the commercial banking industry was already vulnerable. Permitted to lend much more casually than would be allowed today, they had been flourishing in an environment of little regulation and insufficient oversight. A new spate of banking regulations would be promulgated in the aftermath of this debacle. But before that could occur, the number of banks in the United States went from almost 30,000 in the 1920s to less than 15,000 in the depth of the depression. And with the wholesale bankruptcy of the American banking system went the savings of millions of households and firms alike.

If a breakdown in the banking industry is a significant factor contributing to the Great Depression, can we conclude it was causal? We had seen more significant losses in financial markets before and after the Great Crash, without the debilitating effects. We had also experienced recessions before. And firms had responded to recessionary forces with layoffs and mounting inventories. Finally, there were deflations of significant speculative bubbles, too. At no time before has there been such a massive failure of banks and credit markets. The resulting effect of frozen capital markets, lost deposits, and a shaken confidence in institutions upon which millions of consumers relied, is likely the single most important factor for destroying the newly found consumer-led economy.

We have learned to recognize the symptoms that give rise to the problems and we now painfully understand the need to act swiftly and decisively at a sufficiently early stage to retain confidence. What we perhaps forget each time is the need to take away the punch bowl during a fantastic party. We, of course, must hope that free-market ideology does not get in the way too, as it has so often in the past. The interesting questions each time is – will we remember these lessons? And have we gained a sufficient understanding of coordination failures to prevent the next collapse?

It is the resulting decade of shaken confidence of consumers that we turn to next. And it is alarming to realize that everything I described in the run up and immediate aftermath of the Great Crash has its modern parallels, but for one distinction. The stock market did not begin to recover so immediately following the even more dramatic Global Financial Meltdown of 2008. Time will tell if both the Crash of 1929 and the Crash of 2008 have a common aftermath.

19
The Depression-Gripped Economy

Anyone alive during the onset of the Great Depression and its aftermath was forever changed by its collective pain. This was a defining era for more than a generation. The lessons learned are all but forgotten now. The parallels between now and then has renewed interest in the Great Depression era.

If the Roaring Twenties were recalled as an era of technology, productivity, and wealth, the Great Depression left in its wake misery, reform, and caution.

Actually, the aftermath of the Great Crash was actually almost business as usual for a while. Over the year following October 29, 1929, the stock market recovered nicely, and spending by companies and government were both on the rise, after declines in the first half of 1929.

Consumers though were directing the show. The United States had quickly become a consumption nation, so when consumers cut back in their spending by 10%, there were repercussions. To compound the disappearance of consumers, the heartland of U.S. agriculture suffered a severe drought in the summer of 1930. The age of the Dust Bowl had begun.

A crisis of confidence

Consumers were fearful partly because of the losses they incurred in the Great Crash. Significant losses forced many to sell, and to miss the subsequent stock market revaluation. These consumer-investors, no longer as wealthy as before, cut back on consumption and also became more risk-averse.

The distressed selling of stocks by panicking consumers also meant they retired the debt many had borrowed on margin to purchase stocks. The retirement of debt, and the unwillingness of wary consumers and firms to borrow also caused a substantial reduction in the money supply. This money supply, defined as cash and the deposits held in banks, fell precipitously following the Great Crash.

This risk-averse behavior had secondary effects, many of which profoundly affected the banking industry. The retirement of debt as consumers withdrew from the stock market caused banks to lose portions of their loan portfolio. Banks also owned assets that declined in value with the Great Crash, damaging their bottom line again. Businesses, too, suffered as asset values declined and bankruptcies and closures accelerated rapidly.

The fall in asset prices, in stocks, homes, businesses, and farms even resulted in an effective increase in inflation-adjusted interest rates. With the deflation that began to take hold in 1930, borrowers realized they would have to pay back any debt in more scarce and valuable dollars. This had the same effect as raising the interest rate, and discouraged borrowing by already wary consumers, businesses, and farmers. And with a steady decline in the number of banks, households compounded the problem by hoarding their cash.

From 1929 to 1932, industrial production plunged by almost half, new home construction declined precipitously, and almost 5,000 banks went out of business. With more than 10 million workers joining the unemployment ranks, few had confidence the economy would recover anytime soon. And, no agency or entity seemed to have a prescription for an ailing economy. It is no wonder that fear set in. And once fear gripped the economy, all bets were off on what might happen next.

A self-fulfilling prophecy

We shall see that the emerging panic and gloom became a self-fulfilling prophecy. These very acts of consumer frugality weakened the economy and the banking industry significantly, justifying and reinforcing consumers' worst fears. They had simply lost confidence in financial markets and banks alike. Banks fell as a consequence. Bank runs and bankruptcies became commonplace as the banking industry contracted and money became scarce.

Bankers, too, became caught up in the panic. They saw consumers' fear accelerating each day, witnessed the runs on some banks, and realized the capacity of borrowers to repay loans could become seriously constrained in the future. They responded by calling in loans to save their own banks, cut back on the credit they were willing to offer, and accelerated the downward spiral in turn.

By consumers hoarding cash and banks calling loans, there was simply little investment capital left to purchase assets, even at fire sale prices. Ironically, the very act of consumers to become more frugal and to reduce their debt further accelerated the decline of their asset wealth.

We now have a much better understanding of this vicious downward spiral of asset value fueling liquidation and hoarding, which in turn accelerates asset declines still further. This dynamics has even repeated itself, to a smaller degree so far, in the Global Financial Meltdown of 2008.

But, we were flying blind in 1930. While there was little experience and sophistication in the fledgling Federal Reserve at that time, the modern Fed has as its chairman Ben Bernanke, an economist who has spent an entire academic career understanding the asset deflation cycle in 1930. So while the Fed stood idly by as The New York Bank of the United States failed in 1929, the Fed could not afford to let that happen with Citibank in 2008.

Old school

We get ahead of ourselves, though. There was so much about panic, fear, and consumer psychology we did not understand during the Great Depression. The self-fulfilling prophecies of the new-found consumer-investors had not been modeled until well into the depression. And President Herbert Hoover, the U.S. leader who presided over a depression that began in the United States but spread around the world, steadfastly maintained an ideologically based faith that the market would heal itself. His belief in the old-style classical economics, despite new problems never before witnessed, even induced him to balance the budget with tax hikes and spending reductions in 1932, further tightening the downward spiral.

Hoover was merely a product of the then prevailing economic school of thought. The notion was that markets reach equilibrium without intervention. Supply was thought to create its own demand. This idea that supply creates its own demand is known as Say's Law, named after Jean-Baptiste Say, a nineteenth-century French economist and political philosopher.

Say's Law argues that the production of goods and services creates new wealth. This wealth is paid to the workers that make the new products, and hence gives them the collective means to purchase these products. According to this classical economic theory, there is little that any institution needs to do, beyond creating a fair and level playing field that would allow private companies to thrive.

This sentiment was particularly strong in the Roaring Twenties as the innovations and growth led to a renewed faith in meritocracies, economic and social Darwinism, and the Horatio Alger-esque notion of rags to riches in pursuit of the American dream.

Too simple by one half

This classical and fatally simplistic theory of Say's Law was insufficient to account for the complexities of a modern economy. It assumed that production would be purchased by the monolithic recipients of payments to the factors of production. These factor owners are workers (the factor of labor), property owners (resources), and capitalists (owners of the factories and patents, and recipients of the profits).

Of these three groups, only workers would plough back into consumption almost everything they earn. And if this group received a smaller share of the earnings and preferred to hoard their earnings rather than consume, Say's Law fails. With the richest 1% owning 40% of the wealth in 1929, some of the newly amassed wealth did not necessarily find its way into the purchase of goods in the marketplace. It is this growing concentration of new wealth in the hands of a very few over the Roaring Twenties that likely contributed to the repeal of Say's Law.

The Federal Reserve also stood accused of failing to grow a money supply that was contracting because debt was retired and defaulted, and households began to hoard their cash. While noted economist and Nobel Memorial Prize winner Milton Friedman argued forcefully that the Great Depression arose because of a failing in monetary policy, we realize now that monetary policy is relatively ineffective if consumers have lost their confidence in banking and monetary institutions. The Great Depression would go on to spawn a new era of banking and investment regulation, and would produce a much more activist Federal Reserve. These innovations came too little and far too late to defray the most economic misery afflicted on developed nations in modern history.

The laissez-faire theories of the economy simply proved inadequate to deal with the displacement and distress of a fear-gripped economy. It was inevitable that there had to be a paradigm shift in our understanding of and willingness to intervene in the economy.

Other countries' experience

Most of Europe tumbled along with the United States as it witnessed the Wall Street failure of 1929 and the dramatic decline in demand from U.S. consumers.

Great Britain, still reeling from the aftermath of the Great War, was spared the dramatic growth the United States saw from 1921 to 1928. Mired in strikes and hampered by a decision by Chancellor of the Exchequer (Treasury minister), Winston Churchill, to revalue the pound sterling, it found its competitive position actually decline globally over the 1920s.

With the onset of the Great Depression, Great Britain too followed the misguided balanced budget path initiated by the Hoover administration in the United States It also imposed wage controls to decrease costs, which further accelerated the deflation that was also at the root of the U.S. experience from 1929 to 1932.

Throughout the period, Great Britain already had in place a well-developed set of social welfare programs. These programs became severely stressed during the 1920s, forcing the government to take radical steps to reduce wages and spending still further with the onset of the Great Depression. Great Britain continued to falter up to the point in 1936 when it began to prepare for World War II.

In stark contrast, Japan remained relatively insulated from the Great Depression. Their economy was quite strong in the 1920s, partly because they filled the gap in decreased trade that Britain had experienced as a consequence of misguided U.S. trade policies of the 1920s. Japan also instituted policies that later became known as Keynesian policies. These policies of deficit spending and infrastructure improvement, even before Keynes had fully articulated his new economic theory, allowed Japan to grow as others were declining.

Indeed, Japan was growing so nicely that their leadership was actually fearful of inflationary growth as the Great Depression created deflation and misery elsewhere. Its attempts to reduce government spending on armaments and munitions actually created a backlash that resulted in the resignation of the finance minister and promoted a rise in nationalist sentiment that shifted the balance of political power toward the military.

Japan's deficit spending and armament buildup actually allowed Japan's gross domestic product to double in the 1930s, just as countries like the United States, Great Britain, France, Australia, and Canada were significantly weakening. What emerged from this nationalistic period was a renegotiated sense of global power.

Aftermath of activist policy

The U.S. economy did begin to turn around in 1933, but took a decade to fully recover. Some argue that the recovery was complete only because of the effort to rearm Great Britain for World War II.

Under the leadership of President Franklin Delano Roosevelt, following his March 1933 inauguration, a number of institutions were put in place to remedy the recognized failings of the 1920s. New Deal programs like the Works Progress Administration (WPA) and the Civilian Conservation Corps (CCC) stimulated employment.

On the financial side, the Securities Act of 1933 reformed financial markets through oversight lacking during the Crash of 1929. It promulgated the Glass Steagall Act and the Federal Deposit Insurance Corporation to help renew confidence in a banking industry riddled with failures of overextended banks and with the loss of customer deposits. And the Reconstruction Finance Corporation, actually initiated under Herbert Hoover, helped create the loans for industry and state and local government that had all but evaporated from the traditional banking sources of credit.

More controversial were the National Recovery Act and the National Labor Relations Act, both of 1935. The NRA allowed government to play a much more significant role in controlling economic competition, while the NLRA provided much broader rights for workers to organize in unions. They heralded in an era of labor-management strife that, at least temporarily, reduced the effectiveness of the recovery efforts. As a consequence, the New Deal efforts of FDR began to level the downward spiral, although with somewhat less effectiveness than one might imagine.

These initiatives began to falter, pushing an otherwise slowly recovering economy into a recession in 1937. This was one year after Keynes came out with his important treatise, and helped induce the FDR administration to commit to significant deficit spending to spur on the economy.

Meanwhile, a British economist was developing a novel explanation of consumer spending that explained a phenomenon that was rapidly developing.

20
Along Comes Keynes

As economies unwound around the globe, the British economist John Maynard Keynes was developing an explanation of consumer spending that was spot on for the era. His insights were both timely and profound, and are even experiencing a resurgence given the strong parallels between the Great Crash of 1929 and the Great Crash II of 2008, and between the Great Depression and our current Global Financial Meltdown.

Son of Cambridge economist John Neville Keynes and social activist Florence Ada Brown, John Maynard Keynes was born into the elite, schooled first at Eton, and then studied mathematics and ultimately economics at King's College at Cambridge, England. He began his career as a lecturer in economics at Cambridge but soon found himself appointed as an advisor to the chancellor of the exchequer of the United Kingdom.

His uncanny abilities in foreign exchange markets at a critical time during the Great War catapulted him into the highest levels of British public service. He represented Great Britain at the Versailles Peace Conference in 1919 and became renowned for his writings about the peace agreement and its economic consequences. He even predicted the debilitating and economic destabilizing effects on Germany's economy following the peace agreement, an agreement that ultimately led to the nationalistic movement in Germany between the two wars.

As his influence continued to grow, he began to write about the causes of the post–Great War recession of 1919–1921 and the need for reform of monetary policy. He was one of the first to recognize the problem with deflation and its debilitating effect on credit markets. He realized then what we all know now.

Borrowers love inflation because they can pay back debt with less valuable cash. However, they abhor deflation because they are paying back debt on less valuable assets with more scarce and valuable dollars. Neither inflation nor deflation is healthy for well-functioning credit markets. Before Keynes, though, the phenomenon of deflation was poorly understood.

Keynes' most influential work though came in the *General Theory of Employment, Interest and Money.*[26] In perhaps the single most influential economic treatise since Adam Smith's *Wealth of Nations* in 1776, and certainly the most significant book since its publication in 1936, Keynes spelled out in clearly understood terms why traditional classical economic theory fails when aggregate production seriously falters.

In the foreword to his influential book he pointed to one serious flaw in a modern political and economic system capable of generating great wealth and production. In his *General Theory of Employment, Interest and Money,* Keynes stated:

> The theory of aggregated production, which is the point of the following book, nevertheless can be much easier adapted to the conditions of a totalitarian state...than the theory of production and distribution of a given production put forth under conditions of free competition and a lance measure of laissez-faire.

Keynes was certainly not arguing for totalitarian states, growing from the left in Russia and the right in Germany. Instead, he was pointing out that classical economic tools, based on the notion of individual markets, created by the self-interest of individual producers and consumers, is too simplistic a characterization of the aggregate economy. While these individual markets can be shown to thrive based on noncooperative competition, they fail miserably in the aggregate when economic coordination is necessary.

Nor was Keynes creating a body of work of great intellectual sophistication or mathematical rigor. Some of the ideas he espoused on the use of taxes and debt to fund government spending had been openly discussed by noted economist David Ricardo in his "Essays on the Funding System" in 1820.[27] The mathematics was relatively simplistic too, with his arguments relying instead on lucid rhetoric and a confidence of assertion no doubt developed from his upbringing, elite education, and meteoric rise in the power circles of Britain.

Regardless of the roots of his genius, he was most definitely in the right place at the right time, proposing a prescription to the worldwide depression while at the same time presenting a plausible description for its causes.

He wrote with a certain flourish that perhaps makes his writings less accessible today, despite their common sense analytics and relatively basic level of theory. Nonetheless, at a time when people were searching for explanations and solutions, and were accustomed to lofty and thoughtful rhetoric from their political leaders, Keynes' writings were well received.

While he treated a variety of failures to coordinate in a depression-era economy, we can focus on perhaps his most significant observations. He was the first to espouse the importance of consumer psychology as an underpinning of the modern economic system.

Four new economic sectors

To better understand the essential role of consumption, and why it can become an Achilles Heel when there are strong deflationary forces, let us break aggregate demand in the economy into four distinct sectors. These are international trade, the spending of investors and consumers, and government spending.

Trade as our salvation?

Let us dispense with trade first. Although trade is a big part of most developed economies, and reactionary trade reform certainly hastened the Great Depression, it is not central to Keynes' idea.

Keynes observed that trade has two influential factors. One is the exchange rate. A strong exchange rate makes imports relatively inexpensive and prices exports out of the market by making the exported product relatively expensive. Foreign exchange markets that are not manipulated typically find a level of the exchange rate that keeps trade in goods, services, and financial capital in balance.

The second factor affecting trade is domestic income. As income rises, our penchant to import novel goods also increases. Likewise, with declining income, imports fall, thereby decreasing the amount of cash leaving the country. This decline in domestic cash on foreign exchange markets can actually lift the value of the currency, and likewise weaken exports too, until imports and exports reestablish a balance.

On the surface, any similar policy that restricts imports sounds like it would also encourage domestic production. Certainly, the protectionist crowd that grows with each downturn believes so. However, some of these production gains are then lost because of the reduced exports that result with gains in the exchange rate.

Most economists now argue that trade manipulation is simply not a productive path for growth, especially if it meets the retaliation that the United States witnessed when it imposed the Smoot-Hawley tariffs leading up to the Great Depression. While such a policy certainly appeals to our fears of economic security, we find that these are but one of many counterintuitive responses that ultimately fan rather than quench our economic fears.

If we take off the table trade policy as an antidote to the kind of production gap that deflation and a depression can create, we are left with three avenues for aggregate demand enhancement – investment, consumption, and government spending.

Where were the investors?

Let us take on investment next.

According to Keynes, investment depends on the ability of additional capital projects to generate future profits. Keynes and economists reserve the term investment to mean the purchase of capital goods to produce future income. This is different from the vernacular definition of investment as the purchase of financial instruments, whether or not they result in the subsequent purchase of capital goods such as factories, equipment, inventories, or new homes. Economic investments by definition must enhance the productive capacity of the economy. Financial investment in the stock market rarely does so directly.

In this description of investment, Keynes observes that low interest rates allow producers a greater range of possible projects that can yield profits sufficient to at least cover the interest rate. As a consequence, low interest rates translate into greater investment, assuming banks are willing and able to lend. While Keynes acknowledges that such new investment is intimately related to the interest rate producers can access, this investment also depends on producers' perception of future demand. If they anticipate bleak demand, they will not invest.

Beyond this recognition that investment ultimately depends on the interest rate, Keynes took the investment decision of firms as autonomous, meaning that it was not related to his most important variable, the overall level of income in the economy at a given time.

The first "Age of Consumerism"

The Roaring Twenties saw the age of consumerism transform the underpinnings of the economy. Then, as now, consumers represent the vast majority of spending, accounting for about 70% of aggregate demand in the economy. The remaining spending is made up of the other three sectors of net trade, new investment in productive capacity, and government spending on goods and services.

Keynes noted that consumption actually has two components. Depression or not, rich or poor, there must be a certain fixed amount of consumption to meet the most basic needs of food and shelter. Even if one has no income, one would have to beg, borrow, or steal to maintain at least this level of consumption, labeled autonomous consumption because it does not depend on other variables included in his model.

His crucial and novel insight, though, was to argue that consumption was fundamentally dependent on the total level of income in the aggregate economy. As income rises, consumers can afford to spend more, first covering the debt in maintaining basic consumption and then using a portion of additional income for discretionary consumption.

While this relationship between income and the psychology of consumption sounds eminently sensible, it turns out to have profound implications. If consumers obey their "consumption function" by spending based on income, then if income falls, consumption falls. This reduced level of consumption will in turn reduce the income of others, leading to a further fall in aggregate income and, in turn, a further fall in consumption. This snowball effect continues until consumption, and income, contract equally.

The multiplier effect

The effect of reduced income reducing consumption, which in turn reduces income and consumption further, and so on, is called the multiplier effect. By the time consumption settles to its eventual value, the reduction in income and consumption is much larger than the initial reduction in income that started this snowball rolling down the hill.

Let us illustrate the effect with a simple numerical example. In 1929, the total net value of payments earned Y for producing goods and services purchased in the United States was just over \$100 billion. To make it simple, I round this down to \$100 billon. This was made up of approximately \$75 billion in consumption C, \$15 billion in autonomous investment I_0, about \$10 billion in autonomous government spending G_0, and a negligible level of net exports (exports that exceed imports) NX. Keynes left for the moment investment and government spending as autonomous, meaning the level of these forms of spending were not immediately influenced by the level of income in the economy.

Part of the \$75 billion in consumption was autonomous too, and part depended on discretionary income. Let us assume that \$25 billion was essential autonomous consumption that would be spent in any regard. The remaining \$50 billion was discretionary, and depended on the level of income in consumers' pockets.

If overall income was \$100 billion, this would translate into \$50 billion of discretionary spending for every \$100 billion of aggregate income, or 50% of aggregate income. Keynes called the 50% share of additional income that spurs new consumption the "marginal propensity to consume," labeled here as "*c*."

The psychological consumption function is then as follows:

$$C_p = C_0 + c \times Y = \$25 \text{ billion} + 0.5 \times \$100 \text{ billion} = \$75 \text{ billion},$$

while the remaining components of investment, government spending, and trade add the additional \$25 billion to spending. Total spending of \$100 billion then equals the total income earned and distributed of \$100 billion. The accountants are happy because income equals expenditures. And the economy is in equilibrium because everybody does what they had planned to do. It is here that Keynes made his profound discovery. If income equals spending,

$$Y = C + I_0 + G_0 + \text{NX}, \text{ or}$$

$$Y = C_0 + c \times Y + I_0 + G_0 + \text{NX}.$$

Mathematically, there is only one level of income that can ensure income equals spending, which makes the accountants happy. Solving the equation for Y gives:

$$Y = \frac{C_0 + I_0 + G_0 + NX}{1 - c}$$

Let us see if this works. Those autonomous elements of consumption, $C_0 + I_0 + G_0$ + NX totaled \$25 billion + \$15 billion + \$10 billion, or \$50 billion. The denominator is $1-c$, or $1 - 0.5 = 0.5$. If we divide the numerator of \$50 billion by the denominator of 0.5, we get \$100 billion, the equilibrium level of income, and now the mathematicians are happy too.

The Keynesian multiplier

Things get really interesting if we postulate a change in some of these autonomous components. Let us see what happens if, because of the Great Crash, investors are fearful and decrease their investment in their factories by \$6 billion. In this case, investment would drop from \$15 billion to \$9 billion. Because this decreased investment translates into layoffs of workers who would have produced the inventories, or construction workers who may have built the new factories, there is less income available for consumers. They, too, consume less until income drops by a multiple of the initial drop in income.

In this case, we see only one quantity changed in our denominator. The level of investment I_0 went from \$15 billion to \$9 billion following the Great Crash. Instead of a numerator that totals \$50 billion, we now find it totals only \$44 billion. This \$44 billion is divided by the denominator 0.5 translates into a new equilibrium income of \$88 billion, once the multiplier can do its work.

This numerical example approximates what happened between 1929 and 1930. A drop of investment in new plants, equipment, and housing was approximately \$6 billion. And overall income in the economy, once consumers responded to the decline in construction jobs and equipment making, added a further drop of \$6 billion. In other words, the overall decline in the economy was twice the original \$6 billion decline, a multiple two from $\frac{1}{1-c} = \frac{1}{1-0.5} = 2.$

Another way to look at this phenomenon without the algebra is to recognize that Keynes had invented the concept of the multiplier. This ratio $1/(1-c)$, or the reciprocal of one minus the marginal propensity to consume, is the eventual effect that gives us the multiple of income arising from some initial change in consumption, investment, government spending, or trade. Then, as now, the economy will decline by some multiple of an autonomous reduction in spending. We call this the multiplier effect. And we employ this multiplier effect in reverse to stimulate and expand our way out of subsequent recessions.

The Wealth Effect

Moving from 1930 to 1931, investment and government spending fell still further. By 1931, consumers became very fearful, even reducing some of their autonomous consumption. This tendency for households to adjust to a new and lower permanent standard of living actually was not modeled by Keynes. However, the researchers Franco Modigliani and Milton Friedman later won the Nobel Memorial Prize in Economics by noting that consumption depends not only on income but also on permanent wealth.

If we take the lost wealth arising from the Great Crash and the bank failures into account, we see that consumption actually fell even more in 1931 than predicted by Keynes' model. We now see that the $14 billion drop in wealth following the Great Crash of 1929, and a similar drop in the value of household's housing value, would result in a further $1 billion loss in consumption and a final $2 billion loss in total income arising from the multiplier effect.

In total, the gross domestic product would drop by $12 billion from 1929 to 1930, another $14 billion, the next year, and $18 billion from 1931 to 1932. Total gross domestic product and income dropped by more than $47 billion between 1929 and 1933, with drops in consumption representing two thirds of this decline through the Keynesian multiplier effect and the Modigliani-Friedman wealth effect. While the initial shots were fired on Wall Street, there was a firefight occurring on Main Street.

The multiplier effect in reverse

But Keynes was not finished yet. While he was certainly permitting economics to live up to its label of the dismal science, he had a couple of additional insights to glean.

First, he noted that as discouraging as this dismal prophecy is, it could also work in reverse. If our goal was to stimulate the economy, we do not have to make up the entire shortfall of $47 billion in lost income. We can let the multiplier work in our favor by providing a stimulus of just half that amount and letting the snowball effect work for us instead of against us. Of course, even $23 billion was a huge amount, and more than twice the level of annual spending by government. In desperate times, it was worth a try.

We must next ask who can credibly come up with such a massive shot in the economic arm. It is true that the richest 1% of the population owned 40% of the wealth in 1929. And many of those investors were smart enough to insulate themselves from the worst days on Wall Street. However, the stock market continued to decline until 1933, and they were likely in no mood to plough what they had left for some uncertain bailout of the economy, even if Keynes had produced his treatise by then and could somehow convince them of his algebra. No, the investment community was probably not going to be part of the solution, even if they were part of the problem.

Nor was it reasonable to assume that consumers could simply begin spending willy-nilly again. They were wiped out, unemployed, and fearful, and no amount of cajoling was going to get them to spend again. We tried protectionism to cut imports, and instead found ourselves in a retaliatory trade war as a consequence of the Smoot-Hawley tariffs that were passed in 1930.

There was only one entity left standing that could even conceivably mount such a massive spending program to make up half of the fall of spending. If only they could put half the gap back into the pockets of households, the consumers could do the rest.

While Keynes' treatise had not yet been published in the summer of 1932 as FDR campaigned across the country, he had been commenting in U.S. magazines about the need to pursue proactive fiscal policy. For instance, Keynes writes in *The Nation*, May 10, 1930:

> The fact is – a fact not yet recognized by the great public – that we are now in the depths of a very severe international slump, a slump which will take its place in history amongst the most acute ever experienced. It will require not merely passive movements of bank rates to lift us out of a depression of this order, but a very active and determined policy.[28]

FDR – the first Keynesian president

The soon-to-be elected President Roosevelt seemed to have an intuitive understanding of what needed to be done. And spend he did. From 1933 to 1938, government spending almost doubled, generating an additional $10 billion in national income. Other polices allowed home prices to recover, further spurring consumer wealth and spending, And policies were developed that would stimulate private corporate investment. By 1937, the nation's GDP would recover to $91.9 billion, while deflation had decreased prices by about 15%. In other words, real GDP had approximately recovered by the onset of the arms buildup for World War II.

Keynes was not yet done though. In one of his first major works in economics, Keynes had published a two volume "The Treatise on Money" in 1930 that hinted at his embryonic monetary theory of liquidity preference.[29] His emerging theory of monetary economics concluded that credit markets will break down if overly aggressive monetary policy pushes interest rates so low that households would prefer to hoard their cash under their mattress rather than keep it in banks and the loanable funds market.

Keynes concluded that monetary policy may be an effective tool for tinkering with equilibrium when the economy is approximately operating with full employment. However, such policy is fraught with uncertainty when financial markets are broken down, consumers have no confidence in the banking industry, credit markets have become dysfunctional, and banks are unwilling in any regard to extend credit.

The paradox of thrift

In other words, Keynes concludes that consumer confidence must be restored and fear relegated through prudent and decisive use of government spending to stimulate the economy. He described to us the paradox of thrift, in which we each do what we think is individually prudent in times of economic distress, but which becomes economically debilitating collectively. The solution to this paradox is a collective action to reverse our individual but economically destructive thrift.

Keynes also reaffirms the need for economic leadership, a message that was not lost on the first Keynesian president, Franklin Delano Roosevelt. In a current economic meltdown with eerie parallels to the Great Depression, Keynesian theory is since enjoying a resurgence in popularity and interest. It is uncanny how some of the words of Keynes and others, uttered in the fear-gripped era of 1929 to 1938, still ring true.

It is also uncanny how often the history of fear and panic has repeated itself, as our next discussion shows.

Part VII
Coordination Failures

Each of the past panics shared certain characteristics. They typically arose following a period of strong growth. Each experienced a period of volatility. And in each instance, a herd mentality ensued that created a broader panic. In each case, too, credit markets became dysfunctional, often giving pause for concern about bank solvency.

We next try to better understand the social, economic, and political forces that are part of the problem and could conceivably be reformed to be part of the solution.

We begin with the observation that individuals at times act contrary to our collective interest. This observation is a natural consequence of free markets and uncoordinated individual behavior. In Chapter 22, we see how technology can sometimes amplify these unfortunate human tendencies. We conclude this part by discussing how ratings agencies can help us with the information breaches that give rise to such coordination failures, and how, at times, the ratings agencies can be part of the problem.

21
The Market for Lemmings, or A Tale of Two Cultures

What is it that causes the masses of investors to panic and run for the doors? And who manages to lead the charge?

The investing masses can sometimes be likened to herd animals. They do not have the access to the corridors of power to discover for themselves the inside scoop. And they do not have the resources to independently verify information or analyze the fundamentals of a market or an individual firm. Instead, they focus on two pieces of readily available information: one is the current price of a stock or value of an index and the other is its direction of motion, up or down.

In such an environment, fear can quite easily grip the vast majority of market participants and dictate the ultimate outcome. While the investing majority certainly may not include the biggest players, the sheer mass of their movements can best be likened to herding elephants or trying to control a fast moving river.

For instance, we saw the folly of the panics in 1901 and 1907 when small groups of investors thought they could corner the market in railroad or copper stocks. We also saw this more recently when the Hunt brothers notoriously tried to corner the silver market in 1980. These were attempts to manipulate the great masses of the marketplace for their own personal gain. In these instances, complete market breakdowns resulted. Many other times, such manipulations have no doubt succeeded in moving the masses of the market in the direction that would allow a few individuals to profit.

Herding over a cliff

The instinct that would induce us to be moved in a direction so obviously contrary to our own self-interest rests with our human response to fear. Faced with an emergency situation where humans do not have the luxury of formulating a rational decision, the most primitive mechanism of survival kicks in. We look for clues that indicate to us the decisions of others, under the assumption that they, too, are responding to the same predicament and they have come up with a rational plan.

For instance, if someone shouts fire in a crowded theater and sees hundreds are running in a particular direction, one may defer independent research on the rational course of action and instead join the crowd running for the door.

Panic in markets creates a similar phenomenon. When a market is dropping swiftly, the masses do not have the luxury to contemplate what might happen next. If they do, they may find themselves holding stock that has plummeted in value. And, so the masses bail on the market.

Whether or not the rumor that began the rush is valid, or the motivation of those leading the charge is ethical, the masses of the market have acted. In the final analysis, the masses concluded there was a rush toward the door, and the reality is that an emergency situation emerged, whether or not an emergency situation existed in the first place.

An act of faith

We accept as an act of faith that the free-market system can regulate and right itself from temporary shocks or excesses. Now even free-market zealots such as Alan Greenspan recognize that free markets do not necessarily self-regulate. How is this possible?

A devotee of Ayn Rand, Greenspan was appropriately enamored with the beauty of a system that encourages and rewards innovation. But mixing policy with idolatry is always a dangerous thing. Greenspan recently acknowledged such in his interesting dialog with Congressman Henry Waxman, the chair of the House Committee and Oversight and Government Reform and the subsequently named chair of the House Energy and Commerce Committee.

Testifying to Congressman Waxman's committee, Greenspan stated, "Those of us who have looked to the self-interest of lending institutions to protect shareholders' equity, myself included, are in a state of shocked disbelief."[30] He added that the failure of self-regulation by banks has broken down.

Further chided by Congressman Waxman, Greenspan responded, "I have found a flaw." Waxman asked, "In other words, you found that your view of the world, your ideology, was not right; it was not working." Greenspan responded, "Absolutely, precisely."

What was the nature of the flaw?

A beautiful mind

To recall, in the movie *A Beautiful Mind* about John Nash, a brilliant mathematician, published an absurdly short 27-page thesis in May of 1959. Partly typed and partly handwritten, the thesis earned him a PhD from Princeton University, one of the finest mathematics schools in the world.

His insight was in describing the strategies of what he called noncooperative games. While he had poker in mind, it turns out that he also described the free-market system. His insights were so profound that he became the only pure mathematician to ever win the Nobel Memorial Prize in Economics.

In short, a noncooperative equilibrium describes how various participants develop their economic strategies, given the strategies of other participants. These uncoordinated actions in the self-interest of individual market participants form the basis for the free-market system. It turns out though that these acts, while in the isolated self-interest of individuals, are not in the collective best interest. In other words, we often find ourselves pursuing our self-interest at our own peril. Economic depressions are but one particularly painful example of the dilemma when the pursuit of individual happiness harms the individual and the economy alike.

A prisoner's dilemma

To see how we can get stuck in a nasty noncooperative equilibrium like our current Global Financial Meltdown, let's look at what economists call the Prisoner's Dilemma. Imagine two people running down the street with boxes of stolen DVD players under each arm as a burglar alarm blares in the background. The police arrest the two for possession of stolen goods that would net each of them a year in prison.

The two alleged burglars are brought to the police station and individually interrogated. The police can't prove they broke into the looted electronics store. If they could, the prisoners would get ten years in prison. The police make each of them an offer – if one prisoner confesses and the other does not, the former will get six months in prison and the latter will get the full ten years.

If the prisoners do not confess, they will only face a year in prison, no more or no less. And if each cooperates with the police, they will get the full ten years because the police offered a reduced sentence only if one confesses but the other does not.

John Nash's equilibrium shows us that they will both turn the other in to save themselves and both will consequently serve ten years in jail. How is it that we can individually pursue what we think is in our best interest, but collectively we find ourselves in a bad spot?

The prisoners find themselves acting to better their own position, based on what they think the other will do. If one does not confess and the other does, the first goes to jail for ten years, while the other gets off almost scot-free. And if one states he absolutely won't confess, the other has an even greater incentive to confess. Despite their best efforts, the very nature of individual confessions and actions forces them each into a noncooperative equilibrium that does neither any good.

Fixing coordination failures

How do we prevent our own uncoordinated actions from harming ourselves and others? Either we cooperate in making joint decisions, or we create rules, institutions, or policies that prevent us from pursuing our individual interest at the expense of others. While we may individually find such rules an imposition, they exist for our collective good to prevent a troubling noncooperative equilibrium. For instance, an individual hedge fund or investment bank may resent onerous regulation. However, if regulation helps ensure a healthy banking system, it is a good policy for the industry and individual banks and funds, alike.

For example, our economy is currently stuck in just the persistent noncooperative equilibrium John Nash describes. Each of us has cut back in our spending as a natural individual response to our economic dilemma. The combined decrease in spending reduces demand for domestic production. Employers must lay off workers, reducing income and, in turn, reducing spending further. Our belief in a recession became a self-fulfilling prophecy.

What can get us out of this dilemma? As Keynes noted earlier, a totalitarian state can, in a heavy-handed fashion, force producers to produce and consumers to consume. A free-market economy cannot compel individual firms to produce or individual households to spend. Instead, as distasteful as huge doses of government spending may be in a free market, it is the only entity capable of coordinating our spending and production and pushing us from a bad equilibrium to a normal state of economic affairs.

At first, John Nash did not realize that his theory of noncooperative games could explain the most exasperating nature of the free market. John Maynard Keynes realized this sometimes-fatal flaw in economics a generation earlier, but without the mathematical rigor to prove it. Neither, though, had the solution to prevent a Prisoner's Dilemma from occurring. Given the response of humans to crisis situations, perhaps the dilemma will never be solved.

A theoretical explanation

Researchers have actually produced models that postulate the existence of herd behavior. In an important paper by Bikhchandani, Hershleifer, and Welch,[31] the authors set up the following model. Let's assume that we do not know the true state of the world, but we can see what choices others have made before us. If our subsequent decision turns out to be true, we are rewarded. Our decisions, and the decisions of our predecessors, are chosen from a correct state of the world, or from an incorrect state of the world. Even if we draw our decision from the incorrect state, let's say we could still be correct, for the wrong reasons. Likewise, even if we make our decision based on the correct information, any randomness allows us to still be incorrect, but for the right reasons.

For the first mover, as long as the information drawn from the correct state of the world is quite accurate, their choice is easy. They will likely make the correct choice. However, the second mover has a more difficult decision. This mover, too, sees two sets of information. If the move of the first person seems consistent with the second person's best guess, things are pretty easy. When the move of the first person is at odds with the second person's intuition, the second mover is no longer so certain.

With each subsequent move, we must weigh both our intuition of the correct state of the world and the randomized decisions of others. If there is only a little information to give us a sufficiently strong intuition about the correct state of the world, we may ultimately be led astray by the randomness of the world and jump on a bandwagon going in the wrong direction. In this way, a herd mentality can run the lemmings over the cliff.

Ecopathy

It is frustratingly human to work at times en masse against our collective self-interest, especially if motivated by fear. Can we reasonably expect more ethical or collectively interested behavior from those showing us the direction toward the door? Perhaps not.

If the large group dynamic causes us to herd for the door, as pack animals we follow the directions of the alpha investors among us. I do not mean we seek the alpha in the finance terminology that means we look for excess returns above the risk we take. Rather, I mean we follow the lead of the alpha wolf that is directing the pack.

To use the expression of the Swedish psychologist Torbjörn K. A. Eliazon, financial leaders at times engage in an economic pathology, or ecopathy. Once they have amassed their first billion dollars, their actions can no longer be explained by the need for economic security. Were these investors to stop at the first billion and live their remaining years in luxury, they would still be able to spend perhaps a $100 million a year, or more than $250,000 a day for the rest of their lives.

Instead, financial leaders become motivated by a craving for economic power in itself, rather than for the consumption their riches and economic security can bring. Some individuals become motivated by something that money cannot really buy – control over other human beings. These nouveau riche who are new to wealth exhibit the arrogance and hubris of self-made and successful individuals. Some have not yet acquired the sense of responsibility old money realizes goes with such power.

There are exceptions, of course. Most notably, one of the world's richest men-investor Warren Buffett has every intention of amassing a wealth that will be given away to better humankind. Buffet, and Bill and Melinda Gates have inherited the mantle of philanthropy that measures their worth not by the power flowing from their wealth, but rather from the good they can do with their wealth.

This maturity of wealth is something acquired after a period of contemplation of their responsibilities to the system that made it possible to amass such incredible wealth. These lessons are not learned behind those closed doors where schemes are concocted to benefit a handful of youthful financiers at the expense of the rest of us. Such participants are motivated by a thirst for economic power as a measure of their self-worth. Because they are responding to a certain animal instinct that may have little regard but for the survival of the economically fittest, our rational models of economics or human nature fail to explain their behavior. And so we do not anticipate the need to create institutions that prevent them from pursuing their self-interested schemes.

Indeed, a society that develops institutions and regulations through a process of debate and discussion has a hard time even predicting what scheme may be lurking behind the next financial instrument.

In such an environment where it is difficult to know who is shouting fire and why, it is natural to assume that fear will, once in a while, get the best of us and panic will result.

We next see that technology will not always come to our rescue to maintain that rational even keel we usually assume.

22
The Role of Machines and Programmed Trading

World financial markets also went through a gut-wrenching financial decline in October of 1987. Sometimes called Black Monday, stocks began to trade steeply downward, first in Asian markets, then in Europe and Africa, and finally in the Americas. When trading was over at the end of that day, New Zealand's market fell by almost 60%; Australia's and Hong Kong's fell off by more than 40%, and markets in Europe, Canada, and the United States were down by between 20% and 35%. The drop in the Dow Jones Industrial Average at 22.6%, represents the largest plunge in its history. Some argue that it was technology that led the markets down.

Technology certainly played an essential role. With networked computers and the Internet came the ability to monitor trading in real time all around the world. It did not take long for actual trades to be executed instantly worldwide. For global trading, such execution speeds are essential, to time opportunities to obtain shares in a particular market or corporation and certainly, in this case, to quickly get out of a market that is deteriorating.

Technology was also employed to take some of the minute monitoring and trading away from humans. For instance, a bank or insurance company may employ a stop-loss strategy that follows a prudent investment policy. If the value of an asset in the portfolio falls to the degree it no longer meets underwriting requirements as collateral, a computer can step in and liquidate their holding automatically. Other computer programs might be used to detect momentum shifts in a stock and buy as it begins to turn upward. Still other programs sense when there is a gap between the price a futures market indicates a stock will head and its current price and buys or sells to take advantage of this potential arbitrage opportunity.

Barring a computer glitch, we should first look at some very human explanations that brought on the dramatic decline.

The United States had been experiencing a year of reasonably good fortune in the first half of 1987. It had recovered from a deep recession earlier in the decade, and interest rates on bonds were relatively low, despite large-scale federal government borrowing to fund President Reagan's Star Wars and an economic push to finish off its Cold War opponent. The U.S. trade deficit was in poor shape, especially with Japan, the major beneficiary of U.S. trade imbalances.

Two decades earlier, the term "made in Japan" represented inferior quality. By the 1980s though, it meant superior products from Sony, Honda, Toyota, Toshiba, and many others. Japan was building a better mousetrap and American consumers were beating down its door to buy them. Of course, it did not help that oil prices were on the rise and the U.S. car manufacturers were not offering a product mix designed for that reality.

Unfortunately, U.S. products did not represent the same sort of quality in the eyes of Japanese consumers. Japan was selling much more than it was buying and was building up a huge excess of U.S. dollars in the process. We see this dynamic reoccurring today, but with China. And just as China used much of that surplus to buy U.S. bonds in an attempt to keep the U.S. party going, so did Japan.

This willingness for Japan to invest in the United States allowed the U.S. Treasury to keep interest rates relatively low. These low interest rates were a boon for 18 years of growth. They also sowed the seeds for an incredible speculative bubble that would generate the worst panic since the Great Crash of 1929.

A decade of scandal

At the same time, Wall Street was experiencing scandal after scandal. From major arrests of floor traders and financiers for cocaine abuse, to tax conspiracies, to the downfall of rogue financiers and market manipulators Ivan Boesky and Michael Milken, it seemed that Wall Street was in the news every day. Except for the good earnings reports, much of the scandalous news was bad. It appeared that Wall Street, too, was suffering from the excesses of the 1980s. Even Church Street was having its challenges, with one of its populist leaders, the former Reverend Jim Bakker caught in a sex scandal. Public cynicism was hitting new lows.

Meanwhile, the lobbyists of "K Street" in Washington were also busy on the sidelines. Some were lobbying congressmen to protect the U.S. automobile industry by imposing trade barriers. These barriers would also have the politically opportunistic effect of reducing the trade deficits the United States maintained with Asian countries, especially Japan.

The U.S. automobile industry, having met Honda's challenge of the Civic with nothing better than the K-car (presumably not named after the lobbyist's street), was experiencing a slump, and many blamed Japan. In the pique of populist sentiment, a Democratic Congress passed a trade amendment that was intended to punish Japan for its export prowess.

In response, Japan stated it would no longer participate in the weekly treasury auctions that were funding the U.S. party. The interest rate on government bonds began to rise significantly, moving into double digit rates reminiscent of the stagflation recession that began in the previous decade.

On October 14, 1987, market cynicism was beginning to weigh heavily. On a weakening dollar against the yen, rising prices, a worsening trade deficit, and some profit taking from a historically high Dow, selling set in. Between October 14 and 15, the Dow dropped 12% from its historical high in August. The Dow dropped another 4% on the Friday, October 16. The Treasury Secretary James Baker had voiced concern about market volatility and market overvaluation and the world was now watching.

Meanwhile, military tensions with Iran were heightening, causing concern about the reliable flow of oil through the critical Suez Canal. All these mounting concerns came to a head when the first markets opened, in Australasia on Monday, October 19, 1987. The drops spread like a tidal wave circling the world as markets opened in sequence. When all came to rest, most markets experienced their single largest one-day drop in history.

Markets go global – the Weekend Effect

One phenomenon that occurred was the Weekend Effect. Then, as now, a bad Thursday and Friday on Wall Street offered Asian traders an entire weekend to brood and, ultimately, to fan the flames of fear. When Friday turns ugly on Wall Street, we now often see things turn downright fearful in Shanghai or Hong Kong on Monday. The snowball, wavering at the top of the hill on Friday, is forcefully pushed downward, picking up speed and creating an avalanche by the time U.S. markets open on Monday. The carnage begins in East Asia, spreads to South Asia and Europe, and echoes to Wall Street, often inflicting even further damage.

Before computerized trading, markets simply acted less rapidly, giving some time to reflect and perhaps to avoid the herd instinct that takes the lemmings over the cliff. The second phenomenon was programmed trading. For some time, critics of such trades executed by computers predicted that such a cascading of selling may someday occur.

One of the principal critics of programmed trading was Congressman Edward Markey. He had been leading a debate in Congress for two years, rallying against unmonitored and unregulated programmed trading and its perceived destabilizing effects on markets and volatility. Fearful of congressional action, both the New York Stock Exchange and the Chicago Mercantile Exchange almost immediately imposed emergency circuit breakers that would halt trading temporarily if the market swung too wildly. These measures have been in place ever since, and the possibility of their automatic deployment is frequently mentioned at times of extreme market volatility.

A cascade effect by programmed trading occurs only if there is something else troubling the market, such as the macroeconomic factors discussed earlier. Technology does not start the turmoil, even if some argue that it may exacerbate volatility and the decline.

Another explanation was portfolio insurance. Large investors could hedge their bets by purchasing insurance. The underwriters would then have to look at the risks by measuring the difference between stock futures and stock prices today and spread the risk accordingly between the two periods. In those days in October, the long-term mood was negative, meaning that future prices were actually lower than current prices. This forced many insurers to sell their stock used to insure portfolios almost simultaneously so that they could maintain liquidity. This added to the downward selling pressure.

Finally, the market suffered from a herd mentality. With nerves already frazzled because of the high market volatility of late, few casual investors wanted to wait and see what happened. If one could, the best strategy was to respond to fear and get out early. After all, no one could predict how low the market could go.

While this crash goes down in history as the largest single day drop, the market actually recovered very rapidly. By December 31, 1987, the market actually closed higher on the year. The market dodged that bullet – for the moment.

Too much of a good thing?

In economics, we generally assume additional information is a good thing. Certainly technology allows every market to see information worldwide, in real time, and simultaneously. However, the creation of vast amounts of additional information does not always produce better decisions. Perhaps as we are afforded the time to absorb so much information, markets converge to a more accurate long-term valuation.

And perhaps, too, this convergence can occur quicker. But, in that moment, when split-second decisions must be made, additional and conflicting information may be unhelpful. Continuing with the analogy of running for the door of the theater when one shouts fire, too many flashing exit signs may cause more confusion than coordination. This is without even having time to address the question of whether there is indeed a fire in the first place.

Markets may, indeed, be suffering from information overload. Machines may help us process information. Ultimately, though, it must be humans that make the final decisions. Clearly, in the meltdown of credit markets in 2007, our models were telling us that these new fangled collateralized debt instruments were a good thing to buy. It took humans too long to realize that this information was faulty. And, by then, it was too late for the global economy.

It is sometimes argued that the high volatility of less mature and emerging stock markets is a sign of inexperience in processing risk. Perhaps that conclusion is well-founded. However, it may be equally true that oversophistication of the world's most mature and developed securities markets may be equally problematic. Time will tell. In the meantime, we have developed a certain market cynicism for the agencies that are to clarify our uncertainties, reduce our risk, and dispel our fears. These agencies have served us poorly, as we see next.

23
The Ratings Agencies – More Perfect Information?

Risk assessment is a highly technical problem. If each bond investor was to try to estimate the downside risk of each asset under consideration, it would be likely that few investors would be qualified to buy bonds or other risk bearing fixed income securities. If such were the case, those issuing the bonds would have few buyers, and would then have to offer a commensurately higher interest rate to attract sufficient interest and raise sufficient capital. With such uncertainty and such an advantage to most skilled analyses, it would be smart for the bond issuers or investment houses marketing the bond issues to hire a risk-assessment agent to analyze the proposed security and give it a letter grade that would signal the level of risk to the marketplace. This is the job of the ratings agencies.

But, like all principal-agent problems, we must figure out precisely who is representing whom. If not, we may have the proverbial fox in the hen house. We now know that we got it wrong most recently – with devastating results.

Someone watching out for us

There are three major risk assessment agencies and another ten smaller agencies worldwide that assign credit scores for corporate and investment house assets. The primary agencies are Fitch Ratings, Moody's, and Standard and Poor's. These big three allow purchasers of risky assets to more reliably position themselves on their capital allocation line, thereby improving returns while reducing risk. The market is willing to pay well for this tremendous service by these agents.

Risk assessment is a conservative enterprise, borne out of the green-shaded actuaries of the insurance industry. These risk-assessment specialists traditionally used conservative economic models to explore the likelihood and costs of various detrimental scenarios, based on observations of past liabilities. They cannot model, though, what they have never seen before.

And if one analyst cannot, or will not, model risk, well, we will just have to keep looking until we find someone who can. All the better if, in the process, we generate a bit of competition for the analysis we want. This environment of letting the market choose who would assess the risk of the next new instrument designed to make a lot of money for the investment houses is just the scenario that has set us up for failure. We should not have been surprised.

Measuring risk

In the ratings world, a triple-A (AAA) rating is the gold standard. Ratings agencies assign letter grades to riskier bonds, from a rating of Aaa, through BBB, and all the way to junk status, allow us to choose the instrument risk, and the commensurate return to fit our level of risk aversion.

Two problems arose. One was the ability to assess risk for a new instrument that no one has experienced before. The other was the gamesmanship that clever financial marketers employed to package combinations of these instruments in ways that ultimately obscure, rather than illuminate, risk.

The first of these problems of accurately assessing risk is difficult. The situation that gave rise to the Credit Crunch and then the Global Financial Meltdown was in assessing as low risk assets we now call toxic. These assets were collections of mortgages aggregated from new subprime mortgagees. On the positive side, these home purchasers were buying into a market that had been consistently and dramatically rising nationwide.

The problem, though, was that mortgage brokers were increasingly having a difficult time finding new potential mortgagees. Knowing they would be taking some additional risk, first they began to offer mortgages at 100% or more of housing value. Traditional mortgages often imposed higher interest rates for any home financed for greater than 80% of housing value. In times of rising prices, though, brokers and risk assessors argued that this was a risk they could manage.

Then they began to suspend the requirement that potential home buyers must verify income. Instead, the brokers would hire accountants to verify that the job title the mortgagee proffered could indeed yield the income the mortgagee claimed. Why they would cut this corner by not simply asking the mortgagee for a tax return or W2 slip is a red flag.

Nonetheless, these so-called liar loans or NINJA (no income, no job or assets) loans satisfied the risk-assessment specialists for two reasons. One was the external verification of potential income, and the other was the assumption that mortgagees could always sell the home at a profit and pay off the mortgage should they ever come under distress and wish to protect their (likely worthless) personal credit rating.

Another problem was in the models themselves. The housing models used by the raters had not been adequately proofed and tested because never before had homeownership been expanded to this market of new mortgage clients. The moral hazard problems of renters finding themselves as homeowners but still acting as renters because they were permitted to buy a home with no money down was problematic.

There was also an adverse selection problem. Some say that there are owners, and there are renters, for a reason. Those who are interested in maintaining their properties find it advantageous to build up sweat equity by maintaining their homes. Renting is more advantageous for those who are not interested in maintaining a home or do not have the experience of resources to do so.

Then there was an emerging problem with financial gamesmanship. Let's assume the ratings agencies could accurately assess risk, even based on some faulty assumptions. The agencies could place some mortgages in the AAA category and others in the BBB category. The financial marketer would then go back to the raters and, in an effort of financial alchemy as labeled by Nobel Memorial Prize winning economist Joseph Stiglitz, ask the raters the question – If we took the AAA mortgage pool and inserted in the pool some of these inferior BBB mortgage assets, just how many BBBs could we insert without sacrificing the overall AAA rating?

Tell me what I want to hear

There is a facetious joke among accountants that goes like this. A new accounting grad goes in for an interview and the partner at the accounting firm holds up a number. When asked what number is printed on the card, the new grad reads "7." The partner says, "Thank you, we'll get back to you."

A second accounting grad comes in for the interview and the partner again holds up a number. Again, the grad reads "7." The partner says, "Thank you, we'll get back to you."

Finally, a third accounting grad comes in for the interview and the partner again holds up a number. This time the grad says, "What number do you want it to be?" The partner says, "Thank you, you're hired."

The financial marketers could also shop around and have the ratings agencies compete until the marketer eventually found a ratings agency that would allow the investment house to bundle as many high risk BBB mortgages as possible in the AAA package without sacrificing the AAA overall rating.

The big three ratings agencies doubled their income from 2005 to 2007 by tagging these new ratings on new collateralized debt obligations and mortgage-backed securities. The market purchased some $5 trillion of these instruments through banks, mutual funds, hedge funds, and pensions, and the presidents of the big three ratings agencies collectively earned $80 million from 2002 to 2008.

The level of hubris in this gamesmanship almost became comical. Subpoenaed emails from the executives at these ratings agencies at one point claimed in April of 2007 "that deal is ridiculous.... It could be structured by cows and we'd rate it." Meanwhile the collateralized debt obligation departments in these organizations flourished, growing in some cases by 5,000% and generating huge profits for the ratings firms.

No one wanted the party to stop. Not the brokers accepting the commissions, but not bearing the risk, for selling these new types of mortgages. Not the ratings agencies that raked in billions of dollars of new business, but not bearing any of the risk. Not the investment houses that sold these instruments, for big commissions, and no risk. And not the buyers that were happy to get AAA rated investment instruments that paid well above the paltry returns they would earn by investing in Treasury bonds.

There were a number of critics who suggested this was all a house of cards. However, if there is one thing we have learned from these dramatic run ups, it is that nobody wants to listen to the party pooper when everything is going so swimmingly.

We might ask the appropriate question when confronted with a situation which, in retrospect, everyone should have known better. Where were the regulators? After all, in the aftermath of this fiasco, the resulting untouchable toxic assets froze credit worldwide, precipitated the Credit Crunch of 2007, and eventually caused the Global Financial Meltdown of 2008. Surely an ounce of prevention would be worth a pound of cure? We must ask – where were the regulators?

Part VIII

Social Responsibility as an Antidote to Fear

Each of the past panics shared certain characteristics. They typically arose following a period of strong growth. Each experienced a period of volatility. And in each instance, a herd mentality ensued that created a broader panic. In each case too, credit markets became dysfunctional, often giving pause for concern about bank solvency.

We next try to better understand the social, economic, and political forces that are part of the problem. Our understanding of the dynamic may allow us to reform these problems into solutions.

We begin by asking where the regulators were over two decades of economic excess. We go on to ask in Chapter 25 whether there is a certain ethical responsibility that would prevent individual actors from undermining the common good. We conclude with a challenge to the Friedman hypothesis that corporations have no responsibility but to make profits.

24
Where Were the Regulators

There is one thing that has become most apparent from the Global Financial Meltdown of 2008. We must certainly remedy the problem of regulators that are underpaid, understaffed, overworked, or are a bit too cozy with the institutions they are asked to regulate on our behalf.

This point was certainly brought home recently when we discovered that the government regulator implicated in a savings and loan scandal in the 1980s has also been linked to shenanigans in another major bank failure of late. He defended his regulatory role as one of acting as a consultant hired by the government to help banks out.

This newfound sense that the mice were now the customers of cats may not have been restricted to savings and loans regulators. It was recently revealed that the Federal Aviation Administration began to view themselves as consultants to their airline customers. The model of regulators as enforcers was waning in the post–Reagan era of deregulation.

A necessary adversarial relationship

Unfortunately, a certain adversarial relationship can actually be most productive in ferreting out the information that can keep the playing field even and promote the public trust.

We understand that companies are wary of regulators and regulation. And so they should be. The goal of companies is to make a profit on behalf of their shareholders. They must do it without polluting the environment society has created for them to succeed, or without violating the responsibilities of the legal franchise that permits a corporation to contract as a person and walk away from its obligations when liabilities exceed assets.

The cat and mouse game companies play with regulators implicitly assumes that the competitive model is predicated on full and complete information. They believe too much information divulged to regulators diminishes their market power and competitiveness. Certainly, they do not believe the regulator is there to help them, as a government sponsored consultant, despite the testimonies of some regulators. In the end, corporations operate with an assumption that the goals of public policy are at odds with their goals to make a profit. This tension creates the necessity of regulation.

Reasons for regulation

We have become painfully aware that economic chaos creates risk and invokes fear and panic in individuals. We must rely on regulators to ensure that there is a level playing field that maintains the integrity and advantages of the free-market system, while at the same time protects us from its excesses and failures.

We also rely on regulators to protect our property and the fruits of our hard work. If there were no institutions that protected our property and our economic rights, we would each have to devote more of our energy to protect what we have rather than produce what we can. These protections are not limited to tangible property. We also rely on regulators and government to enforce the rights to our intellectual property, knowing that in the absence of such protections, we would either produce less or keep our best ideas to ourselves.

Regulators can also ensure that markets are created when and where they are needed, and are equally accessible to all. Transparency in such markets is essential for both their efficiency and for the protection of our interests. We rely on regulators to keep markets open, transparent, and efficient. Ultimately, the markets, too, rely on regulators because a failed market does nobody any good.

Finally, we need regulators to overcome market failures that arise from such issues as insider trading, incomplete information, problems of moral hazard, excessive transactions costs, or unfair competition and monopolization. Sometimes regulators even have to step in and create markets that could not exist or be efficient on their own. In this respect, markets at times are public goods. Some such goods are not efficiently provided by private markets but are nonetheless necessary for our economic welfare.

Of course, we should maintain a healthy scepticism about regulation. It is human nature for any agency, regulatory agencies included, to want to broaden their budgets and their scope of influence and power. But as with every activity, there is a point where enough is enough. Regulatory expansion for its own sake must be balanced against the diminishing, and even chilling effect on innovation that regulation inevitably provides.

Regulatory problems

Regulation can even impose certain distortions. For instance, it can create a certain "cat and mouse" gamesmanship between the regulatory agencies and the regulated bodies. There is no doubt that paper shredders are an important technology to protect intellectual property and trade secrets. They seem to be increasingly employed, though, to erase the paper trail of firms concerned with regulations or regulators.

The systems of competition and free enterprise are built upon the notion of private property. With more and more of our gross domestic product devoted to services, the value of intellectual or human services is growing. For instance, almost a third of the world's output is now in services. The share of the gross domestic product in services in the United States and the United Kingdom now exceeds 70%. The total value of such services worldwide in 2008 was estimated to be almost $30 trillion.[32]

A share of these services cannot be protected by the traditional protection of tangible property. And many of these services can be transacted over the Internet, or by easily transmitted media. It is more difficult to inspect such services. We now require of regulators constant vigilance and innovation to merely keep pace with the innovations of service providers.

The first wave of regulatory reform

Following the Great Crash of 1929, the public was almost inconsolable. They had lost all confidence in the banking institutions chartered with federal and state governments. Reeling from the aftermath of a wild and wooly period of laissez-faire economics in the Roaring Twenties, the public had grown frustrated by the apparent lack of regulatory responsiveness of the Herbert Hoover administration from 1929 to 1932. Franklin D. Roosevelt was swept to power in 1932–1933 with the promise of restoring trust in our financial institutions.

And trust was sorely shattered. In 1932, as the Great Depression was getting its grip, the Match King, Ivan Kreuger, was bankrupt and committed suicide, leaving thousands with worthless stock. His empire, built up by bribing national governments to permit him a monopoly for match production in their countries, was reportedly worth more than $100 billion dollars, in today's dollars. He had been the toast of towns, and had consulted President Hoover at the White House. The Great Crash left his matchmaking and construction empires on shaky foundations, which he covered up in a pyramid scheme not unlike the recent Bernard Madoff incident.

To then, securities regulation was left to state governments under the so-called Blue Sky Law. These laws were easily avoided simply by using the mail system to exchange securities across state lines, leaving the securities industry largely unregulated. Roosevelt's New Deal reforms squarely dealt with this regulatory failing.

It is believed that Kreuger committed suicide in 1932, although conspiracy theories abound. This massive financial failure is also said to have motivated the Securities Act of 1933, the Securities Exchange Act of 1934, and the formation of the Securities and Exchange Commission in 1934. With the appointment of Joseph P. Kennedy Sr., the father of a later president John F. Kennedy, as its first commissioner, the era of financial regulation had begun in earnest.

Born out of failure

The effectiveness of the Securities and Exchange Commission is questioned each time we have failures like the Madoff affair in 2008. Bernard Madoff was apprehended for one of the most massive financial frauds ever perpetrated by an individual. Some calculate the losses and diversions to be in excess of $50 billion over more than a decade. And while whistle-blowers had informed the main regulatory body, the Securities and Exchange Commission, of some of the alleged wrongdoings, there was little or no regulatory oversight to prevent this massive fraud.

This was just the last in a decade-long wave of regulatory failings. One of the largest failures in regulation before the Madoff affair was with Enron.

The end of laissez-faire?

The French language term laissez-faire means, quite literally, "Let it do, or let it be." It is most often invoked in the context of the desirability of free markets. This principle cannot be used too blindly, though. The underlying premise of the term is that people should be free to pursue their own economic well-being, conditioned under the assumption that no one else is harmed in the process. It is not a blind approval to get ahead regardless of the damage one's recklessness imposes on others.

The notorious corporation Enron was decidedly in the camp of "success, even at the expense of others." Their corporate culture grew out of a legitimate and successful strategy of buying and selling future deliveries of energy commodities, most notably natural gas. It went from an energy broker to a financial powerhouse. And something went astray in the process.

Enron's roots in the energy production and transportation business eventually moved into the business of energy speculation, but with a twist. Not only did they realize they could speculate in energy markets, but they also began to directly control the supply of energy in these markets.

For instance, Enron controlled some electric power plants in California. They also bought and sold energy up and down the West Coast of the United States. They soon realized that, in periods of very high demand, they could sell energy at a rate of five times the usual going rate by simply creating a temporary shortage. All they needed to do is shutdown one of their energy plants for maintenance at these critical times, and they could predict with almost perfect confidence that the spot price on the market would rise substantially. They could even buy up other supply in advance, essentially becoming the sole supplier in markets that became critical at times of their choice.

By using this novel, unethical, and fraudulent policy, they managed to extract, some even say extort, billions of dollars in profits. Once the manipulations became public, a company that had been valued by the market at over $30 billion went bankrupt.

Stockholders, the pensions of more than 20,000 employees, and the energy buying public, lost tens of billions of dollars. Fines and restitution went unpaid, and even the sentencing of a few high level executives was an insufficient deterrent from such a ploy occurring again. The failure ultimately brought about the demise of a couple of the world's leading accounting and consulting firms.

The Enron era saw similar scandals from MCI/Worldcom, Global Crossing, Tyco International, and others. These scandals resulted in a clarion call for increased regulation of corporations so the public could hold chief executive officers responsible for the ethical misconduct of their companies.

Most notable of this era of partial repeal of laissez-faire was the Sarbanes-Oxley Act, and its European counterparts. Unfortunately, such regulation ultimately costs the vast majority of honest corporations dearly for the ethical and regulatory failings of the tiny but highly costly and visible minority.

Ultimately, though, these costs are borne by us all.

The second wave of regulatory reform

In the aftermath of the Enron meltdown, the public was angry, Californian energy consumers had lost billions, and thousands of newly unemployed professionals, many of whom had lost their entire pensions, were distraught. Congress was forced to act. And act they did. They passed the Public Company Accounting Reform and Investor Protection Act of 2002 with relative swiftness. Known more commonly for their congressional sponsors, Sarbanes-Oxley, or SOX for short, produced a number of reporting innovations.

These innovations were designed to substantially improve financial transparency and with that, reduce investor fear and uncertainty. Most notably, it required the chief executive of all publicly traded companies to personally vouch for the accuracy of the financial statements emanating from their companies. Of course, all of us who are certainly held accountable for any representations of our personal financial affairs might have assumed that this would be the case all along.

The other provisions are equally important. The Sarbanes-Oxley Act contained 11 titles that further regulate public companies. These include the creation of a Public Company Accounting Oversight Board to provide independent oversight of corporate auditors as its first title. Title II requires that these auditors must follow standards that ensure independence and limit possible conflicts of interest. Auditors are also prevented from acting as consultants to the public companies they audit.

Title III of SOX specifies the level of responsibility for various corporate officers, boards, and committees; while Title IV specifies what must be reported and how, to the various parties that rely on the accurate flow of corporate information.

Title V is designed to restore confidence of investors in the analyses of securities professionals by requiring these experts to disclose conflicts of interest and to follow a code of conduct. When we hear a financial expert tell us about his or her stock picks and also reveal to us that they own some of these stocks, the analysts are following the provision of the Sarbanes-Oxley Act. Title VI goes on to outline how analysts may be barred from acting as a broker because of perceived conflicts.

Title VII requires the Securities and Exchange Commission and the Comptroller General to periodically study the state of regulation and report to the public their findings. Title VIII specifies the penalties for violation of SOX and offers protection for whistle-blowers. Title IX recommends sentencing guidelines for infractions, while Title X specifies that the chief executive officer must sign the corporate tax return. Finally, Title XI specifies corporate fraud and records tampering, including the mammoth levels of paper shredding following the downfall of Enron and its consultants, as a criminal offense.

SOX has been broadly praised by the investing public for its emphasis on corporate responsibility and its command for greater reporting accuracy and timeliness. It has also been praised for improvements in the participation of senior management, audit committees, and boards of directors in more proactive ways.

SOX has even created an apparent new industry in "financial restatements" designed to correct previous misstatements on financial reports as chief executive officers come to realize they are criminally liable for the accuracy of these statements. As a consequence, the number of corrections by publicly traded companies doubled the year after the provisions took effect and are now the routine in almost one in ten companies.[33]

Not all love SOX

There is no universal appreciation for the value of more accurate information through SOX, though. Smaller publicly traded companies may incur costs upward of 2% of revenue to cover the added layers of control and accurate reporting. Because more sophisticated companies most likely had more sophisticated accounting information systems, the cost for larger firms may represent but 0.1% of revenues. And yet, the scandals that gave rise to SOX were not formulated on kitchen tables or over the desks of executives of small- to medium-sized companies. They emanated from the board rooms and plush executive suites of mammoth companies that can easily afford the regulatory burden that so burdens smaller companies.

Not all agree in the appropriateness of these added costs to U.S. corporations. A December 21, 2008 editorial in the *Wall Street Journal* doubts that the provision of SOX and other regulations have prevented fraud. Instead, they may have managed to induce companies to offer their initial public offerings on exchanges elsewhere, or not list publicly at all. They argue that declining public offerings and a greater number of companies assumed by larger corporations are failing because of increased regulation.

SOX also encouraged a new "mark to market" approach to the valuation of assets on balance sheets that had some tragic, unintended consequences. The provisions, adopted by the U.S. Financial Accounting Standards Board (FASB) and its international counterparts, required firms to accurately reflect the current value of their assets on their books. In the wake of the subprime meltdown, when banks were left with underperforming assets with little marketability, financial institutions around the world were quickly deemed insolvent. Bankruptcies ensued, plunging economies to the depths of recession not seen since the Great Depression. Part of the international recovery effort was the recognition that mark-to-market is destabilizing when markets are dysfunctional. Mark-to-market has been placed in partial abeyance.

These regulatory changes may simply be a consequence of poor market conditions arising from a failure of laissez-faire economics. It is very easy to see the costs of regulation, but much more difficult to measure the value of market confidence arising from more honest, accurate, timely, and transparent reporting.

A new wave of financial regulation?

Following the Enron meltdown and the birth of the Sarbanes-Oxley era, we were met with another crisis. This is less a crisis created by a few too-clever people in one room, but is a more broad-based conspiracy to deceive. And many more than the hundred or so direct perpetrators ended up participating, including every person permitted to buy a home without the ability to pay for it.

Flip That House

When something seems too good to be true, it almost always is. One can't blame another for wanting to realize the great American dream of home ownership. As a matter of fact, the rate of home ownership is often invoked as a measure of the triumph of the U.S. consumer. And when the demographics were just right to ensure a steady improvement of homeownership demand as baby boomers reached the age of home affordability, almost everyone thought that prices could only go up.

However, when syndicated television shows like *Leave It to Beaver* were replaced with shows on how to make a quick profit in real estate like *Flip That House*, trouble could not be far away.

Just as housing prices began to take off, the smart people on Wall Street figured out ways to create both the supply of, and demand for subprime loan mortgage instruments. To create the demand for these loanable funds, mortgage underwriters packaged promissory notes they knew to be good with some that they could have known, if they wanted, would go astray. This permitted them to solicit new homeowners that would prefer to not reveal income, credit, or even employment. And on the supply side, they could raise the money for these loans by convincing investors the products were sound, and even insured.

This perfect storm was complete once the pyramid scheme began to run out of new buyers. Growth in housing prices could only occur as long as the underwriters could keep finding new people to buy homes. But once everyone who could conceivably buy a home, job or not, income or not, and credit or not, had one, demand sputters and prices declined.

At that point, the market collapsed. But it lasted long enough for the mortgage underwriters to make their commissions, the ratings agencies and investment banks that rated and assembled these instruments to collect their fees, and the marketers to sell them to an unwitting public deceived by claims of insurance, AAA ratings, and better returns than found elsewhere.

The public – the new residual claimant

We all were ultimately left holding the bag. These toxic assets just about brought down the banking and credit industries, and bailouts will cost us for decades. And that is the best case scenario. Some argue that things could get much worse than a simple failure of credit.

There will no doubt be clarion calls to reregulate financial markets, perhaps even more intensively than ever before. The pendulum had moved to a high level of deregulation and shall likely swing to the other side. How far it will swing we do not yet know. We do know that regulation must address market integrity, information, and incentives. If regulation can do that, we will go a long way in restoring confidence. If it turns out to be too little and too late, fear will continue, and panic will likely erupt again.

The deregulation that was de rigor since the Reagan era of the 1980s is premised on the belief that financial markets were self-regulating and were dominated by smart investors who could figure out any problems for themselves. This was an era when people still had pensions from their companies and all had confidence in social security. The wave of wealth and the acknowledgment of financial independence over the 1990s created many more investors who were not of the old money, Wall Street ilk. These investors were the proverbial babes in the woods.

The market now depends on the confidence of these investors though. Their interests are our interests. And the public interest can likely not be protected by the Wall Street types who can also profit from our collective missteps. Only agents representing the public can be the cops on the financial beat.

Ultimately, all benefit from healthy financial markets. Securities prices depend crucially on well-functioning markets with accurate market prices. SOX tries, at least, to remedy some of the pitfalls of information distortion by disincentives to deceive. However, we are still left with the moral hazard problems created by executive compensation schemes, the benefits of insider trading so difficult to detect, and the tremendous cost of toxic assets forcing out good assets.

Don't we have enough regulation?

Of course, many of the antics that have brought markets to their knees and fanned the flames of fear are illegal. Many more are unethical. Why do we need more regulation?

Certainly we now see the cost of poor or ineffective regulation. Do not the perpetrators weigh these costs when they decide to act against the public interest? In a word, no, they do not. They cannot, as a matter of simple math.

Let us consider the current Global Financial Meltdown, brought about by the actions of a few that designed these toxic assets, a few dozen that rated them, and a few hundred that sold them. For the benefit of the doubt, let us say that a thousand people, some in the same room, most not, created this toxic asset problem.

We see now that the Credit Crisis of 2007 and the resulting Global Financial Meltdown of 2008 have reduced worldwide wealth by almost $30 trillion. Let us generously spread that cost over a thousand people, of varying degrees of knowledge and malice. The distribution comes to $30 billion per conspirator.

Of course, none of these crimes on the economy rises to the level of a capital crime (no pun intended). How can one be deterred from committing a $30 billion crime? Even someone like Bernie Madoff, by all accounts a respectable, responsible, well-educated, and honest person, except for that little $50 billion investment fraud thing, was enticed into a huge scandal with apparently insufficient deterrence.

Once damages move beyond any level we could even possibly dream of deterring, criminal sanctions become relatively ineffective. This is especially true if the potential wealth one could amass is sufficient to hire enough of the top lawyers in the world to create some plausible deniability. Courts are, of course, willing to impose treble damages to try to deter these acts. Would a $150 billion fine have deterred Bernie Madoff from his $50 billion fraud? Probably not. And treble damages still not compensate the investor who has lost all confidence and has become cynical about high finance. Ultimately, the broad market and the consumer are left holding the bag.

Regulators to the rescue?

Can the ounce of prevention prevent the pound of cure? We spend fractions of a penny on the dollar to try to regulate the marketplace. For instance, the budget for the Securities and Exchange Commission is less than a billion dollars. That is about the amount of trading in the first few minutes of opening on U.S. stock exchanges in a single day. Their budget of late has not even kept up with inflation. And employees earn very low six-figure salaries and must regulate very high eight-, nine-, or ten-figure-salary chief executive officers and financiers.

Regulators are constantly playing catch up too. Just as our security experts are not in the room when terrorists plot attacks, financiers loathe to share their next strategy with regulators. And just like terrorists, financiers have to only realize one colossal failure for regulators to have failed spectacularly in their mission. In such an environment of secrecy, it is impossible for regulators to get things right all the time, especially when the odds are so stacked against them.

Even when regulators can get ahead of the problem and induce Congress to pass the legislation to prevent the next global financial meltdown, the industry immediately hires a big room full of the smartest lawyers and financiers in the world to immediately figure out ways to legally circumvent the new laws.

Regulators can, though, offer the reassurance not unlike cops on the beat or officers at airports. They can give the reassuring sense that someone is watching out – and in doing so, can go a long way to ally the panics of a fear-gripped market. Against this yardstick and the $25 trillion cost of the Global Financial Meltdown of 2008, a greater investment in regulation is likely a luxury we can afford.

A call for ethics

Ultimately, the solution cannot flow entirely from an even more elaborate cat and mouse game. Potential future perpetrators of the next scheme that will cost us trillions must instead be deterred by a realization that their antics will cost all of us, including the perpetrators themselves, trillions in the long run. Reputation and ruin may be a more effective deterrent than an army of new regulators. And we will likely not change the sentiment raised by an industry leader fearful of a wave of reregulation.

25
Ethics and Social Responsibility

The Global Financial Meltdown is also a meltdown in business ethics. How could this be? And what can we do about it?

Having developed and taught a course in business ethics, I had to endure the jokes about business ethics as an oxymoron like jumbo shrimp and military intelligence. I am currently working with a colleague to determine if indeed a business ethics education changes behavior, or at least perceptions of right and wrong. It seems like a safe assumption, though, that an education in business ethics will allow our business graduates to discern between right and wrong. The next step, of course, is to be sure they act on this knowledge. After all, most of the major ethical breakdowns that have cost us so dearly were perpetrated by graduates of our business schools. As a former business school dean, this is a realization I find quite troubling.

It is becoming increasingly evident that ethics, or our ability to discern between right and wrong and act accordingly, has a strong cultural aspect. For instance, Prof. Dan Ariely, the Alfred P. Sloan Professor of Behavioral Economics at MIT, recently related a story of an experiment on a class of business students at Carnegie Mellon University in Pittsburgh, Pennsylvania.[34]

Students were asked to complete a quiz. They were paid depending on how many answers they got right. They were paid in two different ways though. Half the students were paid in advance, and merely had to return some of their earnings for each wrong answer, on an honor basis. The other half were paid after the quiz by presenting to the instructor their correct answers.

One interesting observation is that the students who were paid in advance and merely had to refund some of their earnings on the honor basis did statistically better than the students who had their results confirmed and were paid after the exam. This result, that the honor system seems to break down, is not too earth-shattering.

The researchers then added a twist. They had an actor sit down with the large class of students. Just a few moments after the quiz began, the actor stood up and publicly announced he had finished the quiz, got all the answers correct, and then proceeded to walk out of the class with his envelope of earnings in clear view. Obviously, everybody in the class saw he had cheated. But their response depended on whether he was wearing a Carnegie Mellon sweatshirt in this class of Carnegie Mellon students, or if he was wearing a sweatshirt from the competing school, University of Pittsburgh.

If the actor wore a Carnegie Mellon sweatshirt, cheating still occurred as before. But if he wore the sweatshirt of the arch-rival school, deemed an inferior school by Carnegie Mellon students, cheating dropped off dramatically.

In other words, a cohort's willingness to cheat depends on whether they believe that cheating, or bending the rules, is an accepted norm of the group to which they belong. In essence, to a cheater, the retort that everybody does it makes it alright.

A culture of cheating

The ethical failures of the 1970s, 1980s, and 1990s, from financier Ivan Boesky to Michael Milken, and even from the pardoned former President Richard Nixon to disgraced football star O. J. Simpson may have created an environment where people believe everyone cheats or deceives, and sometimes even without penalty. Lucrative book and movie deals even further enriched their crimes or ethical breaches. We may have left a whole generation with a perception that they can catch as catch can. Perhaps they believed the real chumps are the ones that got caught in an unethical pursuit of greed.

This experiment and the portrayal of successful cheats reinforce the institutionalization of ethical or unethical behavior. Even the willingness of reputable accounting firms and consultants to endorse the behavior of unethical corporations or reputable banks to market the toxic assets of unethical lending practices gives an institutional stamp of approval on behavior we cannot tolerate.

This observation of the cultural norm of unethical behavior explains one odd bit of data. Many wondered why the wheels of justice came down so heavily on Martha Stewart, a well-known television personality, and former trader, who was convicted on actions stemming from a relatively small amount of insider trading. Surely, it was argued, there were plenty of bigger scams to prosecute, especially given the stretched enforcement budget of our financial regulators.

The beauty of the Martha Stewart conviction was not in securing a bit of jail time. It was in sending out a clear and very public message that unethical behavior will not be tolerated. The Securities and Exchange Commission perhaps spent hundreds of thousands or millions of dollars prosecuting a case involving insider trading and a stock transaction that netted Martha Stewart $45,673.[35] The true value of the case was in the chilling effect such a very public trial would have on the calculations of others contemplating insider trading. It presented a norm of honesty, and created a rather unattractive picture of the club one would join if one engages in insider trading.

The compliance and sentencing provisions of the Sarbanes-Oxley Act of 2002, and even the sentencing guidelines included in Federal Sentencing Guidelines for Organizations in 1991, certainly sensitized chief executive officers to the importance of the creation of a culture of ethical behavior. Most major companies have ethics or compliance officers whose job it is to ensure that ethical behavior permeates the organization.

These compliance officers develop policies to educate employees on a regular basis about the ethical expectations of the corporation, to create examples and norms for expected ethical behavior that are realistic and accessible by employees, and to back up these programs with monitoring and with penalties for ethical violations.

Often these compliance officers are at the same time tied to enforcement of other corporate policies, such as the advocacy of diversity or the prevention of acts that contribute to a hostile work environment. As a consequence, the officers are sometimes received in a cynical manner as advocating policies that reduce lawsuits for the corporate office, rather than as advocates for the right thing to do. Such cynicism is magnified if the corporate leadership is subsequently accused of unethical behavior.

Instead, ethics must be presented as a desirable norm in a way that agents of the corporation can relate and strive to imitate. Actions and positive examples set a much clearer tone.

Is ethics education effective?

Business ethics as a stand-alone course in business programs is still relatively new and uncommon. As a consequence of the various ethical breakdowns occurring throughout the 1980s and 1990s, the main accrediting body for business schools, the Association for Advancement of Collegiate Schools of Business International, recently developed standards for ethics in accredited business school curricula. Most schools argued that ethics is infused across their entire curricula, but had difficulty actually documenting the veracity of their claims. Others created courses dedicated to instruction in ethics. Such courses offer researchers the opportunity to determine if ethics can be learned.

Most studies demonstrate that the moral and situational awareness can be enhanced in students. For instance, Nguyen et al. show that ethical instruction makes students less likely to report that they would find themselves behaving unethically if confronted with an ethical dilemma.[36] However, it is more difficult to determine whether training in ethics actually translates into an enhancement in actual ethical behavior.

Given that the evidence suggests ethics are created through a cultural norm, the relatively few students immersed in an ethics education are unlikely to transform larger corporate cultures. If an ethical education is demonstrated to be effective in creating ethical behavior and if a sufficiently large number of our graduates have been immersed in ethics education, it would remain an open question whether business truly embraces, and insists upon, ethics as a predominant corporate value.

Is corporate responsibility an oxymoron?

The problem is that ethical behavior is presumed to be at odds with the primary goal of a corporation, to make a profit on behalf of their stockholders. Some have argued that this profit-making goal is paramount, and instead, ethics behavior must be invoked through punishment of transgressions. For instance, Nobel Memorial Prize winning economist Milton Friedman argues that social responsibility should not be a value of the firm, but instead can be pursued individually by the shareholders of the firm, if they wish.[37]

Others are increasingly arguing that ethics and social responsibility are good business, leading to gains in reputation and an enhancement in market share.

Still others believe that ethics and social responsibility are an essential and integral value of a firm, quite separate from any profits these values may generate. While Friedman argues that a firm should not develop values for itself that may conflict with the value of profit making for which all shareholders can agree, proponents of inherent ethical values argue that the firm is a legal person with its own set of ethical values. Shareholders would then invest in this firm because it is attracted to the firm's balance of ethics and profit as a natural extension of the individual investor's personal philosophy.

Ultimately, firms are a microcosm of a broader society. If society insists upon ethical behavior, and requires such behavior of its individual and corporate citizens alike, ethical behavior is more likely to prevail. Working against such a culture, though, is the sense of secrecy that also permeates corporate culture. Lack of transparency is at odds with ethical behavior.

Transparency and the New York Times Test

For instance, I offer my students various tests that help them create their own moral compasses. One of my lessons for students is "The New York Times Test." Barring any issue of legitimate protection of the security of an employer or others, if the student would not like their behavior printed on the front page of the *New York Times*, they may be behaving unethically.

It is the need for secrecy, for organizational silos, for the punishment of whistle-blowers, and for the creation of groupthink that challenges ethical behavior. However, transparency, the creation of paths of mobility across the organization, and diversity of thought, race, cultures, incomes, and genders, enhances corporate ethical behavior.

Indeed, the most compelling case for diversity is not in the opportunity it affords disadvantaged groups. Such policies are on shaky ground if they purport to require an institution to subjugate its interests to a broader social interest. Instead, the more compelling case is that diversity of thought and experience makes the institution better able to integrate with the values of society and the marketplace. Because diverse individuals also bring a diversity of ethical norms to the institution, the institution is forced to constantly confront its own ethics rather than fall into a norm that may inadvertently confound its own long-term ethical interests.

We can ask ourselves, as well, whether there is a collective responsibility of our leaders, our educators, and our media to help guide our increasingly complex economy. The onus is great, but the price of failure is even greater.

26
Wall Street, Main Street, and the Social Contract

It is somewhat ironic that we associate the capitalist model with financial capital and Wall Street. The domination of Wall Street is a relatively recent economic phenomenon.

Just after the Second World War, the financial services industry represented 2% of gross domestic product. At its current 8% share of GDP, the finance industry has doubled in two decades, and has experienced a fourfold increase in just 60 years. This trillion dollar a year industry now attracts the best of our business school graduates, with promises of six- or seven-figure bonuses, fast cars, nice apartments in Manhattan, and retirement by the age of 40.

In the third quarter of 2007, just before the Credit Crisis began to take hold, profits in the financial industry accounted for fully a third of all domestic profits in the United States. Profits in the financial industry rivaled manufacturing, wholesaling, and retailing combined.[38] Yet, in 2006, the financial sector only employed 8.4 million people in the United States, representing just 5.6% of employment. With 5.6% of those employed generating a third of the profits nationwide, it is no wonder that this industry attracted our best and brightest graduates.[39]

Now, fewer than 15% or 22.5 million U.S. workers are engaged in nonagricultural production of goods. We have grown from a country of farmers and manufacturers to one of services producers, especially in financial services. In reality, the production of goods and services has, in no small part, been replaced by the production of capital.

The fear premium

With profits in the financial industry in these most volatile of times exceeding $400 billion annually in the United States, the profits accruing to those that produce the goods and services is depleted. One out of every three dollars of profits now accrues to the financial industry rather than to the industries that make the products. Greater volatility means greater redirection from production to finances. In other words, the price that producers of goods and services pay to the financial industry increases with increased volatility and fear. This fear diverts resources from production, and toward increasingly complex financial instruments and derivatives that increasingly place us in even more fear.

Capitalism with a big C or a little c?

It is actually incorrect to assume that capitalism refers to the financial capital industry. The root capital in the term capitalism refers to the actual factories, machines, hardware, and software, etc., that the owners of capital, the capitalists, purchase so that we can produce goods and services. Because they purchase this important factor of production, and hire the workers and buy the resources to work with the capital, they earn the profits that the capital generates.

Of course, there are other models. For instance, the owners of human capital could assemble, and buy the machines and resources to produce goods and services.

Such worker collectives are but one additional model to organize the production of goods and services. We have seen from history, though, that such a collection of workers/owners creates some problems in developing a shared manufacturing strategy. Unless the enterprise is relatively small, this model proves difficult to compete with the more efficient coordination possible under the physical capitalist model.

While the capitalist model allowed the owners of physical capital to earn the profits of their investment, a most substantial industry of its own in the raising and lending of financial capital was, until recently, a secondary enterprise in support of the capitalist model.

Now, though, capitalism has come to be symbolized by the construction of financial empires, with the bulk of a nation's profits now going to those who can move financial capital around, rather than those that can use physical capital to produce the goods and services we value.

The excesses of financial capitalism

We saw earlier that the financial industry thrives on volatility. Sophisticated financial models allow their managers to earn profits as markets rise, and also earn profits as markets fall within a reasonable range. The industry even stands accused of encouraging volatility to spur these profits.

For instance, in a paper titled "Do Hedge Funds Profit from Mutual-Fund Distress?" economists Joseph Chen of the University of Southern California, Samuel Hanson and Jeremy C. Stein of Harvard University, and Harrison Hong of Princeton University demonstrated in 2007 that hedge funds are able to profit from the predictable actions of distressed investors. Hedge fund managers are able to make market moves before the rest of us. They can sell short with a great deal of leverage, to profit from our panic selling. Our fear is their profit.[40]

If it is volatility that produces consumer misery and excessive volatility that can plunge us into panic and fear, is there a greater social responsibility of these financial capitalists to society? In other words, does the financial capital industry have a responsibility beyond the Milton Friedman concept of returning the maximum profits, at any cost?

Corporate responsibility?

If we accept the Freidman postulate that the financial industry has no obligation but to make profits on behalf of the shareholders of these firms, we violate a central tenet of economics. The gains of hedge funds in the example above are not made out of thin air. They come at a cost to the rest of us. In effect, the hedge fund industry has grown tremendously by employing thousands of highly paid experts who devote their efforts to capturing a piece of our economic pie.

This is in stark contrast to traditional forms of production. We pay a performer to entertain us, a banker to keep our money safe, an automaker to build us a car, or a contractor to build us a house. We believe the good or service they produce and we buy is valuable to us and presumably more valuable than the cash we have to give up to purchase the good or service. The seller and the buyer, both, are enhanced by the transaction and the economic pie grows.

On the contrary, an industry that devotes significant effort into snatching other's piece of the pie, rather than growing the pie themselves, is actually anti-economic. Interestingly, economists would have little problem with such grabs if there was no effort devoted to the enterprise. One side gains, the other loses, but no production is lost in net. For instance, a game of poker between four willing participants is benign because one's gain is another's loss. Nothing is lost in the process except the energy to play, which the participants would not do unless the entertainment value exceeds their effort.

An industry, on the other hand, that is designed to devote tremendous talent and resources to capture others' pieces of the pie provides no social or economic reward. Rather, the talent that goes into this enterprise is wasted, compared to what it could do in a productive activity.

Some of these high-flying financiers have a sense of immortality, fueled by their own power, that may cause them to underestimate risk and overestimate reward. Their large wealth, ability to spread risk over many projects, and addictive or testosterone-fueled personalities, all lead them to choose points much higher on the return-risk-based capital allocation line than most investors. These high fliers are almost predestined for risky behavior, some of which may stray beyond the merely unethical and into the downright criminal.

Worse yet, if such activities also destabilize financial markets and, at times, the volatility induces fear and plunges us into recessions, their costs to society are even more significant. These factors negate Milton Friedman's argument that there is no responsibility to society than to make a profit. His statement was based on a world where all production was actually productive. It seems that those times are gone.

A mammoth scale

We argued that "investment" in the derivatives market, through swaps, futures, collateralized debt, and the like does little to facilitate traditional markets and the real economy. These markets do not represent ownership of production. Instead, they are often little more than betting instruments that derive their value from other more fundamental instruments. Just as a bet on a horse does not cause the horse to run faster, trades of derivates have little effect on the underlying instruments.

Even if they arguably contribute to some efficiency in the stock, bond, and loanable funds markets, the mammoth scale of these derivatives markets is disproportionate to any possible positive benefits. On a given day, markets in derivates may account for more than 60% of overall market activity.

They also create downside risk that certainly outstrips any positive benefits. It is ironic that derivatives argued to decrease risk were instrumental in the financial market crash that led to the Global Financial Meltdown. These instruments also were at the root of the ethical breaches that destroyed consumer confidence and irreversibly changed the way we view Wall Street.

The huge sums, outstripping the total value of trades in traditional markets in a given day, create a certain culture that has proven to be dangerous. And just as betting on horses creates the temptation to fix races, or betting on boxing may have produced the occasional dive, the sums involved in the derivatives markets have had a deleterious effect on bond raters and traders. Without the discipline of the real economy, this gamesmanship over the pieces to a fixed economic pie was ignored – at least until we realize it would ultimately cost us all dearly.

Life, liberty, and the pursuit of happiness

By enshrining protections for private property, the free-market system affords us all an opportunity to pursue our own self-interest in pursuit of happiness. Society protects our property from being impounded and allows us to focus on producing things others value rather than protecting things we have accumulated or purchased from others. Society also gives similar rights to corporations and firms, which it considers to be legal people. Society asks for something in return.

For the opportunity to earn and to create economic security, we pay taxes. These taxes pay for the physical protection of our property by police and the laws of courts; the services we need to be productive, such as roads, schools, and a modicum of health care; and the services of government that can respond to our changing needs.

We do not pay for the efforts of those who created the free-market system by which we benefit, or the rights and constitutions that create the free-market system. We all buy into our collective system, and we aspire to use the system to allow us to create our own economic security.

In turn, we all have a responsibility to protect the notion of a free-market system that allows us to keep what we have earned, and provides the opportunity for us to produce the better mousetrap that may, in turn, benefit us all. The free market system has empowered us and we, in turn, must continue to empower the system by protecting it from the abuses that allow others to usurp our production through financial shenanigans.

Philanthropists such as billionaire financier Warren Buffett well understand this responsibility to give back to society some of the earnings that society's laws have given to them. Andrew Carnegie, in his book *The Gospel of Wealth,* uttered these words 120 years ago:

> He who dies rich dies disgraced.[41]

Carnegie recognized what Friedman would refute. We all have a responsibility to put something back into a world that has given much more to us than we could have done for ourselves. While we also have a right to give to those we love and wish to protect, it is not unreasonable to expect that society can enforce regulations that prevent industries whose goal is to take from others. It is this reasonable expectation that commands greater regulation of industries, such as finance, that have the potential for doing so much good, but which also can be led astray by greed or by capitalizing on the fear of others.

Part IX

Institutions That Ameliorate or Amplify Fear

Fear and panic need not be part of our modern economy. Nor need the flames of fear be fanned by the institutions we trust. We next discuss the roles of the media, politics, and leadership in controlling and sometimes manipulating our fears.

We begin with a discussion of the role and responsibility of the media. Just as there has been a speculative bubble in financial markets, there has at the same time been burgeoning growth in the media. And just as financial markets can be poisoned by bad assets, the media can be tainted by poor or uninformed reporting. I argue that the media has some responsibility to our economy, and is in a better position than most to educate and guide us in our collective economic decisions.

Chapters 28 and 29 go on to discuss the role of economic leadership in keeping the economy on an even keel.

27
The Media as an Antidote to Fear

The media is the conduit that allows us to create order in an increasingly complex civilization. It seeks out the information it believes we need to know and processes that information so that it is most accessible and relevant to us. Sometimes, though, in an effort to compete, it substitutes entertainment under the guise of information. Unfortunately, fear catches our attention better than almost any other emotion. The cultivation of fear allows the media to sell advertising so that it can remain competitive.

The range of media outlets has grown phenomenally over the past century and especially over the past couple of decades. The world's first newspaper was a pamphlet that began publication in 1605. More than four centuries later, in 1920, the first radio newscast spread the news of the election of President Warren Harding. This new medium expanded our range of choices beyond newspapers, magazines, pamphlets, and books.

Fifteen years later, the German government began the world's first public television service, followed by the United Kingdom the next year, and the United States two years after that. Soon, television newscasts eclipsed radio.

The Genie is out of the bottle

But while newspapers have spread the news for more than four centuries, radio for nearly a century, and television for more than half a century, journalism really changed for good in 1980. Before then, each outlet was a member of an oligopoly of perhaps no more than half a dozen significant competitors in a given market. With the first broadcast of the Cable News Network (CNN) in 1980, the competitive landscape changed considerably. In one fell swoop, every news outlet instantly had competition that was global, ubiquitous, immediate, and around the clock.

While CNN may not have had the multiple bureaus of news services like the Associated Press or Reuters, or the bureaus of the major networks, it had access to wire reports and the reports of local stations desiring the occasional national or international audience. The news industry has been much more competitive ever since. We must ask though whether this competitiveness has produced a substantially better product.

Other cable news outlets began to compete with CNN. However, few anticipated the next innovation – the Internet. Beginning soon after the widespread use of the Internet, Internet news sources had surpassed newspapers as the second most common source for national and international news.[42] And for people under 30, Internet news overtook the television as the top news outlet. News competition has become even more intense, and at the same time more diverse.

This diversity of media may be a positive thing. However, it has complicated our lives in other ways.

Ultimately, humans crave order. It gives us security, allows us to understand how our decisions will affect our fate, and ensures that what we do today will have some positive effect tomorrow. We live in an uncertain world, though. With this uncertainty comes anxiety. And when the uncertainty threatens our livelihood, we respond to this risk with fear or panic.

Our efforts to create order in an uncertain world also forces us to focus on only the subset of information around us that tends to support and reinforce our current views. This tendency of human nature in a risky environment fuels our fears and induces our panics. The same tendency to incorporate the information that reinforces our outlook also induces us to see only good news and reject the rest when the prevailing mood is optimistic.

Tell us what we want to hear

And the media gives us what makes us comfortable and conforms to our world view, for better or worse. Gone are the days when newscasters gave us the information it felt we really needed and has been known to withhold from us the news it felt would not illuminate us. Now, news wants to capture our attention so that it can succeed in raising more revenue from the advertisements it solicits.

This shift from informational content to more entertaining or sensational content has likely forever changed commercial broadcast and cable news, and has forced more serious news junkies to noncommercial outlets like public broadcasting or the Internet.

Commercial television stations, long feeling the pinch of increased competition, have adopted a new strategy to capture our attention. It appeals to our most primordial core emotion of fear. We see that on every short-news blurb broadcast on the hour between prime time shows. Fifteen-second blurbs like "New threats at our local airports," "Storm of the century on the way," or

"Biohazards in your kitchen cupboard" are designed to compel us to watch the "News at 11" for fear that missing it will forever damage our economic security or health.

Of course, after a few such shocks, we realize these earth-shattering teasers are invariably benign. In any regard, we know we can always switch on the cable news to find out if the looming threat to all things we cherish is for real. But while such invocations of fear and panic may be good for late news broadcast ratings, they also have the side effect of creating a constant sense of low level panic.

This low level panic and fear has the effect of distorting our rational decision making. Author Barry Glassner, in his book *The Culture of Fear: Why Americans Are Afraid of the Wrong Things,*[43] describes how the media that blows our news out of proportion induces us to believe that airplane travel is much less safe than automobile travel, violent crime is on the increase, child abuse is everywhere, and road rage could erupt at any time.

In doing so, we reduce the deliberative process to anecdote rather than evidence. And because generations have been programmed to trust what appears in the mass media, we collectively suspend our skepticism. After all, if it is on the news, it must be true.

By distorting the news and inducing us to live in a state of low level fear and panic, we become less thoughtful, less discerning, and more dependent on the filtering of self-professed experts. These experts have created an industry of their own, with the most successful experts the ones that can capture our attention with statements designed to do so. Even issues as important to us all as politics and economics are simplified, sensationalized, and now suspect.

It is more than just entertainment

How can an atmosphere of fear distort how we regard information? We know the information is complex and often ambiguous. To recall, Bayes Rule states that when we confront information that is uncertain, we partition that information based on our interpretation of the state of the world.

For instance, when confronted with a value-free piece of information like "The Securities and Exchange Commission investigates a hedge fund," we can conclude either that the SEC remains diligent in keeping our markets on a level playing field. Or we can alternately conclude that the market is rife with corruption, depending on our beliefs.

In one era, we may be overcome with irrational exuberance, absorbing all news that is good and rejecting dark clouds as mere anomalies. We have seen this attitude before. It is the same culture that induced the raters of toxic assets to grant their seal of approval because, after all, housing prices always go up, except in those anomalies when housing prices go down.

In these times, though, every piece of news is another omen of a downturn. It has been shown that friends of those who have taken their money out of the bank will likewise do so. And in a "six degrees of separation" kind of way, this attitude spreads like a virus, eventually bringing down an industry. The medium that spreads this self-fulfilling prophecy is often the media.

In a recent interview with the *New York Times*, economist Dan Ariely, author of *Predictably Irrational*, stated:

> When everyone is talking about a recession, we feel like something has to change, even if nothing has changed for us. The media messages that are repeating doom and gloom affect everyone, not just people who really have trouble and should make changes, but people who are fine. That has a devastating effect on the economy.[44]

At times, the media, with its reports amplify our worst fears, seems to recognize its responsibility. *The Economist* magazine recently noted that the rate at which *The New York Times, The Times (of London)*, and the *Wall Street Journal* used the word "depression" in economy-related articles doubled on average after the brief Crash of 1987 and a little more than doubled since the recent Global Financial Meltdown in 2008.[45]

While "the D word" has been on the tip of many economists' tongues since early in 2008, and many more since October of 2008, few were willing to mention it. We talk about a severe, long, and deep recession, but few talk about their fears of a depression.

Perhaps economists are less fearful of job losses for themselves during a depression. After all, if financiers got us into this mess, presumably it would have to involve economists to get us out. In these times, maybe economics is one of the only growth industries.

In fifteen seconds or less

One unfortunate problem is that economics is a complex subject. It is a most technical and subtle social science, and it is nearly impossible to express these subtleties in 15 seconds, much less 15 minutes. And no story gets more than 15 minutes per session, in mainstream media, these days.

Let us imagine how effective the media might be in a subject that is more remote to our economic security. As the Global Financial Meltdown took its grip, the new Large Hadron Collider, built near Geneva, Switzerland, was started up on September 10, 2008. Designed to accelerate ions to 99.999999% of the speed of light at a cost of $5 billion, the facility was built to detect the theorized Higgs boson. It may also allow physicists to determine the process for electroweak symmetry breaking. Some postulated that it could generate a tiny black hole that would destroy the planet.

That got your attention. Imagine if you watched a 15-minute report on this impending doom. I am pretty sure that you could watch ten such interviews, in ten different media outlets, and still not be able to sort out the truth for yourself. Worse yet, you may only hear a 30-second report from an anchorman, or maybe even ten seconds at the top of the hour, stating "The world to be destroyed. Film at eleven."

To avoid forcing the reporters to actually understand the subtleties of particle physics, they usually employ the talking heads approach. Two experts, one pro, and one con, debate the issue in front of us. If we are inclined to already believe we are doomed, we would probably believe the pro speaker, or is that the con? If we are a bit more optimistic, we would conclude otherwise. If we are neither, we might make our conclusion based on who seems most credible, who has tied his or her tie the best, or perhaps we could flip a coin. Not always, though, is the truth in the middle.

Too much balance

After presenting both sides of the story in a balanced way, the impression left is that the planet could go either way. Given that almost no physicists actually believe the world will come to an end, an effort to provide "fair and balanced" journalism is neither fair nor balanced. It is difficult for us to gauge the true risk in this situation. We are instead left in fear, and are sure to watch the film at eleven.

Media reports on the economy are no different. Unless the interviewer is sufficiently skilled and educated about the economy to successfully explore the intricacies of the problem with the guests, the audience is left baffled. And because the differences between economists may be, as often as not, based on different politics rather than different theories of economics, we must differentiate between politics masquerading as economics.

To solve this dilemma and gain a better, healthier, and more accurate individual perspective, we can expect our correspondents to be trained in economics, or we must be trained ourselves. A certain economic education is necessary so that we can differentiate between the best theories, and the rest.

Even if we can enhance economic literacy to the point where all citizens can gauge for themselves the quality of economic information, we must still insist upon a certain economic sophistication from our reporters and interviewers. They choose the talking heads and provide for the appropriate balance that ensures we are left with the proper perspective.

There are some that offer us this service. Paul Solman of the Jim Lehrer *NewsHour* on the U.S. Public Broadcasting Service combines his keen understanding of economics with his careful choice of experts who demonstrate to us complex economic theories. His well-constructed and produced pieces are but one side of the spectrum of quality in economic reporting. Many reports, by oversimplifying complex problems either leave us with the impression that the solution is equally simple, or leave us with more uncertainty and fear. In a Gresham's Law of media, the bad economic reports force out the good, and the factoids replace facts. And we are left none the wiser.

For instance, it is part of the economic folklore that Black Tuesday of 1929 induced many Wall Street brokers to jump from windows. John Kenneth Galbraith points out in his book *The Great Crash: 1929* that reports of mass suicides to be an "imaginary carnage."[46]

On the contrary, at least three suicides were linked to the panic of 2008. Adolf Merckle, one of Germany's richest men, was killed by throwing himself in front of a train after his fortune of $12.8 billion was wiped out. Rene-Thierry Magon de la Villehuchet committed suicide after he lost more than a billion dollars following discovery of the Bernard Madoff fraud. And Reuters reports that the World Health Organization warned of a possible wave of economically motivated suicides in the year following the 2008 Global Financial Meltdown.[47] Kirk Stephenson, a London chief executive officer of the hedge fund Olivant, was also killed by a train. His death, too, was determined to be suicide. A commodities trader in Brazil and a money manager in Los Angeles also killed themselves after losing millions.

Taken out of context, and without an ability to compare these sensational incidents to similar incidents under less trying times, we could easily conclude the recent Global Financial Meltdown induced a wave of suicides. The media is in the best position to keep these incidents in perspective on our behalf.

If facts are becoming more difficult to differentiate from factoids, the opinion of the uninformed is now passed off as news. A major new feature of cable news is the survey. Just because 61% of viewers cast their "vote" that we are in a recession does not make it so.

A recession is a technical determination, not one of opinion. It is equally invalid to conclude after listening to the physics talking heads that the earth will end tomorrow, based on the opinion of viewers.

Ultimately, we must take responsibility for our economic education, expect more from those entrusted with providing us with information, and ask the experts and our economic leaders a sufficient number of questions until we understand and are comfortable with the answers. Only our increased economic literacy will reduce our economic fear.

We should also rely on our economic leaders to educate us about the market and, in doing so, assuage our fears. Until the U.S. presidential election of 2008, the mantle of economic leadership was the destiny and the hallmark of the last leader forced to confront economic calamity. Move over, President Roosevelt. There is another Economic Communicator in town.

28
Politics That Fan the Flames of Fear

President Franklin Delano Roosevelt of often slightly misquoted as saying "There is nothing to fear but fear itself." But a dash of fear sure makes leadership easier. There is an advantage to fear, from a political perspective. It makes for a more compliant citizenry.

Sharon Begley of *Newsweek* magazine recently reported how an international student asked the then presidential primary candidate Barack Obama about the post September 11, 2001 political climate of fear. Obama went on to outline the myriad ways in which fear has entered the political discourse, and implored those listening to break the fever of fear.[48]

President Obama recognized that fear was being used as a tool to manipulate citizens to trust the authority of their leaders without question. Fear mongers recognize that fear makes us more risk-averse, and greater risk aversion makes us more conservative with what we have and more resistant to change, even if change may be for the better.

The author and political psychology professor Drew Westen, in his book *The Political Brain: The Role of Emotions in Deciding the Fate of a Nation,* explains how such fear is used to manipulate voters.

The politics of fear always maintains a kernel of credibility. President George W. Bush's administration used a forged document claiming Saddam Hussein was trying to procure yellowcake, an unrefined form of uranium, to justify the invasion of Iraq, for fear that if we do not, they would build a weapon of mass destruction that would be used to attack the United States. In an earlier administration, his father, President George H. W. Bush, under the direction of fear strategist extraordinaire Lee Atwater, convinced many that Governor Dukakis, if elected president, would free felons from prisons who would subsequently unleash violence on an unsuspecting public.

There have only been three Democratic presidents who have been reelected in the past 175 years. Prof. Westen explains that Democrats mistakenly assume voters make rational decisions based on the issues.[49] Westen concludes it is the emotional issues that sway us. Candidates inevitably return us to Panksepp's core emotions of fear, seeking, rage, panic, play, lust, and caring, that are hard-wired to our biological brain. Of these emotions, fear is the easiest to tap, and has the most immediate and profound response.

So profound is the effectiveness of fear in politics that a generation of political consultants has defined their careers around fear. It is this fear of having someone take from us what we have toiled to save that creates a built-in tailwind for the traditional conservative political platforms. This fear of protecting something we have earned trumps the hope of creating something we can only imagine. And it led the Republican French Prime Minister Georges Clemenceau to reputably conclude "Not to be a socialist at twenty is proof of want of heart; to be one at thirty is proof of want of head."

In the *Newsweek* article, Begley also quoted the political scientist Edmund Burke (1729–1797), who concluded "no passion so effectually robs the mind of all its powers of acting and reasoning as fear." These fears are particularly powerful when our fate is placed in the hands of others.

For instance, we all know people who are perhaps not the safest of drivers and who drive on dangerous highways. Yet these same drivers who take their own lives in their hands while driving to the airport are frozen with fear as they entrust their lives to highly trained pilots flying airplanes that have a strikingly better safety record per mile traveled than automobiles. The American Public Transportation Association, in their 2008 *Public Transportation Fact Book*, reports that airlines have a fatality rate of 0.02 fatalities per billion miles traveled, while automobiles have a fatality rate of 7.4 fatalities per billion miles traveled, or a rate that is 370 times higher than air travel.[50]

The difference, of course, is control. We are more fearful of those issues in which we feel we have little control. This may even strengthen our association with the politicians of our choosing. Our willingness to believe in their agenda, at the most basic level, gives us a connection to their authority, and assuages our fears.

The elections of 1932, 1960, and 2008 demonstrate that candidates can be elected on a platform of hope. We shall see whether this hope can continue and can allow a candidate to be reelected. We can be sure of one thing though. Fear has not been banished from the political lexicon.

Hopefully, we can also renew the sense of corporate responsibility to return our economy to the necessary fundamental of true production, rather than the virtual production of increasingly sophisticated but dangerous financial instruments. And we can create the financial institutions and protections necessary to decrease what we find to be rapidly accelerating financial market volatility. These reforms will require significant economic leadership.

29
Is There More to Fear than Fear Itself?

While fear from a misled populace has taken a bad turn and created a downward spiral, merely soothing the fear at this point will not be sufficient to return us to better days. Why not?

Fear certainly has created a life of its own. Even if prosperity returned tomorrow, households will remain gun shy – permanently more cautious and more conscious of the risk and precariousness of even the most buoyant economy. It took the market 25 years to recover to the level before the Great Crash in 1929. And it took generations to forget the memories of thrift and the burden of debt. These memories are imprinted with suffering, and are far more resilient than the celebrations of happier times.

This asymmetry, to remember pain more acutely than prosperity, is simply a natural consequence of our risk aversion. We have shown that the pain of a financial downturn exceeds the joy derived from an equal upturn. This may be a broader comment on the human spirit as well.

There are things that we can do to repair some of damage, even if we cannot reboot our memory. But as Mark Twain tells us:

> We should be careful to get out of an experience only the wisdom that is in it – and stop there; lest we be like the cat that sits down on a hot stove-lid. She will never sit down on a hot stove-lid again – and that is well; but also she will never sit down on a cold one any more.[51]

We can be cautious in the future to not fall into the same trap of the past, but in the process, our recollections of a past fear will make us cautious in unrelated and unproductive ways, too. Pain can invoke a certain timidity and caution that is also not in our interest.

Let us nonetheless assume we can remedy the psychic damage caused by the Global Financial Meltdown. But what must we fix in the economy to get us back on the road to recovery?

A three-step program

First, we must get banks lending again.

The modern decentralized economy depends crucially on credit. Growth, even growth toward a sustainable economy, cannot proceed without capital investment. And investment cannot occur on a sufficient scale without the pooling of capital from savers to permit the creation of new institutions, industries, and innovations for tomorrow.

Without investment, we cannot realize the American dream of home ownership. Homeowners serve a most productive function in society; their fixity builds community, and their sweat equity adds to the value of the housing stock. These social and economic benefits represent a significant part of our gross domestic product that makes a healthy housing sector essential for our collective economic well-being.

Without credit markets, we also see the breakdown of all financial markets, as we witnessed in 2008. And without financial markets, industry loses the signal that indicates what investments are prized, and what activities are obsolete. We need the market to participate in these important decisions. Without such signals, we are forced to rely on the individual decisions of a few rather than the wisdom of the many.

There are some signs that credit markets are beginning to free up again. The TED Spread, the difference between the rate at which banks will lend to each other in the short-term and the risk-free Treasury return, hit historical highs during the Credit Crisis, but have since come down to near normal levels below a percentage point.

But while this drop tells us that banks are willing to lend to each other again, it does not tell us that banks are willing to borrow from each other. Instead, we could interpret the recent drop to affirm only that banks are sitting on excess cash with no place to go – at least until they are willing to lend to the rest of us again.

Second, we must avoid a deflation.

While deflation sounds like something as outdated as the panics and crashes of the nineteenth century, it remains a very real threat.

Deflation is simply a decline in the general price level and is the opposite of inflation. Actually, deflation is not always problematic and is actually quite common for some goods. Improvements in technology and manufacturing productivity allow a decline in price and often an increase in quality, too. Manufacturers can translate these improvements in efficiency to increase profits and productivity, and consumers can use the money they save to perhaps purchase other products or to save.

The type of deflation that is dangerous is the decline in prices motivated by sellers who are desperate and buyers who are fearful of making purchases.

Unable to lower its wages and production costs, these fire sales induce producers to drive down inventories, lay off workers, and further fuel the economic uncertainty that makes us cut back on purchases even further. This type of deflation arising from a decline in aggregate demand creates a downward spiral that cannot be reversed unless something stimulates the aggregate demand.

It is this type of deflation that gives rise to the necessity of government spending. Few would advocate that we defer to government the responsibility for centrally planning a large share of our aggregate expenditures on our behalf.

Perhaps the essential beauty of the free-market system is in its ability to signal those avenues of production most valued to households and voters. And while the government can sometimes play a role in directing investment to those areas in the public interest, this spending should be confined to the implementation of national industrial policies or the creation of a public infrastructure we all value but which is too expensive for private firms to feasibly provide.

The other dangerous deflationary effect is when it depresses asset prices. Consumption is spurred at a rate of approximately five dollars for every thousand dollars of financial and housing wealth. Significant declines in market value and housing prices depress the consumption spending that can plunge the economy into a deficient aggregate demand-led spiral. While government spending can fill that gap too, market health is proportional to healthy financial and housing markets. It is for this reason that many clamor for the shoring up of housing markets through the reversal of increasing home foreclosures.

Housing markets are notoriously sensitive to even slight imbalances in housing supply and demand. Even a small increase in the size of the vacant and available housing stock can have a dramatic effect on home prices. These foreclosures can also generate a downward spiral as the decline in housing prices induces more households to walk away from homes that have been devalued than the mortgage on the homes. Policies that keep people in their homes are important less because of sympathy over a shattered American dream, but rather for the pragmatic realization that a housing market in peril places the entire economy in peril.

Finally, we must get people spending again.

If we are able to get credit markets going again, so people can once more buy cars, homes, and consumer durables, and producers can build new factories and inventories, we can again generate the jobs that provide households with the income to spend. In simpler times, the creation of goods and services created the jobs that, in turn, created the purchasing power that allowed producers to sell their wares.

The level of coordination necessary to ensure these links work smoothly is now so elusive that Say's Law is no longer completely relevant. In this more complicated modern economy that is no longer so transparent that all can see its inner workings, consumer confidence is a necessity. And consumer confidence depends crucially on the psychology of the macro economy.

This psychology points to the value of economic leadership. Consumers filled with fear for their economic security understandably, but unfortunately, follow an instinct that leads us all astray. Our paradox of thrift in such times creates a self-fulfilling prophecy that manages to confirm our fears by creating the downward economic spiral. The steadying rhetoric from our economic leaders can reassure consumers that there is a grand plan.

These words may not be anything more than a statement of resolute tone that our leaders stand prepared to do all things necessary to bolster demand and prevent an economic collapse. There will be plenty of time later to analyze the circumstances that caused the breach in confidence and create the institutions that protect consumers from a similar decline again.

If we are able to do these things, we can begin to recover. While at the time of writing, we are only a little more than a year after the Global Financial Meltdown brought about by two decades of financial decadence and two years of credit panic, it is obvious that, like at no other time since the Great Depression, the economy preoccupies us all. The call for reform, regulation, corporate responsibility, and moderation over greed, will likely be heard. A new administration campaigned on that promise, and it represents a new generation of leadership, both literally and figuratively.

This new generation is neither tied to the privileges of the past, nor the blind ideologies of either laissez-faire capitalism on one side, or unbridled labor on the other. Instead, the new mantra is to discover pragmatic, resilient, and sustainable solutions for complex problems. Such an approach that vaults rationality above ideology may be less passionate than either extreme, but may also put some of our fears to rest.

Part X

Solutions to an Economic Quagmire

We have seen that there is plenty of responsibility to go around, if we are to prevent fear and emotion from dictating market movements. Despite the economic forces that fan our deepest economic fears, there is good reason to be optimistic. There is now a cacophony of voices demanding solutions. And our leaders are listening.

In this part, we document the realm of the possible, and the replacement of fear with hope. I begin by documenting the important role President Franklin Roosevelt played in quelling the fears of a depression-laden society. I note that President Obama is continuing within this Roosevelt school of thought. I continue in Chapter 31 with some policy prescriptions to move markets and the economy to a more rational set of fundamentals.

30
Economic Leadership as an Antidote to Fear

When the global economy last faced the fears of a financial meltdown, it responded in the way that humans typically respond to fear. It blamed other countries and imposed trade barriers. Countries adopted Marxism, Fascism, and Totalitarianism in frustration with prevailing political systems. Capitalism was rescued only by the promise of Keynes and President Roosevelt that the economy could be reformed, albeit at a cost of much more government control. This contract with capitalism, through government spending and regulation, was unbroken until the deregulations that began when President Reagan unwound much of the New Deal policies.

In his inaugural address on March 4, 1933, President Roosevelt threw down the gauntlet by promising "leadership of frankness and vigor" to ward off the "unjustified terror which paralyzes needed efforts to convert retreat into advance." He was promising new, bigger government if the people could replace their fear with faith and rationality:

> I am certain that my fellow Americans expect that on my induction into the Presidency I will address them with a candor and a decision which the present situation of our people impel. This is preeminently the time to speak the truth, the whole truth, frankly and boldly. Nor need we shrink from honestly facing conditions in our country today. This great Nation will endure as it has endured, will revive and will prosper. So, first of all, let me assert my firm belief that the only thing we have to fear is fear itself – nameless, unreasoning, unjustified terror which paralyzes needed efforts to convert retreat into advance. In every dark hour of our national life a leadership of frankness and vigor has met with that understanding and support of the people themselves which is essential to victory. I am convinced that you will again give that support to leadership in these critical days.[52]

President Obama is taking a cue from his predecessor, Franklin Delano Roosevelt, by invoking the danger to the economy when fear dictates our response to economic hardship. In his speech to a fear-gripped nation on January 8, 2009, he recalled Roosevelt by saying:[53]

> More than any program or policy, it is this spirit that will enable us to confront this challenge with the same spirit that has led previous generations to face down war, depression, and fear itself.

He went on to invoke the hope espoused by President John Fitzgerald Kennedy when he implored:

> That's why I'm calling on all Americans, Democrats and Republicans and independents, to put – to put good ideas ahead of the old ideological battles, a sense of common purpose above the same narrow partisanship, and insist that the first question each of us asks isn't what's good for me, but what's good for the country my children will inherit?

In appealing to our sense of rationality over fear, and to our emotion of caring over fear, President Obama was gambling that the American people can be led through their minds and hearts, rather than by the primitive emotion of fear. This case is obviously much more complicated to make. The sense of hope requires constant reinforcement. It also requires some evidence of the fruits of hope.

The case for rationality may even be more difficult. Rationality requires knowledge, assertions that can be demonstrated and proved, and the willingness to educate the citizenry. We see in the style of President Obama that he makes an effort to educate in almost every speech. Perhaps a lifetime of having to prove himself based on the strength of his ideas and to debunk fears or prejudices because of the color of his skin has served him well. The ultimate transformation, though, will be to see if he can assuage the fears of a world plunged into war, strife, and financial ruin.

Obama can take some relief from the response to President Roosevelt's economic leadership. Following his first fireside chat, he told the nation that he was imposing a two week bank holiday. While there remained over 20,000 banks in the country in 1933, he stated that each would be audited, over a two-week period. Of course, this would be impossible. His rhetoric, though, gave the population a sense that something would be done. Somebody was in charge and was charting a new course.

At the end of the two-week period, consumers returned in droves to redeposit their horded cash. And the stock market rebounded. Mere rhetoric was successful in garnering support for a population that wanted to be led.

However, mere rhetoric was not sufficient. It created an expectation for change. And it is change that must successfully navigate political resistance.

Presidents such as Roosevelt Eisenhower, Kennedy, and Clinton succeeded by giving the public a sense that they lie shoulder to shoulder with their public. The symbolism is important, even in cases when it is sometimes time, not economic leadership, that heals our economic woes. Obama has left a nation and a world with a sense of hope.

Throwing down the gauntlet

After pulling out war, pestilence, evil, burdensome labor, and evil from Pandora's box, there was only one thing left – hope. The challenge in promising hope is that there is nothing remaining, should hope fail. While the sentiment is noble, the risks are high, and the eyes of a nation are on Obama.

In a recent speech, Obama stated:

> And where we are met with cynicism and doubt and fear and those who tell us that we can't, we will respond with that timeless creed that sums up the spirit of the American people in three simple words – yes, we can. [54]

Obama has raised expectations and hope over fear. And now the stakes are most high, while the cost of failure is immense. Perhaps this realization will focus our efforts.

31
A Dozen Prescriptions to Take Back the Markets

If we acknowledge the importance of investor confidence, and can deal with market failures and fear head-on, we can prevent the Global Financial Meltdown from reoccurring. To do so will necessitate some changes that can reduce market fear.

Many of these recommendations will meet stern resistance from the financial industry. Some of the recommendations will require more of us, or more of our institutions. All, though, will improve the overall health of the economy and our potential to grow. And none are designed simply to take from one group and give to another.

Tax reform

There are two types of taxes – those that are designed to make the economy more efficient and those that are designed to redistribute wealth. The first set of taxes expands the economic pie and the second invoke a sense of equity to redistribute the economic pie. This latter goal, of redistribution, should best be left to the political process. However, expansion of the economic pie is a legitimate goal of an economic policy.

Currently, we tax most heavily on the profits of producers, next most heavily on the earnings of the wealthy, and least heavily, if at all, on those who earn little.

The irony is that producers are taxed heavily, despite our observation that it is true production which creates our economic pie. This relatively high tax on the profits of producers is ultimately passed onto consumers, in this and other countries, in the form of higher product prices. Globally, it makes our products more costly, and reduces our competitiveness, especially in light of the fact that few countries tax corporations at the rate we do.

This is not an issue with corporate taxation from a philosophical perspective. Indeed, many of the wealthiest corporations are able to evade corporate taxes, to a large degree. Rather, this is an argument of encouraging global competiveness.

The next group, the wealthy, too are taxed heavily, but able to evade taxation that may place their effective tax-rate below those of the middle class.

The wealthy are increasingly likely to earn greater earnings from capital gains and dividends. Each of these has garnered reduced tax rates, arguably to spur investment. However, relatively little of the additional investment occurring as a consequence of reduced taxation actually results in true economic investment of the kind that leads to additional production.

Artificially low tax rates on assets valued solely because of financial market demand, rather than the production of a better mousetrap, simply helps inflate a stock market prone to excess, and allows traders to churn stock and play other nonproductive games at little cost.

Such a reform will not affect our pension accumulations as they are held in tax deferred accounts, in the case of Independent Retirement Accounts (IRAs), and are tax-free, in the case of the Roth IRA. This reform may again put the emphasis on productive wealth rather than paper wealth.

Transparency

While I am certain that investors such as Bernie Madoff, hedge funds, and investment banks will resist full financial transparency, the markets would benefit considerably by requiring all securities and derivatives trades to be public. I agree that there may be a small share of such trades that are done in pursuit of a corporate strategy. However, these would be few and far between. Most are designed for short-term profits, which the public ought to know, or for long-term gains, which are likely discoverable eventually anyway.

Some hedge funds and investment banks may balk at transparency of all trades because it prevents them from performing the market manipulations outlined by Joseph Chen et al. Others may argue that the very wealthy would like to have the size of their wealth and their investment strategies remain confidential, from us and from regulators.

However, every economic decision the average middle-class consumer makes is scrutinized and analyzed by credit reporting agencies, credit card agencies, or even our local supermarket through our customer loyalty cards. It is not unreasonable for those transactions that can bring down markets, like the antics of Madoff or the marketers of toxic assets, to face similar openness as is required of the rest of us.

The Tobin Tax

Nobel Memorial Prize in Economics winner James Tobin has long advocated a very small tax on foreign exchange transactions. This tax, in the order of 0.1% to 1% per trade, would be designed to provide some disincentive to trade on derivatives without any intention of actually taking delivery of the foreign exchange. These markets are often simply the gambling house of the megabanks and investment houses.

A slowing down of such churning of currency derivatives would not prevent the larger necessary movements of foreign exchange. However, this innovation would dramatically reduce the level of activity in these markets, which have grown exponentially in recent years.

I would recommend extending this innovation to all derivatives. Traditional securities markets are now dwarfed by the activity of derivative markets. But while securities markets represent the actual ownership of firms or of promissory notes, derivatives are simply bets on the direction of movement on the underlying securities. A modest tax to discourage such trades would instead direct more of this gambling money to more legitimate investments.

Nations around the world have embraced the Tobin Tax. However, nations recognize that any unilateral imposition of such a tax would simply force gamblers to trade elsewhere. Such a tax would thus require global coordination.

Taking tax

A growing amount of our economy is now based on effort devoted to taking income from one group and giving it to another. Of course, this is a legitimate role of government. However, we all understand that government redistributes income. They also do so through taxation, at a relatively low cost.

However, the nation's collective effort in lobbying of Congress to obtain favorable consideration, the resources spent by hedge funds to take advantage of less-sophisticated investors, and even the legal costs of frivolous lawsuits or lawsuits not in the public interest, are resources poorly spent.

A tax on such forms of "production" that are not in the public interest could instead be used to reduce taxes on those more productive enterprises that at one time were the bread and butter of an industrialized country.

The imposition of such a tax would require global coordination, in some cases. If one country imposes a tax on manipulative financial market investment, it would simply force such transactions to some tax haven elsewhere. This tax would require us to discriminate against some transactions, and in favor of others. The tax system already has determined myriad ways to discriminate between various classes of income earners.

Regulation

There is a wave of consensus regarding the necessity of reregulation after decades of deregulation. No longer do people believe that regulation is the root of all evil. Even the common belief in the beauty of a cat-and-mouse relationship between regulators and regulatees has likely fallen out of vogue. We have collectively lost trillions, and the days of game playing with regulators are over.

We must regulate wisely though. Regulators are human too, and are prone to creating regulatory empires. Just like the corporate executives who create a culture based on power, regulators can create organizations that lose their responsiveness to the initial goals of regulation. We must regulate smart, in ways that make the market more efficient, rather than regulate to make transactions more difficult. We should also regulate in a way that can keep us ahead of the toxic assets, the Bernie Madoffs, and the Enrons of the world.

Circuit breakers

After the Crash of 1987, we realized that the combination of programmed trading and investor fear can create market panics. In the aftermath, the major exchanges accepted the recommendation of halting trading for a short period if the market begins to fluctuate wildly. These circuit breakers are designed to slow market transactions down when they become too jumpy. They allow the market time to calm down and take time to reflect.

Since 1987, many more investors participate in the market. Innovations such as Internet trading also make it much easier to jump on the fear bandwagon. These reduced transaction costs and increased trading speed may require us to adjust our circuit breakers accordingly.

Liquidity maintenance

We recognize that markets of all sorts require sufficient lubrication to keep the gears turning. Too little lubrication prevents trades, and too much lubrication causes the machine to spin out of control.

The Federal Reserve well understands the need to ensure sufficient monetary liquidity. Too loose monetary policy can cause speculative bubbles and inflation. Too tight monetary authority can cause unemployment and possibly even recessions and deflation.

The banking system, too, must ensure liquidity to credit markets. In a large part, the Global Financial Meltdown was caused by creditors' unwillingness to extend credit. In times like these, the Fed has increasingly realized it must step in to ensure liquidity not only in the monetary system, but also in the credit system. They must institutionalize their ad hoc efforts of late to ensure credit too remains liquid. After all, credit is now the new paper money.

Taking credit liquidity still further, it may be necessary to expand the quasi-public institutions of Fannie Mae, Freddie Mac, and Sallie Mae to other credit markets. These private organizations are offered special privileges and access to credit because we recognize their ability to create credit in housing and student loan markets is invaluable for continued investment in housing and human capital.

This principle should also be extended to help spur other forms of credit that flow to investment of the productive sort. At the height of the credit crunch, lenders approved only a third of the car loans that would have been approved the previous year. The interest rates are higher too, despite lower prevailing interest rates in the economy. We must develop institutions that ensure investment in automobiles, small business, agriculture, and strategic industries that can promote sustainability.

Hedge funds and leverage

Many of the excesses of the past decade can be traced to excessive leverage. Hedge funds and investment banks are the new financial alchemists, creating wealth out of thin air. The problem is that this wealth is not truly created. Rather, it is simply grabbed from others and leverage helps them profit spectacularly.

These firms have been able to leverage themselves thirty to one or more. This means that for every dollar of their own investment, they have borrowed thirty dollars from others. The returns they would have earned with their own individual investment are then multiplied by thirty one. After paying interest on the loans, they have still been able to profit spectacularly.

Hedge funds are also destabilizing. While a 5% return, above and beyond the interest they must pay on debt, is multiplied by thirty one to yield a 155% return on their original investment, a 5% loss completely wipes them out. It wipes them out far beyond their ability to pay, forcing funds into bankruptcy, and leaving their creditors holding the bag.

We have experienced such behavior in the past. Companies could reap huge profits extracting resources, and then declare bankruptcy when it comes time to mitigate their damage to hillsides or their pollution in rivers. Strategic bankruptcy creates privatized gains and socialized losses. Bankruptcy insurance would force them to pay premiums in the good years to ensure we can clean up the mess they create in the bad years.

Global coordination

We have pursued a period of isolationist policy. At one time, economic superpowers could afford to do so, in essence dictating rather than dealing in our foreign economic policies. This Global Financial Meltdown has demonstrated one thing. There are no remaining economic superpowers that can ignore their effects on the world, or the world on them.

A new Bretton Woods global economic agreement is absolutely necessary. The original Bretton Woods agreement, forged in New Hampshire by the developed countries of the 1940s, created a blueprint for global economic cooperation. It has become too costly for one nation to pursue an economic strategy that is reversed or undone by another. With capital able to flee so easily to low regulation nations, it is also important to work in unison. Finally, a coordinated effort can have the effect of magnifying our individual efforts and help ensure a coordinated success. Ultimately, we can no longer afford not to coordinate.

Media reform

The media has made a Herculean effort of late to report to households every twist and turn of financial markets. However, more often than not, they likely promote fear rather than understanding, if perhaps inadvertently. Just as it is irresponsible to shout fire in a crowded theater, it is equally irresponsible to broadcast bad news without also creating the ability for viewers to correctly understand and process the information.

The media must better understand and embrace their role in the public trust. Yes, they must give us the information we need. They must also anticipate how the fearful mind might respond to the information and must provide us with an avenue to respond appropriately. Just as Orson Welles raised a national debate when he aired the radio show *War of the Worlds* on Halloween in 1938 with such realism that people were convinced the world was being invaded, Hitler used the resulting induced panic as an example of the irresponsibility of democracy, and thousands of newspaper articles subsequently argued it was an irresponsible form of entertainment.[55]

While few of us would be fearful of a simulated news broadcast portending a war of the worlds, many were induced to do just as Keynes feared. We embraced the paradox of thrift, and cut our spending to the point our fears became a self-fulfilling prophecy. A more informative and educated media could have helped us with this, early and often. It can no longer consider its sole role to entertain, or to pander to us by confirming our prejudices, just as it cannot be the sole goal of corporations to make a profit even if at odds with the public interest.

Economic literacy

Of course, there are many we can blame for the Global Financial Meltdown. We know that it invoked fear, and we responded to this fear, immediately, in misguided but completely reasonable efforts to protect our own economic security.

We, too, must better understand the workings of an increasingly complex economy. Our economic leaders will need to ratchet up the quality of the national discourse if they are to rely on households to help in the collective push necessary to get the global economy back on the tracks. We must do our part because there is barely a moment we can afford to waste.

Economic leadership

Finally, we must recognize that our leaders are also our economic commanders in chief. This is something that the last president confronted with such turmoil, Franklin D. Roosevelt, understood implicitly. The need to lead at this critical juncture is pragmatic rather than ideological. We no longer have that luxury of ideology. Instead, we must expect a lot of our leaders. And if they cannot put politics aside in the interest of the nation, we may have to find better leaders.

In any regard, these are difficult times, and will require sophisticated and challenging solutions. Our leaders must bring us all together so that we can each make the necessary sacrifices. To degenerate into the politics of self-interest at such a calamitous time is both dangerous and irresponsible. And only our leaders can set the example and illuminate the path.

Conclusions

Humans are hardwired to protect our economic security and crave order. Any threat to our economic security is considered risky, and as humans we are, by our very nature, averse to risk. As the world becomes increasingly uncertain, there is greater occasion to threaten our economic security and fan our fears.

In a fearful environment, we retrench, isolate, prejudge, narrow the scope of our understanding, and devote more energy to anxiety than production. These responses are not in our rational self-interest. They are wholly human, however. Recognizing this, we must respond to greater uncertainty not through fear but through genuine understanding and rational thought.

This book was written to explain the current economic situation. It is also hoped that a blunt discussion of the process of fear, and the elements that promote our fears will afford us an opportunity to deal with them as we would any difficult emotion in a time of necessity. The shining light is the best antidote to what fearful things might lurk in the dark cave.

Certainly, we have let our individual and collective fears take us too far astray in this crisis. Our leaders have been confused, or have not been speaking from the same script, thereby creating a greater sense of uncertainty, anxiety, and fear. We have lost a lot of time as a consequence, and have likely made the current Global Financial Meltdown much worse than necessary. This does not obviate the need for us to do something now, and to expect more and better for the future.

Fear too can be a motivator. Its biological roots were designed to ensure that a dangerous condition captures our immediate attention. The irreversible biological imprint also warns us if we come across similar situations in the future and preprograms us for a successful response next time. It is important to verbalize our fears if, by doing so, we are less likely to let the least productive aspects of history repeat themselves.

We have seen crashes come and go, some relatively short-lived and benign, and others life transforming. We have not seen the degree of panic and displacement we see now for more than 75 years. This period is too long for most of us to recall in our own lifetime. And that is perhaps the problem. Our saving grace is that the severity of the Great Depression is so firmly imprinted on a global psyche that some lessons are not too unfamiliar. It is also helpful that the macroeconomic tools of Keynesian economics developed as a consequence of the Great Depression have been employed and further developed since.

These tools of rational analysis are the same antidotes humans always employ in fearful situations. Pilots, when confronted with an emergency, put their fear aside and rely instead on their training. Of course, pilots also have the luxury of constantly rehearsing and simulating possible calamity to the point that their responses become relatively routine.

We do not have to fly blind through our fears. While we do not have the luxury to put our economy through simulated panics, we can nonetheless study and remember our past, and plan for our future. By doing so, I am fully confident we will get through this. We may even be able to figure out a way to snatch a victory or two from these jaws of defeat.

We may even decide to redesign our economy so that it is less vulnerable to the manipulations of some that could cost us all. I think we will even find that we can figure out how to harness our fear as a motivator for some badly needed changes. After all, when there is little left to protect, we have less to fear and a little more freedom to take some risk toward a more durable and sustainable economy.

While hope is sometimes a dangerous thing, it is not inappropriate to express some optimism. The full recovery of the economy may be slow and painful. However, it can hopefully be rebuilt better, more sustainable, and more robust. We can also learn from the failure so that we can recognize similar prospective potential failures earlier, with the hope of preventing future crises. Perhaps most helpfully, we can better understand the role of fear in market turmoil, and the potential for economic leadership in guiding consumers in these most challenging times.

Notes

1. The others are seeking, rage, play, lust, and caring. See Panksepp, J., *Affective Neuroscience: The Foundations of Human and Animal Emotions*. Oxford: Oxford University Press, 1998.
2. See for instance http://psychology.about.com/od/theoriesofpersonality/a/hierarchyneeds.htm, accessed January 11, 2009.
3. Mattil, James F., "What in the Name of God?: Fundamentalism, Fear & Terrorism" [article on-line], http://www.flashpoints.info/issue_briefings/Analysis%20&%20Commentary/Analysis-Religion_main.htm, accessed December 8, 2008.
4. This quote is often attributed to the Reverend Reinhold Niebuhr, from Niebuhr, Reinhold, *The Essential Reinhold Niebuhr: Selected Essays and Addresses*, edited by Robert McAfee Brown. New Haven: Yale University Press, p. 251, New Edition, September 10, 1987. However, a recent article casts doubt on this attribution. See for instance Shapiro, Fred R., "New Evidence," *Yale Alumni Magazine*, July/August 2008.
5. Kübler-Ross, E. and David Kessler, *On Grief and Grieving: Finding the Meaning of Grief through the Five Stages of Loss*. New York: Simon & Schuster Ltd, 2005.
6. Calculated from data obtained from the World Federation of Exchanges, http://www.world-exchanges.org/statistics/ytd-monthly, accessed December 9, 2008.
7. Modigliani, F., and Miller, M. "The Cost of Capital, Corporation Finance and the Theory of Investment," *American Economic Review*, 48 (3), 1958, pp. 261–297.
8. http://www.world-exchanges.org/statistics/ytd-monthly, accessed January 14, 2009.
9. http://www.iapf.ie/Publications/IrishPensionsMagazine/2004/Article2,1163,en.pdf, accessed December 9, 2008.
10. http://www.bis.org/publ/rpfxf07t.pdf?noframes=1, accessed December 9, 2009.
11. Bradsher, Keith, "China Losing Taste for Debt From U.S.," *New York Times*, January 8, 2009.
12. Coates, J. M., and J. Herbert, "Endogenous Steroids and Financial Risk Taking on a London Trading Floor," *Proceedings of the National Academy of Sciences*, 105 (16), April 22, 2008, pp. 6167–6172.
13. Stein, Rob, "Born to Be a Trader? Fingers Point to Yes," *Washington Post*, January 13, 2009.
14. Gollier, Christian, "Time Diversification, Liquidity Constraints, and Decreasing Aversion to Risk on Wealth," *Journal of Monetary Economics*, 49, 2002, pp. 1439–1459.
15. Waggoner, John, "How Long Can Households Sustain Negative Savings?" http://www.usatoday.com/money/perfi/general/2006-03-01-savings-cover-usat_x.htm, accessed December 26, 2008.
16. Arrow, K. J., *Aspects of the Theory of Risk-Bearing*. Helsinki: Yrjö Hahnsson Foundation, 1965.
17. Brinig, Margaret, "Why Can't a Woman Be More Like a Man? or Do Gender Differences Affect Choice?"manuscript, 1994.
18. Hersch, Joni, "Smoking, Seat Belts and Other Risky Consumer Decisions: Differences by Gender and Race," *Managerial and Decision Economics*, 17 (5), September, 1996, pp. 471–481.
19. Jianakoplos, Nancy Ammon, and Alexandra Bernasek, "Are Women More Risk Averse?" *Economic Inquiry*, 36 (4), October 1998, pp. 620–630.

20. Bayes, Thomas, in "An Essay towards Solving a Problem in the Doctrine of Chances. By the Late Rev. Mr. Bayes, Communicated by Mr. Price, in a Letter to John Canton, M. A. and F. R. S.," p. 5. http://www.stat.ucla.edu/history/essay.pdf, accessed December 21, 2008.
21. Shafir, Sharon, Taly Reich, Erez Tsur, Ido Erev, and Arnon Lotem, "Perceptual accuracy and conflicting effects of certainty on risk," *Nature*, 453 (7197), June 12, 2008, pp. 917–920.
22. Akerlof, George A., "The Market for 'Lemons': Quality Uncertainty and the Market Mechanism," *Quarterly Journal of Economics*, 84 (3), 1970, pp. 488–500.
23. http://www.ourfuture.org/blog-entry/2008104324/greenspan-shocked-disbelief, April 18, 2009.
24. Keynes, John Maynard, *The General Theory of Employment, Interest, and Money*, New York: Harcourt Trade, 1964, p. 160.
25. Keynes, John Maynard, *The General Theory of Employment, Interest, and Money*, New York: Harcourt Trade, 1964, p. 160.
26. Keynes, John Maynard, *The General Theory of Employment, Interest, and Money*, New York: Harcourt Trade, 1964.
27. See for instance, McCulloch, J. R., *The Works of David Ricardo. With a Notice of the Life and Writings of the Author.* London: John Murray Publishers, 1888.
28. See http://www.maynardkeynes.org/john-maynard-keynes-treatise-general-theory.html, accessed January 1, 2009.
29. Keynes, John Maynard, "A Treatise on Money. Vol. 1: The Pure Theory of Money," reprinted in Keynes, *Collected Writings. Vol. 5*, and "A Treatise on Money. Vol. 2: The Applied Theory of Money," reprinted in Keynes, *Collected Writings. Vol. 6*, New York: Cambridge University Press, 1978.
30. http://www.pbs.org/newshour/bb/business/july-dec08/crisishearing_10-23.html, accessed April 18, 2009.
31. Bikhchandani, S., D. Hershleifer, and I. Welch, "A Theory of Fads, Fashion, Customs and Cultural Change as Information Cascades," *Journal of Political Economy*, 100, 1992, pp. 992–1026.
32. http://en.wikipedia.org/wiki/List_of_countries_by_GDP, accessed January 7, 2009.
33. http://www.glasslewis.com/downloads/Restatements2005Summary.pdf, accessed January 7, 2009.
34. http://marketplace.publicradio.org//display/web/2009/01/05/pm_cheating/?refid=0, accessed April 9, 2009.
35. http://www.sec.gov/news/press/2003-69.htm, accessed January 7, 2009.
36. Nguyen, N. T., M. T. Basuray, W. P. Smith, and D. N. McCulloh, "Ethics Perception: Does Teaching Make a Difference?" *Journal of Education for Business*, November/December, 84 (2), 2008, pp. 66–75.
37. Friedman, M., "The Social Responsibility of Business Is to Increase Its Profits," *The New York Times Magazine*, September 13, 1970.
38. http://www.bea.gov/newsreleases/national/gdp/2008/txt/gdp308f.txt, accessed January 9, 2008.
39. http://www.bls.gov/emp/empmajorindustry.htm, accessed January 9, 2009.
40. http://www.princeton.edu/~hhong/front-runner.pdf, accessed January 9, 2009.
41. http://en.wikisource.org/wiki/The_Gospel_of_Wealth, accessed January 9, 2009.
42. http://pewresearch.org/pubs/1066/internet-overtakes-newspapers-as-news-source, accessed January 8, 2009.
43. Glassner, Barry, *The Culture of Fear: Why Americans Are Afraid of the Wrong Things.* New York: Basic Books, 2000.

44. From article by Carr, David, "Stoking Fear Everywhere You Look," *New York Times*, December 8, 2008.
45. "The 'D' Word," *Economist Magazine*, October 2, 2008.
46. Galbraith, John Kenneth, *The Great Crash: 1929*. New York: Mariner Books, 1997.
47. http://www.reuters.com/article/lifestyleMolt/idUSTRE5065R220090107, accessed January 8, 2009.
48. Begley, Sharon, Anne Underwood, Richard Wolfe, Suzanne Smalley, and Jeneen Interland, "The Roots of Fear," *Newsweek*, December 24, 2007.
49. Westen, Drew, *The Political Brain: The Role of Emotions in Deciding the Fate of a Nation*. New York: Public Affairs 2007.
50. http://www.apta.com/research/stats/factbook/documents08/2008_fact_book_final_part_1.pdf, accessed January 8, 2009.
51. Twain, Mark, *Following the Equator: A Journey Around the World*, http://www.gutenberg.org/files/2895/2895.txt, accessed January 15, 2009, epigraph to chapter 9.
52. http://avalon.law.yale.edu/20th_century/froos1.asp, accessed January 8, 2009.
53. http://www.mainstreamweekly.net/article1021.html, accessed April 8, 2009.
54. http://www.cnn.com/2008/POLITICS/01/26/obama.transcript/index.html, accessed, April 8, 2009.
55. Hand, Richard J., *Terror on the Air!: Horror Radio in America, 1931–1952*. Jefferson, NC: Macfarlane & Company, 2006.

Glossary

Bond A debt instrument that lists a redemption value at maturity and prescribes the pattern of interest payments.

Collateralized Debt Obligation A bundle of like loans into a common pool that can be bought and sold as shares.

Credit Default Swap An insurance policy on an underlying asset, but with one important distinction. The buyer of the policy does not actually have to own the asset. One party agrees to pay a fee in return for a periodic payment if there is a default on some specified asset.

Derivative Investment vehicles that are priced based on an underlying asset. Derivatives do not represent ownership of the asset, but rather are contingencies that are rarely converted to the underlying asset. They can be used to hedge risk or for speculative purposes.

Exchange A market for the trading of securities. These exchanges were once physical, but now can be virtual, with trades via the Internet matched through computers.

Externality The consequence of a decision that is not enjoyed or suffered by the decision maker or transactor. Consequences that benefit others who do not pay are called positive externalities, while negative externalities are decisions made or transacted that cost others.

Federal Reserve Discount Rate The interest rate the Federal Reserve will charge if it lends funds directly to commercial banks.

Federal Funds Rate The interest rate banks pay to borrow some of the required reserves held by other commercial banks in the United States. The Federal Reserve can target this federal funds rate by controlling banks' reserves through open market operations.

Hedge Funds A fund under a special provision of the securities law that allows wealthy individuals to pool investment capital to increase their trading clout. The term hedge is a misnomer, originally meant to indicate a trading strategy that reduces risk by purchasing instruments that would allow a profit in either a rising or falling market. However, hedge funds are able to employ most any legal trading strategy, often without significant regulatory oversight.

Index A calculation of the representative price of a collection of stocks. The most commonly quoted index, the Dow Jones Industrial Average, is a collective price of 30 stocks traded on the New York Stock Exchange.

LIBOR The London Interbank Offered Rate is the average interest rate banks will lend to each other in the dollar denominated London interbank market.

Moral Hazard The inefficient behavior that occurs when an agent does not internalize the risk he imposes on others.

Mortgage-Backed Security Pools of mortgages that have been assembled and packaged to be sold in the secondary mortgage market.

Open Market Operations The buying and selling of government securities by the Federal Reserve to raise or decrease the level of federal cash reserves held by commercial banks.

Options The right to buy or sell a security or commodity at a predetermined price and date in the future. The seller of this option does not actually have to own the security.

Prisoner's Dilemma The phenomenon in which uncoordinated actions between players leave them all worse off compared with a coordinated response.

Rate of Time Preference Sometimes called the discount rate by economists, it is the rate we discount the future. Alternately, it can be considered as the rate we value the present when compared to the future.

Sarbanes-Oxley Act Officially called the Public Company Accounting Reform and Investor Protection Act of 2002, this law imposed significantly higher reporting requirements for the activities of publicly traded companies. It also required the chief executive officer of publicly traded companies to be responsible for the financial statement.

Stock A security that represents fractional ownership of a publicly trading company.

TED Spread The gap between the LIBOR rate banks charge each other for interbank lending of three months and the yield on short-term Treasury bills. It has been as low as one-fifth of a percentage point, to more than three percentage points, depending on the level of treasury interest rates and banks' willingness to lend to each other.

Toxic Assets Various mortgage-backed securities mostly owned by banks, investment houses, and pension and mutual funds that have proven to be inaccurately rated and of dubious value.

Treasury Bill A short-term debt instrument issued by the U.S. Treasury with a maturity of 30, 90, 180, or 360 days. Unlike Treasury notes and bonds, they do not issue interest payments. Instead, they are sold at a discount, usually allowing one to receive the face value on the redemption day for a smaller amount today.

Treasury Bond A bond issued by the U.S. Treasury with a maturity greater than Treasury notes, upto 30 years and with face value denominations between $100 and $1 million.

Treasury Note A bond issued by the U.S. Treasury with a maturity of two, five, or ten years, and with face value denominations between $100 and $1 million.

VIX An index on the Chicago Board of Options Exchange that tracks market volatility. Sometimes called "the fear index" because it measures the uncertainty of future prices, it is calculated from the price of options for S&P 500 stocks. Because options capture expectations of future prices of a security, market volatility translates into shifts in the price of these options.

Volatility A statistical measure of past deviations of a stock from its average.

VXO Another volatility index calculated by the Chicago Board of Options Exchange based on the narrower S&P 100 options.

Index